POCKET NATURE
WILD FLOWERS

POCKET NATURE
WILD FLOWERS

NEIL FLETCHER

DORLING KINDERSLEY

LONDON, NEW YORK, MUNICH,
MELBOURNE, AND DELHI

DK LONDON
Senior Art Editor Ina Stradins
Project Art Editor Vanessa Thompson
Senior Editor Angeles Gavira
Editor Georgina Garner
DTP Designer Adam Shepherd
Picture Editor Neil Fletcher
Illustrator Gill Tomblin
Production Controllers
Elizabeth Cherry, Melanie Dowland
Managing Art Editor Phil Ormerod
Managing Editor Liz Wheeler
Art Director Bryn Walls
Category Publisher Jonathan Metcalf

DK DELHI
Designers Shefali Upadhyay,
Sudhir Horo, Kavita Dutta,
Romi Chakraborty
Editors Dipali Singh,
Sheema Mookherjee, Glenda Fernandes
Editorial Consultant Anita Roy
Editorial Support Chumki Sen,
Sunrita Sen, Bhavna Seth
DTP Designers Sunil Sharma,
Balwant Singh, Jessica Subramanian
DTP Co-ordinator Pankaj Sharma
Cartographers Ashwani Tyagi,
Suresh Kumar
Managing Art Editor Aparna Sharma

First published in Great Britain in 2004 by
Dorling Kindersley Limited
80 Strand, London WC2R 0RL

A Penguin Company

ISBN-13: 978-0-7513-3873-7
ISBN-10: 0-7513-3873-7

Reproduced by Colourscan, Singapore
Printed and bound by South China
Printing Co. Ltd, China

Disclaimer Culinary, herbal, or medicinal uses
mentioned in the book are purely anecdotal.
They are not recommendations of the author or
the publisher and should not be undertaken.

see our complete catalogue at
www.dk.com

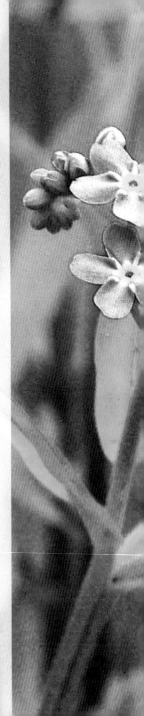

CONTENTS

How this book works

This guide covers the 440 most commonly seen wild flower species in northwest Europe. At the beginning of the book is a short introduction which focuses on the process of identification in the field. For ease of access, the species are then organized into four chapters based on flower colour: Green–White, Yellow–Brown, Red–Pink, and Purple–Blue. Within these colour groups the flowers are broadly organized by family, so that similar plants are kept together for ease of comparison.

SCIENTIFIC NAME

▽ **GROUP INTRODUCTIONS**
Each of the four chapters opens with an introductory page describing the group's shared characteristics. Photographs of representative species show the diversity in the group.

HABITAT PICTURE
Shows the species in its natural habitat.

HABITAT CAPTION
Describes the habitat or range of habitats in which you are likely to find the plant.

PROLIFERATES in damp, open sites, such as river banks, reedbeds, lake margins, ditches, and marshes.

Yellow–Brown

Flowers with yellow petals, such as the Fringed Water-lily below, seem to be particularly attractive to pollinating insects, including flies, beetles, butterflies, and bees. Studies have also shown that many bees are able to detect ultraviolet light and that yellow flowers, such as Tutsan, are among those that reflect it. Some plants even exhibit darker lines in this part of the spectrum that guide bees to the pollen at the centre of the flower. Brown flowers are much less conspicuous, relying on scent to attract insects or, as in the case of Reed Mace, wind pollination.

SCALE DRAWING
To give an indication of the plant's height, a drawing of the plant is set next to an illustration that represents this guide. See panel top right.

PERENNIAL

shallow notched petals

lance-shaped leaf

DETAIL PICTURES
These tinted boxes show individual parts of the plant in greater detail, and may include leaves, flowers, or fruit.

PLANT HEIGHT 1–1.8m.
FLOWER SIZE 1.5–2.5cr
FLOWERING TIME June
LEAVES Mostly opposite, whorled, lance-shaped, c
FRUIT Capsule with four
SIMILAR SPECIES Rosebo (p.211), which has flowere

INHABITS sheltered spots on woodland margins, along ditches, hedgerows, and old walls; also in gardens.

▷ **SINGLE-PAGE ENTRIES**
Species that exhibit greater or more complex features, or are of special interest, are given a full page.

Wild Marjoram

Origanum vulgare (Lamiaceae)

Commonly cultivated as the herb oregano, this hairy, bushy plant often grows in large colonies, filling the air with its strong scent. The culinary herb marjoram comes from two similar, related plants of the Mediterranean, *O. majorana* and *O. onites*. The leaves are a simple oval shape, untoothed and short-stalked, and covered with tiny glands. Numerous flowers, with protruding stamens, are borne in dense clusters on the much-branched reddish stems. The lilac-tipped pink petals are surrounded by prominent crimson sepals and bracts.

blooms in single, dry perennial, woodland, and scrub; also along roadsides, hedgerows, and embankments; and often on steep, grassy chalky soil

flat-topped clusters of purple-pink flowers

NOTE

NOTES
*Describe striking or unique features that will aid identification, or provide interesting background information. **Please note**: Culinary, herbal, or medicinal uses mentioned are purely anecdotal. They are not recommendations of the author or the publisher and should not be undertaken.*

▽ SPECIES ENTRIES

The typical page describes two wild flower species. Each entry follows the same easy-to-access structure. All have one main photograph of the species, which is taken in the plant's natural setting in the wild. This is supported by one or more detail pictures that show the individual parts of the plant in close-up. Annotations, scale artworks, a distribution map, and a data box add key information and complete the entry.

SCALE MEASUREMENTS

Two small scale drawings are placed next to each other in every entry as a rough indication of plant size. The drawing of the book represents this guide, which is 19cm high. The plant illustration is an accurate drawing of the species featured in the entry. The scale represents average height.

Book height 19cm

Average plant height 20cm

CHAPTER HEADING

Villowherb

um (Onagraceae)

d robust plant forms large patches at the Born in racemes, the saucer shaped nk with four-lobed creamy white stigmas. ong, downy fruit capsules, with four back to reveal many arrow

COMMON NAME

FAMILY NAME

DESCRIPTION
Conveys the main features and distinguishing characteristics of the species.

PHOTOGRAPHS
Illustrate the plant in its natural setting.

ANNOTATION
Characteristic features of the species are picked out in the annotation.

MAP
The shading on the map indicates the potential occurrence of the species in the region, although the species may be occasional in some areas of the range and more prolific in others.

COLOUR BANDS
Bands are colour-coded, with a different colour for each of the four chapters.

sules split
ngthwise

eaved
herb

anum (Onagraceae)

semi-shaded places, this willowherb ew pale pink flowers with four deeply ranged in a cross. Despite the oval leaves are not but are broader than those pecies. The rounded, stems are reddish.

PERENNIAL

few flowers in loose clusters

toothed margin   4-lobed stigma   notched petals

strongly veined leaf

PLANT HEIGHT *30–75cm.*
FLOWER SIZE *6–12mm wide.*
FLOWERING TIME *May–August.*
LEAVES *Opposite, toothed, strongly veined.*
FRUIT *Long, slender capsule, with purplish tinge, producing fluffy seeds.*
SIMILAR SPECIES *American Willowherb (E. ciliatum), which has narrower leaves.*

SCALE LABEL
The label under the scale artwork indicates the growth habit or life cycle of the plant.
ANNUAL *The plant completes its life cycle in a single year and then dies.*
BIENNIAL *The plant germinates in the first year, then flowers, fruits, and dies in the second year.*
PERENNIAL *The plant survives and flowers year after year, over-wintering above or below ground.*

⌐ OTHER KEY INFORMATION
These coloured panels provide consistent information on the following points:
PLANT HEIGHT: *the plant's height range.*
FLOWER SIZE: *the length or width of the flowers or flowerheads.*
FLOWERING TIME: *the months during which the plant produces flowers.*
LEAVES: *a brief description of the leaves, giving leaf arrangement, shape, surface or margin features, and, where of interest, colour.*
FRUIT: *a brief description of the fruit, giving fruit type and, where of note, colour and size.*
SIMILAR SPECIES: *lists plant that look similar to the featured species, often describing a distinguishing feature to help tell them apart. May list plants not profiled in this book, in which case a distinguishing feature is always given.*

Anatomy

Flowering plants have evolved in different ways to cope with a wide
variety of local conditions, adopting different lifestyles and developing
different physical characteristics in order to compete for resources.
Some plants, for example, are annuals, others perennials or biennials;
most get their energy from photosynthesis, but some parasitize other
plants or adopt a carnivorous lifestyle; some use tendrils to climb up
towards the light, others develop tall stems to rise above surrounding
vegetation. Each plant part has a specific function. For the vast majority,
the leaves are the food factories that enable the plant to store energy;
the roots provide anchorage and absorb water and essential minerals;
and the flowers are the plant's reproductive parts. Using the correct
terms will add precision to your descriptions and help identification.

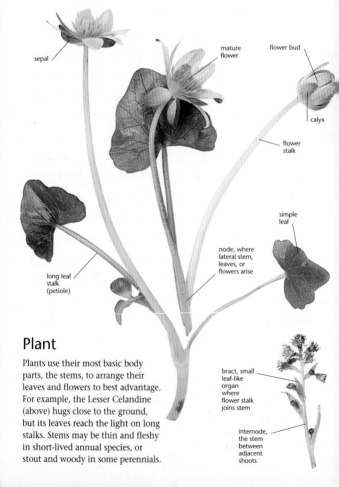

sepal

mature
flower

flower bud

calyx

flower
stalk

simple
leaf

node, where
lateral stem,
leaves, or
flowers arise

long leaf
stalk
(petiole)

bract, small
leaf-like
organ
where
flower stalk
joins stem

internode,
the stem
between
adjacent
shoots

Plant

Plants use their most basic body
parts, the stems, to arrange their
leaves and flowers to best advantage.
For example, the Lesser Celandine
(above) hugs close to the ground,
but its leaves reach the light on long
stalks. Stems may be thin and fleshy
in short-lived annual species, or
stout and woody in some perennials.

Flower

All parts of the flower work together to promote fertilization. The female ovary, found at the base of the style and stigma, is fertilized by the pollen, which is produced by the male anthers. The sepals, collectively known as the calyx, and petals surround and protect the reproductive parts. Flowerheads are made up of small flowers called florets. Insects pick up pollen and distribute it to the stigmas of other flowers.

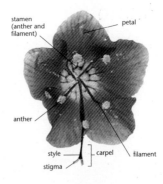

stamen (anther and filament)
petal
anther
style
stigma
carpel
filament

FLOWER

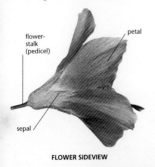

flower-stalk (pedicel)
petal
sepal

FLOWER SIDEVIEW

ray floret
disc floret

FLOWERHEAD

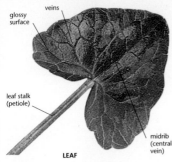

glossy surface
veins
leaf stalk (petiole)
midrib (central vein)

LEAF

Leaf

Green chlorophyll in the leaves harnesses the sun's energy to manufacture sugars and sustain growth. Leaf shape and stem arrangement evolve to maximize available light, and reduce water loss. For example, lower leaves often have a long stalk, while leaves higher up the plant may be smaller and stalkless, so as not to shade those below.

Fruit and Seed

Once the ovary has been fertilized, a fruit forms around one or many of the developing seeds. The fruit covering protects the seed as it develops, and often plays a role in its effective dispersal. For instance, an achene may have feathered hairs to aid wind dispersal, pods and capsules split open when the seeds are ripe, and fleshy fruits such as berries attract animals to eat them as a dispersal strategy.

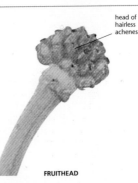

head of hairless achenes

FRUITHEAD

Identification

Occasionally, the flower form or the leaf type alone may be enough
to pinpoint a species but, generally, this kind of identification comes
with the experience of observing the plant many times in the field.
As a beginner, it is important to note all features, including habitat or
flowering season, before finally deciding upon a precise identification.

Growth

Habit is a term used to describe a plant's overall form or mode of growth. It is
a key feature that can sometimes enable identification even from a distance.
The height of individual plants may be affected by such factors as grazing or
mowing, but the habit will usually remain the same throughout the species.

AQUATIC
Amphibious Bistort

PROSTRATE
Creeping Jenny

CLIMBING
Bittersweet

STEMLESS
Thrift

SPREADING
Wood Sorrel

ERECT
Viper's-bugloss

Flowers

Flowers are an obvious plant feature, and their colour can assist identification,
but be aware of those species that exist in several colour forms. Also note how
the individual flowers are clustered together and where, on the plant, they are
borne, as well as the number and form of the petals and sepals.

FLOWER ARRANGEMENT

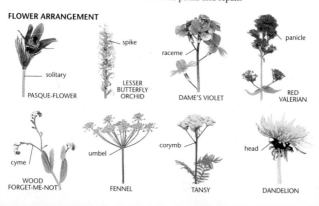

solitary

PASQUE-FLOWER

spike

LESSER BUTTERFLY ORCHID

raceme

DAME'S VIOLET

panicle

RED VALERIAN

cyme

WOOD FORGET-ME-NOT

umbel

FENNEL

corymb

TANSY

head

DANDELION

FLOWER FEATURES

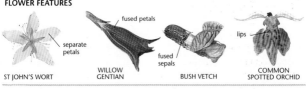

separate petals

ST JOHN'S WORT

fused petals

WILLOW GENTIAN

fused sepals

BUSH VETCH

lips

COMMON SPOTTED ORCHID

Leaves

Assess the colour, texture, and shape of the leaves, how they are divided, whether they have toothed margins, and how they are arranged on the stem. Remember that lower leaves may differ from those above.

LEAF SHAPES

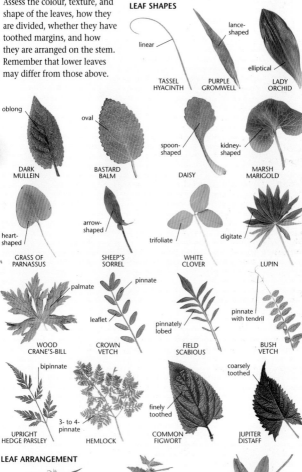

linear

TASSEL HYACINTH

lance-shaped

PURPLE GROMWELL

elliptical

LADY ORCHID

oblong

DARK MULLEIN

oval

BASTARD BALM

spoon-shaped

DAISY

kidney-shaped

MARSH MARIGOLD

heart-shaped

GRASS OF PARNASSUS

arrow-shaped

SHEEP'S SORREL

trifoliate

WHITE CLOVER

digitate

LUPIN

palmate

WOOD CRANE'S-BILL

pinnate

leaflet

CROWN VETCH

pinnately lobed

FIELD SCABIOUS

pinnate with tendril

BUSH VETCH

bipinnate

UPRIGHT HEDGE PARSLEY

3- to 4-pinnate

HEMLOCK

finely toothed

COMMON FIGWORT

coarsely toothed

JUPITER DISTAFF

LEAF ARRANGEMENT

alternate

SMALL YELLOW FOXGLOVE

opposite

YELLOW ARCHANGEL

whorls

WOODRUFF

Fruit

Fruit occur in a huge variety of forms. Closely-related species often develop fruit of a similar type, thus the slight differences between them may be key identification characters. For example, Rape and Charlock (p.113), appear rather similar, but for the longer length of the siliqua growing on the Rape plant. Fruits may also be a useful diagnostic feature if the plant is discovered after the flowers have faded and disappeared.

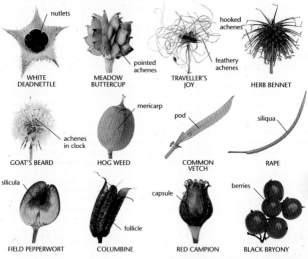

WHITE DEADNETTLE — nutlets

MEADOW BUTTERCUP — pointed achenes

TRAVELLER'S JOY — feathery achenes

HERB BENNET — hooked achenes

GOAT'S BEARD — achenes in clock

HOG WEED — mericarp

COMMON VETCH — pod

RAPE — siliqua

FIELD PEPPERWORT — silicula

COLUMBINE — follicle

RED CAMPION — capsule

BLACK BRYONY — berries

Seasons

Even though the green parts of the plant are visible for a much longer period than the the flowers, the time of flowering can still provide major clues to a species' identity. In general, plants will flower earlier in warm, sheltered locations, as well as at more southerly latitudes.

SIMILAR FLOWERS
Cat's-ear (left) flowers earlier than Autumn Hawkbit (right), but their seasons can overlap.

Distribution

It may be useful to take account of where a species normally occurs, as this can often eliminate potential mis-identification. However, note that sometimes a species may be found outside its normal range, as a vagrant or garden escape, although not usually in large quantities.

WESTERN
Wild Thyme forms creeping mats on sandy and chalky soils in Iceland, Great Britain, and much of western continental Europe.

NORTHERN AND EASTERN
Breckland Thyme is almost identical to Wild Thyme but occurs in eastern Europe and Scandinavia, and a tiny colony in eastern England.

Habitat

Habitat categories can be defined by: geography, such as northerly or southerly latitudes; land-forms, such as mountains or the coast; vegetation, such as grassland or woodland; and human management, such as grazed and farmed land. Plant species have adapted to specific habitats, thus the habitats themselves are identifying features. However, watch out for plants on the margins of different habitats; also, some of the most successful species, such as Bramble, exploit several different habitats.

COASTAL
Sea Holly occurs on coastal sand dunes and shingle. Other coastal habitats include saltmarshes and cliffs.

WETLANDS
White Water-lily prefers open water; other wetlands include marshes, fens, bogs, and ditches.

ALPINE AREAS
Edelweiss favours high altitudes. Northern latitudes share similarly extreme conditions.

GRASSLAND
Red Clover likes meadows and pastures maintained by regular mowing and grazing.

HEATHS
Heather likes the grazed, burned, or cleared habitat of heaths on acid soils.

WOODLAND
Wood Anemone grows in the shady areas of long-established woods with rich soils.

WASTE GROUND
Coltsfoot colonizes the bare soils of disturbed ground. Arable land offers a similar 'pioneer' habitat.

Soil

Soil types are crucial in determining which plant species can grow where. Basic – lime-rich or chalky – soils generally support a greater diversity of species than other soils: their alkaline chemistry provides nutrients more readily for more species.

WELL-DRAINED
Hare's-foot Clover is one of the plant species that has adapted to dry, sandy soils with poor water-retention.

POORLY DRAINED
Marsh Cinquefoil is able to tolerate the waterlogged, airless soils of marshes and flooded grassland.

ACID
Sundew supplements the low-nutrient levels of acid soil conditions by growing leaves adapted to digest insects.

NEUTRAL
Snake's-head Fritillary prefers neutral pH soil conditions that are neither too acidic nor too alkaline.

BASIC
Wild Marjoram is one of the many flowers that grow abundantly on calcium-rich chalk or limestone soils.

Green-White

In early spring, white is the most common flower colour; the comparatively few insect pollinators that are in flight at this time are attracted to the striking contrast of the flower against the foliage. Pale flower colour can also help moths to locate flowers at night. Some plant families have predominantly white-flowered species, such as the carrot family, which includes Wild Angelica (below). This chapter also incorporates plants with green or inconspicuous flowers. In such species, scent is the most important factor in attracting insects.

SUMMER
SNOWFLAKE

COMMON
WINTERGREEN

OXEYE DAISY

HONEYSUCKLE

Hop

Humulus lupulus (Cannabaceae)

The deeply lobed leaves of the Hop are noticeable round the year as they scramble on twisting stems over bushes and hedges. Male flowers form loose panicles; female flowers, borne on separate plants, form leafy, cone-like catkins that develop into the fruit used to flavour beer.

SCRAMBLES *over or through hedgerows, bushes, and woodland trees, on walls, and up telegraph poles.*

drooping flower panicles

rough, toothed leaf

green male flowers

PERENNIAL

twining stems

cone-like fruit

PLANT HEIGHT *Up to 6m.*
FLOWER SIZE *Male 4–5mm long.*
FLOWERING TIME *July–September.*
LEAVES *Opposite, divided into 3–5 lobes.*
FRUIT *Cone, 2.5–3cm long, with overlapping bracts; pale brown when ripe.*
SIMILAR SPECIES *White Bryony (p.36), which has red berries.*

Mistletoe

Viscum album (Loranthaceae)

This evergreen plant, long associated with Christmas, is easily spotted in winter, as its almost spherical form is clearly visible in the bare branches of trees. It is semi-parasitic on its host tree. The small green flowers are less noticeable than the round white berries, whose seeds are distributed by birds.

FORMS *a spherical mass on the branches of deciduous trees, notably poplars, limes, and apples.*

PERENNIAL

forked branches

yellowish green leaves

paired leaves

PLANT HEIGHT *Up to 2m wide.*
FLOWER SIZE *Inconspicuous.*
FLOWERING TIME *February–April.*
LEAVES *Opposite and paired, resembling rabbits' ears, leathery, with smooth margins.*
FRUIT *Berries, 6–10mm wide, borne at the fork of stems.*
SIMILAR SPECIES *None.*

shiny white berries

Common Nettle

Urtica dioica (Urticaceae)

FORMS *colonies on cultivated and waste ground, hedgerows, roadsides, and scrub; on rich, disturbed soil, especially close to manure heaps.*

Also known as Stinging Nettle, this plant is well known to all walkers in the countryside, for the leaves and stems are clothed in stiff, needle-like, hollow hairs which break at the slightest touch, releasing an intensely irritating fluid. There are also many non-stinging hairs, the number varying from plant to plant. The tiny flowers are green, sometimes with a reddish tinge, and have yellow stamens. Males and females are on separate plants; male flowers are borne on long, pendent branches, while the female flowers are in tighter clusters. The plant spreads by rhizomes to form large patches, which may persist for many years.

male flowers in long spikes

coarsely toothed leaves

PERENNIAL

female flower cluster

stiff, erect stem

NOTE

Abundant in chlorophyll, the leaves of the Common Nettle were collected in vast quantities for dyeing camouflage nets during the Second World War; the fibrous stems may be used to make textiles.

PLANT HEIGHT *50–150cm.*
FLOWER SIZE *1–2mm wide.*
FLOWERING TIME *May–September.*
LEAVES *Opposite, heart-shaped, toothed, strongly veined, and hairy.*
FRUIT *Small, rounded achene.*
SIMILAR SPECIES *Small Nettle (U. urens), which is an annual, smaller, and has a less potent sting.*

Sea Beet

Beta vulgaris (Chenopodiaceae)

There is little in the appearance of this plant
to show that it is the forerunner to the
modern beetroot, except that the glossy,
fleshy leaves and stems are often red-
tinged. It has a very prostrate habit,
with long, trailing, flowering stems.
The tiny greenish flowers are borne
in clusters of three on leafy spikes.

slender
flower
spike

SPRAWLS *over shingle
beaches, margins of
salt marshes, old sea
walls, and grassy
embankments. Often
close to the tide line.*

untoothed
margin

flowers
in small
clusters

ANNUAL/PERENNIAL

long flower
stems

long leaf
stalk

PLANT HEIGHT *20–100cm.*
FLOWER SIZE *2–4mm wide.*
FLOWERING TIME *June–September.*
LEAVES *Alternate, fleshy, untoothed, often
red-tinged.*
FRUIT *Corky, swollen segments.*
SIMILAR SPECIES *Fat Hen (below), which
has diamond-shaped lower leaves.*

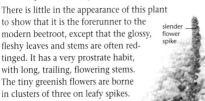

Fat Hen

Chenopodium album (Chenopodiaceae)

The lower leaves of this common weed of arable fields are
diamond-shaped, lobed, and toothed, while the smaller,
lance-shaped upper leaves are usually unlobed
and untoothed. The tiny greenish grey
flowers are clustered in spikes along the
upper branches. Once cultivated as a food
source, the plant is now regarded as a pest
on farms.

flowers in
clusters

PROLIFERATES *on rich
soil of farmyards, field
margins, wasteland,
roadsides, and on
disturbed soil.*

diamond-shaped
lower leaf

lateral
flower
spike

grey-
green
leaves

ANNUAL

toothed
margin

PLANT HEIGHT *40–120cm.*
FLOWER SIZE *2–3mm wide.*
FLOWERING TIME *June–October.*
LEAVES *Alternate; lance-shaped upper
leaves, diamond-shaped lower leaves.*
FRUIT *Seed enclosed within sepals.*
SIMILAR SPECIES *Spear-leaved Orache
(p.18), which has arrow-shaped leaves.*

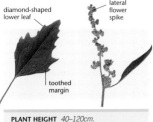

Spear-leaved Orache

Atriplex prostrata (Chenopodiaceae)

GROWS *as a weed on cultivated or waste land, or as a prostrate plant on the coast.*

3 pointed leaf lobes

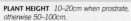

tight clusters of flowers

The oraches are characterized by their weedy appearance and the mealy covering of scales on the leaves, which rubs off as the plant ages. In this species, the upper leaves are narrower than the spear-shaped lower leaves. The clusters of knobbly fruit are more noticeable than the tiny flowers, as they are surrounded by fleshy, triangular bracts.

branched flower spike

narrow upper leaves

ANNUAL

> **PLANT HEIGHT** *10–20cm when prostrate, otherwise 50–100cm.*
> **FLOWER SIZE** *1–2mm wide.*
> **FLOWERING TIME** *July–October.*
> **LEAVES** *Mostly alternate, spear-shaped.*
> **FRUIT** *Achene, 2–6mm long, within bracts.*
> **SIMILAR SPECIES** *Fat Hen (p.17), which has toothed leaves and less knobbly fruit.*

Glasswort

Salicornia europaea (Chenopodiaceae)

PROLIFERATES *in drifts on estuaries, coastal mudflats, and salt marshes.*

This plant is a familiar sight in estuaries, appearing as huge blue-green to red drifts of succulent, upward-pointing fingers protruding from the mud at low tide. The whole plant is edible, although it can be rather woody when mature. The stems are jointed, and the leaves reduced to scales fused to the stem. The flowers are insignificantly tiny, with two barely visible stamens, on fleshy, branched spikes.

scale-like leaves fused to stem

ascending branches

often red-tinged

ANNUAL

> **PLANT HEIGHT** *10–30cm.*
> **FLOWER SIZE** *Spike 1–5cm long.*
> **FLOWERING TIME** *August–September.*
> **LEAVES** *Triangular scales fused to stem.*
> **FRUIT** *Tiny achene.*
> **SIMILAR SPECIES** *Annual Seablite (Suaeda maritima), which has narrow grey-green leaves, and often grows alongside Glasswort.*

Prickly Saltwort

Salsola kali (Chenopodiaceae)

This plant is recognizable by the sharp spine
on the tip of each leaf, unusual for a plant
that is out of reach of grazing animals.
The plant is succulent, much branched,
and bluish green. The tiny flowers, hidden
at the base of the fleshy
leaves, may have a
pinkish tinge.

OCCURS *on sandy
coastal beaches, or in
shingle, often close to
the tide line.*

flowers at base
of upper leaves

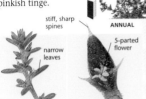

stiff, sharp
spines **ANNUAL**

5-parted
flower

narrow
leaves

ridged stems

PLANT HEIGHT 20–80cm.	

PLANT HEIGHT 20–80cm.
FLOWER SIZE 2–3mm wide.
FLOWERING TIME July–October.
LEAVES Alternate, linear to oval, succulent,
spine-tipped.
FRUIT Achene covered by flower parts.
SIMILAR SPECIES Butcher's Broom (p.29),
which has dull green flowers.

Stinking Hellebore

Helleborus foetidus (Ranunculaceae)

This unpleasant smelling plant is distinctive for its bell-like
green flowers, which hang in clusters in spring. The large
sepals are bright yellow-green and rimmed with purple.
The deep green leaves are palmately lobed, with up to
12 finger-like lobes. The plant
is poisonous.

FOUND *in the light
shade of open
woodland and scrub,
on stony, chalky soil;
also grown in gardens.*

nodding,
bell-like
flowers

deep green
leaves

PERENNIAL

palmate
leaves

narrow leaf
lobes

purple
sepal rim

PLANT HEIGHT 40–80cm.
FLOWER SIZE 1–3cm wide.
FLOWERING TIME January–April.
LEAVES Alternate, palmate with narrow,
slightly toothed lobes.
FRUIT Cluster of three many-seeded follicles.
SIMILAR SPECIES Green Hellebore
(H. viridis) has saucer-shaped flowers.

Lady's-mantle

Alchemilla vulgaris (Rosaceae)

There are many similar varieties of Lady's-mantle that are difficult to differentiate. They all exhibit the same silky, lobed, grey-green leaves with hairs that repel water so that dewdrops collect on them. The yellow-green flowers of this plant have four sepals but no petals.

FOUND *in grassy and rocky places, meadows, woodland margins, and streamsides, at high and low altitudes.*

grey-green leaves

tiny green flowers

palmately lobed leaf

PERENNIAL

flowers in loose clusters

4 stamens

PLANT HEIGHT *30–60cm.*
FLOWER SIZE *3–4mm wide.*
FLOWERING TIME *May–August.*
LEAVES *Mostly basal with clasping stem leaves; palmately lobed, soft, and hairy.*
FRUIT *Small solitary achene.*
SIMILAR SPECIES *This species is an aggregate of many species, with variations.*

Dog's Mercury

Mercurialis perennis (Euphorbiaceae)

This plant may form extensive carpets of green on woodland floors early in the year, before the trees come into leaf. The green male flowers are on long, erect spikes, while the rather insignificant female flowers are formed on separate plants. Like many members of the spurge family, Dog's Mercury is very poisonous.

COVERS *the floors of woodland, coppices, hedgerows, and shady, rocky places. Male and female colonies may be separate.*

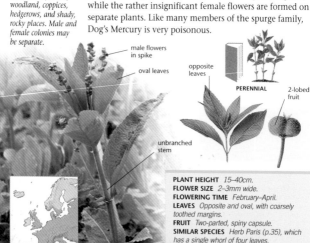

male flowers in spike

oval leaves

opposite leaves

PERENNIAL

2-lobed fruit

unbranched stem

PLANT HEIGHT *15–40cm.*
FLOWER SIZE *2–3mm wide.*
FLOWERING TIME *February–April.*
LEAVES *Opposite and oval, with coarsely toothed margins.*
FRUIT *Two-parted, spiny capsule.*
SIMILAR SPECIES *Herb Paris (p.35), which has a single whorl of four leaves.*

Sun Spurge

Euphorbia helioscopa (Euphorbiaceae)

This spurge produces a clock-like arrangement of yellow-green saucers facing towards the sky, each one made up of whorls of leaf-like bracts that surround the flowers. The flowers themselves are a complex assembly of crescent-shaped glands surrounding the stamens. The smooth, rounded fruit capsule is attached to one side by a small stalk. As with other spurges, the milky juice is very poisonous.

OCCURS *on field margins, cultivated and disturbed land, or wasteland, usually in exposed, dry or sandy situations.*

saucer-like bracts in whorls

flowers borne in umbels

oval leaves

round fruit capsule

fleshy stem

ANNUAL

PLANT HEIGHT 20–50cm.	

PLANT HEIGHT *20–50cm.*
FLOWER SIZE *1.5–3cm wide, with bracts.*
FLOWERING TIME *May–August.*
LEAVES *Rounded bracts in whorls at top; alternate, oval leaves lower down.*
FRUIT *Round capsule on one side of umbel.*
SIMILAR SPECIES *Wood Spurge (p.22); Thorow-wax (p.25) has rounded leaves.*

Cypress Spurge

Euphorbia cyparissias (Euphorbiaceae)

This plant looks like a miniature fir tree with its linear leaves. On slender stems, the flower umbels are encircled by pale yellow-green bracts, which often turn a fiery red in summer. The flower is made up of kidney-shaped glands, surrounded by tiny horns.

GROWS *in rocky sites or open woodland, often at 2,500m in the south of its range.*

soft, needle-like leaves

PERENNIAL

yellow-green bracts

9–18 flowers in umbel

red bracts

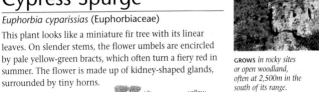

PLANT HEIGHT *20–50cm.*
FLOWER SIZE *8–15mm wide, with bracts.*
FLOWERING TIME *April–July.*
LEAVES *Alternate, linear, and dense.*
FRUIT *Three-lobed capsule with grainy surface.*
SIMILAR SPECIES *Ground Pine (Ajuga chamaepitys), which has two-lipped flowers.*

Wood Spurge

Euphorbia amygdaloides (Euphorbiaceae)

The spurge family consists of around 7,000 species worldwide. The flowers of Wood Spurge, borne in umbels at the end of an unbranched stem, have no petals. Instead, the ovary is surrounded by curious horned glands and cupped by conspicuous yellow-green bracts. The stems may be red-tinged, while the leaves are deep green and untoothed. When the stems and leaves are broken, this spurge like many others, exudes a poisonous milky latex that can be irritating to the skin. Varieties of this plant are grown in gardens.

FORMS *large patches in woodland clearings or coppices, especially among oak or beech. Prefers neutral or mildly acid soils.*

yellow-green bracts

PERENNIAL

oblong, untoothed leaf

bracts form a disc

NOTE

The milky juice of Wood Spurge can aggressively corrode human flesh, and has been used (rather unwisely) in the past to treat warts. Do not try.

PLANT HEIGHT *30–80cm.*
FLOWER SIZE *1.5–2.5cm wide, including bracts.*
FLOWERING TIME *April–June.*
LEAVES *Alternate, oblong and untoothed, tapered towards the base; deep green.*
FRUIT *Capsule, 3–4mm wide.*
SIMILAR SPECIES *Sun Spurge (p.21), which has whorls of leaves; Caper Spurge (right), which has opposite leaves.*

Caper Spurge

Euphorbia lathyrus (Euphorbiaceae)

This spurge has an upright, neat form that makes it recognizable even when young. The grey-green leaves are arranged oppositely up the stem in a criss-cross fashion, and the inconspicuous flowers have leaf-like bracts below. The fruit capsule, which explodes to expel seeds when dry, is very poisonous.

BIENNIAL

CROPS *up by roadsides, field margins, and in gardens where soil is disturbed, usually near human habitation, in semi-shade.*

long, narrow leaf

caper-like capsule

leaf-like bracts

PLANT HEIGHT *80–150cm.*
FLOWER SIZE *3–4mm wide, without bracts.*
FLOWERING TIME *June–July.*
LEAVES *Opposite, lance-shaped, criss-cross up the stem; grey-green.*
FRUIT *Caper-like capsule, 1–1.8cm wide.*
SIMILAR SPECIES *Wood Spurge (left), which has alternate leaves.*

Spurge Laurel

Daphne laureola (Thymelaeaceae)

This small shrub is quite unrelated to the spurges and may easily be mistaken for a small rhododendron bush. In deep shade, it takes on a rather weedy appearance and has only one woody stem. However, it may look more bushy in better light. Its leathery leaves are glossy green and the inconspicuous, four-petalled green flowers are found within the upper leaves. The berries ripen from green to black.

OCCUPIES *shady places, deep within woodland, on dry, chalky soil; also found in rocky places or hedgerows.*

oval black berries

PERENNIAL

clusters of green flowers

leathery leaves

tubular flowers

PLANT HEIGHT *50–120cm.*
FLOWER SIZE *8–12mm long.*
FLOWERING TIME *January–April.*
LEAVES *Alternate; lance-shaped, leathery, clustered towards the top of plant.*
FRUIT *Oval berry.*
SIMILAR SPECIES *None, but can be easily mistaken for a rhododendron.*

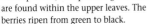

Ivy

Hedera helix (Araliaceae)

CLIMBS *deciduous and coniferous trees, even in dense shade. Trails over walls, buildings, rocks, and hedgerows.*

PERENNIAL

An evergreen, woody climber, Ivy is a familiar sight in woodland, as it scrambles up trees and carpets the ground. The leaves are a shiny deep green but it is only the young leaves that have the classic three- or five-lobed triangular shape. The mature leaves on the flowering stems are quite different, being oval, without lobes. The flowers, in spherical yellow-green clusters, are some of the latest to bloom in the year, providing valuable nectar for bees. These later form persistent, round black fruit.

yellow flowers

rounded flower cluster

oval leaves on flowering stem

rounded fruit cluster

triangular young leaf

pale veins

ripe black fruit

NOTE

The Ivy, often wrongly accused of parasitizing and damaging healthy trees, uses trees only for support, but its weight may bring down weaker limbs.

PLANT HEIGHT *Up to 30m.*
FLOWER SIZE *7–9mm wide.*
FLOWERING TIME *September–November.*
LEAVES *Alternate; three- or five-lobed when young; oval, unlobed when mature, stalked and untoothed, pale veins; deep green.*
FRUIT *Green berries that turn brown, then black when ripe.*
SIMILAR SPECIES *Black Bryony (p.28), which has longer twining stems and smaller flowers; Ivy-leaved Toadflax (p.247).*

Marsh Pennywort

Hydrocotyle vulgaris (Apiaceae)

This plant is recognizable by its perfectly round leaves, which form small carpets like scattered coins, although they may be on long stems if growing among taller vegetation. The inconspicuous flowers, formed beneath the leaves, are in tiny umbels, one of the few features it shares with other members of the carrot family.

FORMS *small carpets in damp grassy places, on muddy edges of freshwater, or slightly brackish, pools.*

coin-like leaves

broadly toothed margin

PERENNIAL

PLANT HEIGHT *5–15cm.*
FLOWER SIZE *2–3mm wide.*
FLOWERING TIME *June–August.*
LEAVES *Basal, rounded with broad, blunt teeth, may be long-stalked; deep green.*
FRUIT *Two-parted mericarp, 2mm wide.*
SIMILAR SPECIES *Navelwort (p.38), which has conspicuous flower spikes.*

stem joins leaf at centre

Thorow-wax

Bupleurum rotundifolium (Apiaceae)

This unusual member of the carrot family has rounded to oval leaves that surround the stem, giving the plant its characteristic look. The lower leaves narrow to form a short stalk before joining the stem. The umbels of small flowers with in-rolled petals have conspicuous, sharply pointed bracts that join at the base, to form a ruff or cup.

GROWS *on cultivated bare land, arable fields, and dry open places.*

yellow-green bracts

ruff formed by bracts

ANNUAL

leaves encircle stem

cluster of yellow flowers

grey-green leaves

PLANT HEIGHT *15–30cm.*
FLOWER SIZE *1–2mm wide.*
FLOWERING TIME *June–August.*
LEAVES *Alternate, oval to rounded.*
FRUIT *Tiny, two-parted, ridged capsule, 3mm wide.*
SIMILAR SPECIES *Sun Spurge (p.21) has whorls of leaves that do not encircle the stem.*

Greater Plantain

Plantago major (Plantaginaceae)

This common weed of wasteland has distinctive thick, dark green leaves that form a flat rosette close to the ground. The plant becomes even more conspicuous when the long, upright flower spikes develop. Varying in length, these bear many tiny green flowers, which for a short while produce purple to yellowish or brown anthers.

FOUND *in bare areas in wasteland, on field margins, and on paths. Also in grassy places that are mown regularly, such as lawns.*

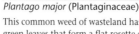

spikes of tiny green flowers

large, rounded leaf

long stalk

PERENNIAL

basal leaf rosettes

PLANT HEIGHT 10–45cm.
FLOWER SIZE 1–2mm wide.
FLOWERING TIME June–October.
LEAVES *Basal rosette, rounded, thick with long stalks, and veined; dark green.*
FRUIT *Small capsule enclosing several tiny seeds.*
SIMILAR SPECIES *None.*

Moschatel

Adoxa moschatellina (Adoxaceae)

A dainty, unusual looking plant, Moschatel is the only species in its family. The tiny flowerhead is quite distinctive with four five-petalled flowers facing each point of the compass and a four-petalled flower on top, facing up. It frequently grows with Wood Anemone (p.44), with which its leaves may be confused.

FORMS *carpets in shade in coppices, damp woodland, rocky places, and among scrub.*

small, terminal flower cluster

PERENNIAL

4 flowers on each side, 1 on top

rounded leaf lobes

4-petalled upper flower

PLANT HEIGHT 6–15cm.
FLOWER SIZE 6–8mm wide.
FLOWERING TIME April–May.
LEAVES *Basal and opposite, divided into lobes, soft; bright green.*
FRUIT *Small green drupe, rarely produced.*
SIMILAR SPECIES *Wood Anemone (p.44), which has solitary flowers.*

Pineappleweed

Matricaria discoidea (Asteraceae)

This delicate plant has daisy-like green flowers, with only the central disc and no ray florets. Not only do the flowers look similar to a pineapple but the plant smells like one too. Although well established in Europe, this is probably a 19th-century introduction from northeast Asia.

PROLIFERATES *on bare paths, in wasteland, and cultivated fields. Despite its fragile appearance, it can withstand trampling.*

finely divided leaves

central disc

domed, bud-like flowerhead

thread-like foliage

ANNUAL

PLANT HEIGHT *10–30cm.*
FLOWER SIZE *5–9mm wide.*
FLOWERING TIME *May–November.*
LEAVES *Alternate, pinnately divided into narrow segments.*
FRUIT *Achenes with a pappus of hairs.*
SIMILAR SPECIES *Scentless Mayweed (p.90), when not in flower.*

Broad-leaved Pondweed

Potamogeton natans (Potamogetonaceae)

The broad leaves of this aquatic plant appear to be hinged at the base, enabling them to float flat on the water surface, while longer, narrower leaves are submerged. The tiny green flowers, which have no petals, are borne in short spikes held above the water. Unusually for a water plant, they are wind-pollinated – contact with water sterilizes the pollen.

COVERS *the surface of nutrient-rich, freshwater ponds, ditches, and slow rivers. May colonize cleaned-out ponds.*

PERENNIAL

flower spike held above water

leathery surface

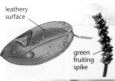

green fruiting spike

PLANT HEIGHT *Water surface, to 1m deep.*
FLOWER SIZE *3–4mm wide.*
FLOWERING TIME *May–September.*
LEAVES *Opposite, broad above water; long and narrow underwater.*
FRUIT *Four small nutlets, each 3–4mm long.*
SIMILAR SPECIES *Frogbit (p.91), which has white flowers; Amphibious Bistort (p.191).*

Crow Garlic

Allium vineale (Alliaceae)

GROWS *in dry, grassy places, commons, dunes, often close to the sea. May be hidden among tall grasses.*

This slender plant may go unnoticed among tall summer grasses. The long, cylindrical, garlic-scented leaves disappear by flowering time, when a papery spathe encloses the developing flowerhead on its long stem. The flowerhead may consist of greenish bulbils, which give rise to new plants, or of small tubular flowers on long stems – or both.

violet flowers

papery spathe

clusters of bulbils

PERENNIAL

long stem

PLANT HEIGHT *60–100cm.*
FLOWER SIZE *Flowerhead 2–3cm wide.*
FLOWERING TIME *June–August.*
LEAVES *Alternate, narrow, and cylindrical.*
FRUIT *Small capsule.*
SIMILAR SPECIES *Field Garlic (A. oleraceum), which has white flowers and two long spathes enclosing the flowerhead.*

Black Bryony

Tamus communis (Dioscoreaceae)

CLAMBERS *over hedges, woodland trees, and scrub; also twines over wire fences; usually at low altitudes.*

The glossy, heart-shaped leaves of this climbing plant are unmistakable. The greenish yellow flowers are borne on long, trailing stems; the male flowers in slender spikes and the female flowers in shorter clusters on separate plants. The shiny red berries are long-lasting but poisonous; although the plant is related to yams, its black tuber is poisonous too.

PERENNIAL

6-lobed flowers

twining stems

male flowers in drooping spikes

cluster of red berries

PLANT HEIGHT *Up to 4m.*
FLOWER SIZE *3–6mm wide.*
FLOWERING TIME *May–July.*
LEAVES *Alternate, heart-shaped; dark green.*
FRUIT *Red, fleshy berries.*
SIMILAR SPECIES *Ivy (p.24), which has flowers in umbels; Hedge Bindweed (p.79), which has trumpet-shaped white flowers.*

Butcher's Broom

Ruscus aculeatus (Liliaceae)

The leaf-like structures of this extraordinarily spiky, evergreen plant are in fact flattened extensions of the stems called cladodes. The stems themselves are upright, and branched on the upper part of the plant. The small green flowers appear directly on the surface of the cladodes and each has three petals and three sepals, the male flowers with purple anthers. Not all the female flowers are successfully pollinated but when one is, a large red berry develops. The whole plant resembles a small holly bush and may grow alongside it.

OCCURS *in ancient woodland, scrub, and hedgerows, even in deep shade. Also in rocky places by the sea. Prefers dry conditions.*

tough, spine-tipped cladodes

PERENNIAL

flowers with 3 petals and 3 sepals

NOTE

So tough and spiky the foliage of this plant that it was once used to sweep butcher's blocks – hence its name.

bright red berry

finely grooved stem

PLANT HEIGHT *25–80cm.*
FLOWER SIZE *3–5mm wide.*
FLOWERING TIME *January–April.*
LEAVES *Alternate, leaf-like structures (cladodes), rigid, elliptical with pointed tips; dark green.*
FRUIT *Bright red berry, 1–1.5cm wide, borne singly.*
SIMILAR SPECIES *None, but may be mistaken for a small Holly (Ilex aquifolium) bush at a glance.*

Sweet Flag

Acorus calamus (Araceae)

INHABITS *the muddy margins of reedbeds, ponds, and slow-flowing streams, often among other similar-looking plants.*

PERENNIAL

The leaves of this plant strongly resemble those of Yellow Flag (p.162), with which it may grow, but they are identifiable by the fact that they are wavy and ridged, usually only on one side of the midrib. Bright green in colour, the leaves are sword-shaped and sharply tapering. The flower spike, borne halfway up the plant, is not always produced and may be difficult to spot among the leaves. It is cylindrical, tapering at the top, and appears at an angle to the flattened stems. It consists of a tightly packed cone of tiny yellow flowers that are divided into six segments with six stamens. Sweet Flag was used to strew floors in the Middle Ages as its leaves exude a fresh citrus smell of oranges when crushed.

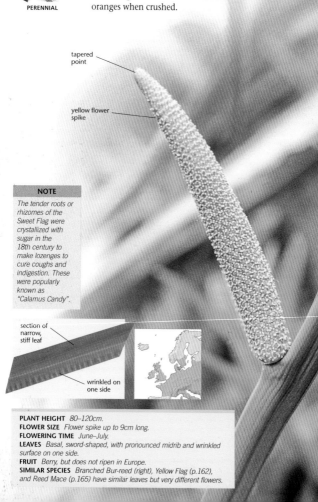

tapered point

yellow flower spike

NOTE

The tender roots or rhizomes of the Sweet Flag were crystallized with sugar in the 18th century to make lozenges to cure coughs and indigestion. These were popularly known as "Calamus Candy".

section of narrow, stiff leaf

wrinkled on one side

PLANT HEIGHT *80–120cm.*
FLOWER SIZE *Flower spike up to 9cm long.*
FLOWERING TIME *June–July.*
LEAVES *Basal, sword-shaped, with pronounced midrib and wrinkled surface on one side.*
FRUIT *Berry, but does not ripen in Europe.*
SIMILAR SPECIES *Branched Bur-reed (right), Yellow Flag (p.162), and Reed Mace (p.165) have similar leaves but very different flowers.*

Branched Bur-reed

Sparganium erectum (Sparganiceae)

The stiff, erect, strap-shaped leaves of this plant are difficult to distinguish from those of other similar plants found on the edges of ponds, such as irises and bulrush. The flowers, however, are distinctive. The branched flowering stem has a number of yellow-green spherical female flowerheads ranged along it, and above those are the smaller male flowerheads in spikes, with attractive white anthers. As the fruit is formed, the female flowerheads swell to become a spiky ball or bur. The plant spreads with the aid of rhizomes.

FOUND *on the edges of freshwater ponds, ditches, lakes, slow-moving rivers, and streams; may grow among other plants with similar leaves.*

PERENNIAL

male flowerheads in spikes

round female flowerheads in clusters

NOTE

Unbranched Bur-reed (Sparganium emersum) has smaller stems and long leaves that may float on rivers.

strap-shaped leaf

white anthers

PLANT HEIGHT *80–150cm.*
FLOWER SIZE *1–2cm wide.*
FLOWERING TIME *June–August.*
LEAVES *Basal, strap-shaped and stiff, usually erect, although some ribbon-like leaves float on water surface.*
FRUIT *Single-seeded drupe, borne on the female bur.*
SIMILAR SPECIES *Sweet Flag (left), Yellow Flag (p.162), Reed Mace (p.165) have different flowers; Unbranched Bur-reed (S. emersum).*

Lords and Ladies

Arum maculatum (Araceae)

FOUND *in shade in woodland or scrub, alongside hedgerows, particularly close to paths and tracks, or on dry banks.*

PERENNIAL

The arrow-shaped leaves of this plant are a deep green colour. They are often, though not always, spotted with dark blotches, and have a wrinkled surface. A large yellow-green bract (spathe) pushes up from the base of the plant and unfurls to reveal the club-shaped, brown flower spike (spadix). This is warm and scented to attract flies down to the true flowers, which are hidden in the bulge below. The green parts of the plant die off but the flowers remain to form berries in late summer, which brighten from green to orange-red.

large yellow-green spathe

club-shaped brown spadix

wrinkled, arrow-shaped leaves

NOTE

Flies visiting the flowers are trapped within the spathe, often overnight, by downward-pointing hairs, to ensure pollination of the flowers.

deep green leaf

green to orange-red fruit

occasional black blotches

berries borne on short stalk

PLANT HEIGHT *15–35cm.*
FLOWER SIZE *Spathe 10–20cm long.*
FLOWERING TIME *April–May.*
LEAVES *Basal, arrow-shaped and wrinkled; dark green, often with dark blotches.*
FRUIT *Red berries.*
SIMILAR SPECIES *Bog Arum (p.94) is smaller; Large Cuckoo Pint (A. italicum) has white-veined leaves and a larger spike of berries.*

Common Twayblade

Listera ovata (Orchidaceae)

This common and widespread orchid bears
only two prominently veined, broad, oval
leaves near the base of the plant and
produces a single flowering stem, at the
top of which is a spike of numerous
yellow-green flowers. Each flower has a
long, grooved, and deeply forked lower
lip. The leaves are more noticeable than
the flower stem, but may quickly be
devoured by insects.

OCCURS *in semi-shaded woods, scrub, meadows, marshy ground, and dunes, on a variety of soils.*

unbranched
veins

numerous
flowers on
upper stem

tall, erect stem

PERENNIAL

forked
lower
lip of
flower

PLANT HEIGHT *20–60cm.*
FLOWER SIZE *Lip 7–15mm long.*
FLOWERING TIME *May–July.*
LEAVES *Basal, simple, two broad, oval leaves on each plant.*
FRUIT *Capsule, containing many tiny seeds.*
SIMILAR SPECIES *Man Orchid (below), which has long, narrow leaves.*

Man Orchid

Aceras anthropophorum (Orchidaceae)

This orchid is not easy to spot as it tends to be hidden
among other vegetation. Its flowers are greenish with red
tinges and borne in a long spike. When seen close up, the
individual flower is highly distinctive – the
elongated lobes of the lower lip look like
narrow arms and legs, while the upper
sepals and petals appear to form
a hood.

GROWS *in fairly open, dry, grassy places such as roadsides, downs, dunes, scrub, and woodland margins, on chalky soil.*

sepals and
petals form
hood

greenish
flowers
tinged red

crowded
spike

lip lobes
resemble
human
limbs

unspotted,
shiny green
leaf

PERENNIAL

long lower lip

PLANT HEIGHT *20–40cm.*
FLOWER SIZE *Lip 1.2–1.5cm long.*
FLOWERING TIME *May–June.*
LEAVES *Mostly basal, narrow and oblong.*
FRUIT *Many-seeded capsule.*
SIMILAR SPECIES *Common Twayblade (above) has a two-lobed green lip; Fly Orchid (p.35) has a dark lip and three green petals.*

Lizard Orchid

Himantoglossum hircinum (Orchidaceae)

An impressive plant, the Lizard Orchid grows to be the largest orchid in northwest Europe. When in bud, the flowering spike resembles an enormous asparagus tip. The oblong lower leaves are unspotted and grey-green, and may be partially withered by flowering time. The flowers have green petals and sepals, which form a small hood, and a short downturned spur and long, narrow bract. The lower lip of the flower is extraordinary, uncoiling like a watch-spring to form a long, twisted, purple-spotted ribbon, on each side of which is a brownish "arm".

GROWS *in grassy places such as scrub, meadows, woodland clearings, road verges, and sand dunes; also found near hedgerows. May form small, loose colonies.*

NOTE

The flowers of Lizard Orchid are designed to attract flies to assist in pollination; to make sure of success they have a strong and rather foetid smell that is reminiscent of goats.

PERENNIAL

numerous flowers in spikes

long, twisted, ribbon-like lip

cowl-like hood

pointed tip

long bract

short spur

"arm" on each side

grey-green leaf

PLANT HEIGHT *50–90cm.*
FLOWER SIZE *Lip 3–5cm long.*
FLOWERING TIME *June–July.*
LEAVES *Alternate; lower leaves elliptical to oblong, upper leaves smaller and narrower.*
FRUIT *Three-parted capsule, containing many seeds*
SIMILAR SPECIES *Man Orchid (p.33), which is smaller and more slender; the flower lacks the long, twisted lip.*

Fly Orchid

Ophrys insectifera (Orchidaceae)

Often hidden in shady undergrowth, this slender orchid can be difficult to spot. It has narrow, pale green leaves and a single long flower stalk bearing a loose spire of 2–12 narrow flowers that look like flies. They have green sepals and a long, three-lobed chocolate-brown lip with a violet patch (speculum).

FOUND in semi-shaded grasses in woodland, coppices, road verges, and scrub; on chalky soil.

PERENNIAL

widely spaced flowers

green sepals

violet patch

lobed lip resembles a fly

slender flower stalk

PLANT HEIGHT *30–60cm.*
FLOWER SIZE *Lip 9–13mm long.*
FLOWERING TIME *May–June.*
LEAVES *Alternate, simple, thin and narrow.*
FRUIT *Capsule containing many tiny seeds.*
SIMILAR SPECIES *Man Orchid (p.33); Bee Orchid (p.189); Early Spider Orchid (O. sphegodes) has a much larger lower lip.*

Herb Paris

Paris quadrifolia (Liliaceae)

This unusual member of the lily family bears a whorl of just four leaves halfway up the stem. Above these it produces a single flower, which has four very slender green petals and sepals, and eight yellowish stamens. The most notable feature is the large blackish fruit capsule in the centre, which splits to reveal red seeds. A low-growing plant, it may also spread by means of underground rhizomes.

FORMS patches in ancient woodland and other shady habitats on chalky soil.

PERENNIAL

round blackish capsule

4 petals and sepals

whorl of 4 oval leaves

8 prominent stamens

PLANT HEIGHT *20–40cm.*
FLOWER SIZE *3–5cm wide.*
FLOWERING TIME *May–June.*
LEAVES *Whorled, oval and pointed.*
FRUIT *Capsule to 1cm wide, containing small red seeds.*
SIMILAR SPECIES *Dog's Mercury (p.20), which is leafier and has flowers in spikes.*

Sea Sandwort

Honkenya peploides (Caryophyllaceae)

This unusual member of the pink family survives on windswept coasts by hugging the ground in mats and by conserving moisture in its succulent leaves. The tiny green flowers, with five sepals and five shorter petals, are insignificant compared to the spherical fruit.

FORMS *mats or large patches on coastal shingles, dunes, and rocks; tolerates salt spray and may grow close to the tide line.*

PERENNIAL

criss-cross leaf arrangement

oval, stalkless leaves

tiny green flower

5 petals

round, yellow fruit capsule

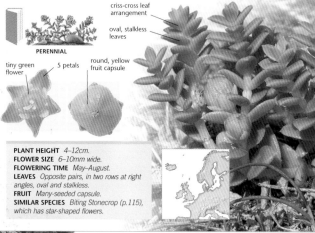

PLANT HEIGHT *4–12cm.*
FLOWER SIZE *6–10mm wide.*
FLOWERING TIME *May–August.*
LEAVES *Opposite pairs, in two rows at right angles, oval and stalkless.*
FRUIT *Many-seeded capsule.*
SIMILAR SPECIES *Biting Stonecrop (p.115), which has star-shaped flowers.*

White Bryony

Bryonia dioica (Cucurbitaceae)

Unrelated to Black Bryony (p.28), this plant climbs by means of tendrils borne near the base of the fig-like leaves. Male and female flowers, both greenish white, are borne on separate plants, the male in longer-stalked clusters than the female, which have the developing berries beneath them. The poisonous berries are bright red when ripe.

CLIMBS *over hedges and bushes in scrub, and at woodland margins, on lime-rich soil at low altitudes.*

5-lobed leaves

PERENNIAL

5-petalled flowers

coiled tendrils

small red berries

PLANT HEIGHT *2–3m.*
FLOWER SIZE *1–1.8cm wide.*
FLOWERING TIME *May–September.*
LEAVES *Alternate; divided into five deep lobes.*
FRUIT *Poisonous, bright red berries.*
SIMILAR SPECIES *Hop (p.15), which has three-lobed leaves and pale brown fruit.*

Field Eryngo

Eryngium campestre (Asteraceae)

This very prickly, spiny plant is thistle-like, but the insignificant flowerheads show that it is actually a member of the carrot family. The tiny flowers are buried within a mass of green bracts, forming a greenish white domed head. The three-lobed leathery leaves are stiff and spiny on much-branched stems, the lower ones further divided.

GROWS *in small numbers in dry, grassy habitats and rough places, often near the coast.*

tiny white flowers

long spiny bracts

prickly leaf margin

dense, thistle-like flowerhead

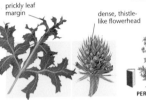

PERENNIAL

PLANT HEIGHT *40–75cm.*
FLOWER SIZE *Flowerhead 1–1.5cm wide.*
FLOWERING TIME *July–August.*
LEAVES *Alternate; leathery, spiny, and three-lobed, lower leaves divided further.*
FRUIT *Two-parted mericarp with scales.*
SIMILAR SPECIES *Spear Thistle (p.180), which has spiny stems; Sea Holly (p.259).*

Cleavers

Galium aparine (Rubiaceae)

A common hedgerow plant, Cleavers is especially well known to walkers and dog-owners because the entire plant is covered in hooked hairs that help it to clamber over other vegetation, but it may also stick (cleave) to clothing or fur. The paired, rounded fruit are also studded with hooked spines to facilitate their distribution. The white flowers are very small and have four petals.

flowers in small clusters

SCRAMBLES *over and through vegetation in scrub or on hedgerows, wasteland, and also cultivated sites. May form extensive patches.*

whorls of narrow leaves

sharp-pointed leaves

4 petals

bristly, paired fruit

ANNUAL

PLANT HEIGHT *30–150cm.*
FLOWER SIZE *2mm wide.*
FLOWERING TIME *May–August.*
LEAVES *Whorls of 4–6, narrow and elliptical.*
FRUIT *Mericarps with hooked bristles.*
SIMILAR SPECIES *Hedge Bedstraw (p.78) and Sweet Woodruff (p.78), which do not have bristly fruit.*

Toothwort

Lathraea squamaria (Fabaceae)

FOUND *in shady parts of damp deciduous woods and hedges, where it is parasitic on roots of trees such as hazels or elms.*

This unusual plant has no green parts or leaves as it is parasitic, deriving its nutrients from the roots of trees, usually hazels. The upright, unbranched stems have one-sided rows of ivory or pink two-lipped flowers, interspersed with scale-like bracts that look like teeth. The bracts are pressed close to the stem.

one-sided rows of flowers

ivory or pink flowers

two-lipped flower

PERENNIAL

PLANT HEIGHT *10–20cm.*
FLOWER SIZE *1.4–1.7cm long.*
FLOWERING TIME *April–May.*
LEAVES *Cream-coloured scale-like bracts.*
FRUIT *Capsule that splits along the middle.*
SIMILAR SPECIES *Common Broomrape (p.164), which is parasitic on herbs, Bird's-nest Orchid (p.166), which has brown flowers.*

Navelwort

Umbilicus rupestris (Crassulaceae)

RESIDES *on cliffs, rocky outcrops, old walls, and stony banks, from sea-level up to 2,500m.*

The coin-shaped leaves of this plant of dry walls are very characteristic, being fleshy and circular, with a dimple in the centre of each leaf where the stem joins underneath. The tall, flowering spikes are also distinctive, with many drooping flowers, each with a five-parted tube, like a miniature Foxglove (p.224). The colour of the flowers varies from cream or green to deep pink.

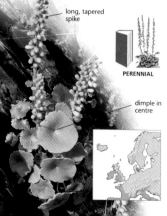

long, tapered spike

dimple in centre

PERENNIAL

shallowly lobed leaf margin

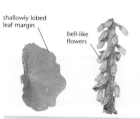

bell-like flowers

PLANT HEIGHT *15–40cm.*
FLOWER SIZE *8–10mm long.*
FLOWERING TIME *June–August.*
LEAVES *Basal rosettes, circular, fleshy, with the stem attached to the centre.*
FRUIT *Group of follicles with tiny seeds.*
SIMILAR SPECIES *Marsh Pennywort (p.25), which has similar leaves, but tiny flowers.*

Ribwort Plantain

Plantago lanceolata (Plantaginaceae)

This common grassland weed can be easily overlooked until its most noticeable feature – the anthers – are mature. These are large and white, forming a conspicuous ring around the flowerhead, whose tiny brown sepals give it a rusty look. The leaves, clustered in a tuft at the base, are long, erect, and tapering, with raised, longitudinal veins on their undersides. The extremely tough and fibrous flower stems are also furrowed. Ribwort Plantain was once used to improve the forage in pastures.

FORMS *extensive patches in meadows, roadsides, pastures, and untended lawns; on neutral soils with little shade.*

PERENNIAL

tapering, rusty flowerheads

ring of white anthers

leafless flower stalks

parallel veins on leaf

tiny flowers

narrow leaf

NOTE

The seeds of this and other plantains absorb up to 25 times their own weight in water, producing a mucilage or gel used in cosmetics.

PLANT HEIGHT *20–50cm.*
FLOWER SIZE *4mm wide.*
FLOWERING TIME *April–October.*
LEAVES *Basal, linear to almost elliptical, with toothed or entire margins, and veined undersides.*
FRUIT *Capsule containing two boat-shaped seeds.*
SIMILAR SPECIES *Spiked Rampion (p.86), which has oval, bluntly toothed leaves.*

Japanese Knotweed

Fallopia japonica (Polygonaceae)

Introduced into European gardens in the 19th century, this weed has become widely naturalized and is now a serious pest in some areas. It is easily recognized by its robust and upright habit, broad, triangular leaves on either side of the zig-zag stem, and short spikes of creamy white flowers at the leaf bases.

INVADES *wasteland, roadsides, river banks, and railway embankments.*

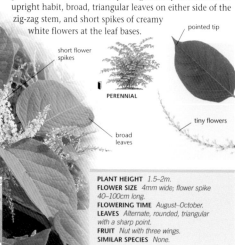

short flower spikes

PERENNIAL

pointed tip

tiny flowers

broad leaves

PLANT HEIGHT *1.5–2m.*
FLOWER SIZE *4mm wide; flower spike 40–100cm long.*
FLOWERING TIME *August–October.*
LEAVES *Alternate, rounded, triangular with a sharp point.*
FRUIT *Nut with three wings.*
SIMILAR SPECIES *None.*

Greater Stitchwort

Stellaria holostea (Caryophyllaceae)

This familiar plant brightens its woodland habitat in spring. Its pure white flowers, in loose clusters, have five deeply notched petals and yellow stamens, with the sepals much shorter than the petals. The rough, oppositely paired leaves persist for many weeks after flowering.

GROWS *in grassy places, such as woodland, shady field margins, roadsides, and hedgerows.*

loosely branched flower stalks

large white flowers

PERENNIAL

yellow centres

linear leaf

deeply notched petals

PLANT HEIGHT *30–60cm.*
FLOWER SIZE *1.8–3cm wide.*
FLOWERING TIME *April–June.*
LEAVES *Opposite, linear to lance-shaped.*
FRUIT *Capsule split by six teeth.*
SIMILAR SPECIES *Chickweed (right), which is smaller, with longer sepals; Common Mouse-ear (right), which has hairy leaves.*

Chickweed

Stellaria media (Caryophyllaceae)

This sprawling plant with weak, straggly stems has star-like flowers with five deeply notched white petals, slightly smaller than the green sepals that surround them. The small, oval leaves are hairless, but there is a single line of hairs running along the stem. Chickweed is a ubiquitous weed throughout Europe, with some medicinal properties, and is often fed to poultry as a tonic.

PROLIFERATES *on cultivated land, road verges, and rubbish tips; in pastures and bare places. Tolerates nutrient-rich soils.*

deep cleft in petal

starry white flowers

ANNUAL

untoothed leaf

sepals longer than petals

PLANT HEIGHT *5–35cm.*
FLOWER SIZE *8–10mm wide.*
FLOWERING TIME *Year round.*
LEAVES *Opposite, oval with untoothed margins.*
FRUIT *Capsule splitting into six segments.*
SIMILAR SPECIES *Greater Stitchwort (left); Common Mouse-ear (below).*

Common Mouse-ear

Cerastium fontanum (Caryophyllaceae)

The most distinctive feature of this plant is the covering of fine hairs on the oval leaves, each looking like a mouse's ear. Like Chickweed (above), its flowers each have five deeply notched white petals, but these are the same length as the white-margined green sepals beneath. The fruit capsule is slightly curved and sits within the sepals, looking like a tiny, half-peeled banana.

THRIVES *in moist areas in grassland, sandy places, and shingle banks, usually on neutral or chalky soils.*

sepals as long as petals

PERENNIAL

opposite, unstalked leaves

oval, hairy leaf

curved fruit capsule

PLANT HEIGHT *5–30cm.*
FLOWER SIZE *6–10mm wide.*
FLOWERING TIME *April–October.*
LEAVES *Opposite, oval, and finely hairy.*
FRUIT *Oblong, curved capsule.*
SIMILAR SPECIES *Greater Stitchwort (left) has large flowers with yellow stamens; Chickweed (above), which has sepals longer than petals.*

Corn Spurrey

Spergula arvensis (Caryophyllaceae)

FOUND *in sandy, arable and cultivated land; also on waste and bare ground where soil has recently been disturbed.*

The leaves of this plant are unusual for a member of the pink family, in that they are fleshy and linear, and form whorls at the swollen joints of the stems. The plant is branched at the base, the stems bending upwards. The flowers, with five white unnotched petals and five green sepals beneath, open in the afternoon.

5 white petals

fleshy leaves

linear leaves

ANNUAL

5–10 stamens

leaf whorls at stem joints

PLANT HEIGHT *5–40cm.*
FLOWER SIZE *4–8mm wide.*
FLOWERING TIME *May–August.*
LEAVES *Whorled, linear, fleshy, and grooved underneath.*
FRUIT *Pendent capsule, split into five valves.*
SIMILAR SPECIES *None.*

Bladder Campion

Silene vulgaris (Caryophyllaceae)

INHABITS *rough ground at the edge of fields and roads, and grassy places; often on dry, chalky soil.*

The conspicuous, inflated sepal tubes of Bladder Campion give its flowers the appearance of bladders or old-fashioned bloomers, making it instantly recognizable. The sepal tubes may be greenish, yellowish, or pinkish, with a fine network of veins, and the five deeply notched petals are white. The flowers become fragrant in the evening. The leaves are oval, pointed, and rather wavy-edged.

branched flower stalks

PERENNIAL

unstalked upper leaves

deeply cleft white petals

inflated sepal tube

prominent midrib

PLANT HEIGHT *40–90cm.*
FLOWER SIZE *1.6–1.8cm wide.*
FLOWERING TIME *May–August.*
LEAVES *Opposite, oval, untoothed, with wavy margins; only the lowermost stalked.*
FRUIT *Many-seeded capsule with six teeth.*
SIMILAR SPECIES *None.*

White Water-lily

Nymphaea alba (Nymphaeaceae)

This unmistakable aquatic plant has often been hybridized to produce many garden varieties and cultivars. The leaves are rounded and dark green, often with a bronze sheen, and are cleft where they join the stem. They either float on or rise above the water surface. The white flowers, which open only in bright sunshine, are held just at the water surface, each with 20 or more fleshy, oval petals and 4–6 green-backed sepals underneath. There are numerous yellow fertile stamens and infertile stamens (staminodes) in the centre, which attract pollinating insects.

COVERS *the surface of still or slow-flowing fresh water in ponds, lakes, ditches, dykes, and streams.*

PERENNIAL

large white solitary flower

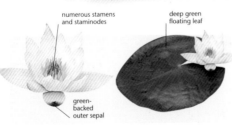

numerous stamens and staminodes

deep green floating leaf

green-backed outer sepal

NOTE

After pollination, the flower sinks below the water surface to develop into a large spongy, warty capsule, which contains many seeds.

PLANT HEIGHT *10cm above the water surface.*
FLOWER SIZE *10–20cm wide.*
FLOWERING TIME *June–September.*
LEAVES *Basal, rounded with cleft, split to the stalk, 10–30cm wide.*
FRUIT *Spongy capsule that ripens under the water surface.*
SIMILAR SPECIES *Yellow Water-lily (p.101), which has larger, oval leaves, and smaller yellow flowers.*

Wood Anemone

Anemone nemorosa (Ranunculaceae)

An early spring flower, Wood Anemone occurs in great sweeps in mature woodland. The white petals, often flushed with pink underneath, open fully only in good light, and follow the direction of the sun. The long-stalked, deeply lobed leaves increase in number after flowering.

FORMS spectacular drifts in deciduous woodland, coppices, meadows, hedgerows, and mountain ledges.

3-lobed leaves

stem leaves in whorls of 3

solitary flower

PERENNIAL

6–12 white petals

PLANT HEIGHT *5–30cm.*
FLOWER SIZE *2–4cm wide.*
FLOWERING TIME *March–May.*
LEAVES *Basal and whorled; long-stalked.*
FRUIT *Head of small achenes.*
SIMILAR SPECIES *Wood Sorrel (p.61), which has heart-shaped leaves; Chickweed Wintergreen (p.75), which has oblong leaves.*

Traveller's Joy

Clematis vitalba (Ranunculaceae)

This scrambling plant produces masses of creamy white flowers in late summer and persistent fruitheads lasting well into winter. These silky, feathery, pompom-like clusters of silvery achenes trail over hedges and trees on long stems that become woody with age, resembling thick rope. The leaves are pinnately divided, with slightly toothed leaflets.

CLAMBERS over hedgerows and scrub, climbing high up on trees or over old walls; on chalky soil.

long stem

twisting leaf stalks

creamy white flowers

PERENNIAL

toothed leaflets

numerous stamens

PLANT HEIGHT *4–30m.*
FLOWER SIZE *1.8–2cm wide.*
FLOWERING TIME *July–September.*
LEAVES *Opposite, pinnate, with oval to lance-shaped, toothed leaflets.*
FRUIT *Clusters of feathered achenes; silvery white.*
SIMILAR SPECIES *None.*

Pond Water-crowfoot

Ranunculus peltatus (Ranunculaceae)

Essentially an aquatic white buttercup, this plant has two kinds of leaves. Those under the water surface are divided into feathery threads, while the leaves that float on the water are rounded, with shallow lobes. The white flowers rise above the water surface on short stems. There are many similar species, but with different leaves.

APPEARS *on the surface of shallow ponds, lakes, ditches, and slow-moving streams, or in mud at the water's edge.*

shallow-lobed upper leaf

ANNUAL/PERENNIAL

thread-like lower leaves

numerous yellow anthers

5 white petals

PLANT HEIGHT *Water surface.*
FLOWER SIZE *1.5–2cm wide.*
FLOWERING TIME *May–August.*
LEAVES *Alternate; rounded and lobed upper leaves, thread-like lower leaves.*
FRUIT *Collection of achenes.*
SIMILAR SPECIES *Frogbit (p.91), which has three-petalled flowers.*

Dame's-violet

Hesperis matronalis (Brassicaceae)

The bold clusters of four-petalled white, violet, or pink flowers of this stately plant are easily noticed. The flowers are fragrant only in the evening. The finely toothed, short-stalked leaves are narrow at the base. A native of southern Europe, Dame's-violet is now naturalized in many places.

FOUND *in damp, semi-shaded places such as woodland margins, riversides, hedgerows, and road verges; often near settlements.*

BIENNIAL/PERENNIAL

4 petals

branched stems

narrow leaf

stalked flowers

PLANT HEIGHT *70–120cm.*
FLOWER SIZE *1.5–2cm wide.*
FLOWERING TIME *May–August.*
LEAVES *Alternate, lance-shaped, toothed.*
FRUIT *Siliquas, 2.5–10cm long, containing many seeds.*
SIMILAR SPECIES *Garlic Mustard (p.46); Cuckooflower (p.199) has pinnate leaves.*

Garlic Mustard

Alliaria petiolata (Brassicaceae)

The large, triangular leaves of this plant appear in early spring. The four-petalled white flowers are borne at the stem tips, in clusters that seem small for the size of the plant. The flowering stem elongates as the long seed pods develop. When crushed, the leaves have a distinct smell of garlic, which is unusual outside the onion family. They can be used for flavouring food, but also give a tang to milk if eaten by cows. The whole plant has many medicinal uses.

FLOURISHES *along hedgerows and roads, in woodland margins and among scrub, in the open or semi-shade, on neutral or chalky soils.*

BIENNIAL

NOTE

Garlic Mustard serves as the foodplant for the caterpillars of the Orange-tip Butterfly. They feed particularly on the seed pods, eating them from the tips downwards.

smaller leaves on upper stem

small flower clusters

triangular, toothed leaves

small white flowers

long, thin seed pods

PLANT HEIGHT *40–120cm.*
FLOWER SIZE *3–5mm wide.*
FLOWERING TIME *April–June.*
LEAVES *Alternate, triangular to heart-shaped, toothed and stalked.*
FRUIT *Seed pods (siliquas), 2–7cm long, splitting lengthwise when dry.*
SIMILAR SPECIES *Dame's-violet (p.45), which has long, finely toothed leaves.*

Horse-radish

Armoracia rusticana (Brassicaceae)

This robust and erect plant, whose root is used as a condiment, is mostly without flowers. However, it is easily identified by its stout, shiny leaves, with wavy margins and pale midribs, which have a faint but distinct horse-radish scent. When flowers do occur, they are white with four petals and borne in dense panicles.

GROWS *in patches on roadsides, wasteland, and river banks, and along farmland edges.*

oblong, toothed leaves

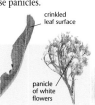

crinkled leaf surface

panicle of white flowers

PLANT HEIGHT *30–90cm.*
FLOWER SIZE *8–10mm wide.*
FLOWERING TIME *May–July.*
LEAVES *Basal, alternate on flowering stem.*
FRUIT *Silicula, 4–6mm wide, but rare.*
SIMILAR SPECIES *Broad-leaved Dock (Rumex obtusifolius), which has similar leaves and habit before it flowers.*

PERENNIAL

Water-cress

Rorippa nasturtium-aquaticum (Brassicaceae)

The glossy, succulent, edible leaves of Water-cress have a characteristic shape, and grow like a ladder up its fleshy stems. Creeping along freshwater habitats, the plant roots into the mud at intervals or floats on the water surface. It may flower for many weeks, forming rows of long, curved seed pods.

SPRAWLS *along ditches, ponds, streams, and wet flushes, sometimes forming colonies.*

tight clusters of flowers

PERENNIAL

oval leaflets

4-petalled white flower

curved seed pod

PLANT HEIGHT *30–70cm.*
FLOWER SIZE *4–6mm wide.*
FLOWERING TIME *May–October.*
LEAVES *Alternate, pinnately divided into oval leaflets.*
FRUIT *Slender, curved seed pods.*
SIMILAR SPECIES *Fool's-water-cress (p.70), which has toothed leaves.*

Hairy Bittercress

Cardamine hirsuta (Brassicaceae)

THRIVES *on wasteland, cultivated and rocky ground, old walls, and in gardens and pavement cracks.*

This common weed of towns and gardens has very small flowers that are easily overlooked. They are in tight clusters at the tips of the gradually lengthening stems, but are usually topped by the long seed pods sprouting from beneath. The narrow, hairy leaves are comprised of well-separated, rounded leaflets in pairs.

long seed pods

ANNUAL/BIENNIAL

large terminal leaflet

tiny flower clusters

four petals

PLANT HEIGHT *5–30cm.*
FLOWER SIZE *3–4mm wide.*
FLOWERING TIME *February–November.*
LEAVES *Mostly basal, upper alternate, with paired leaflets.*
FRUIT *Siliqua, 2–2.5cm long.*
SIMILAR SPECIES *Cuckooflower (p.199), which has larger, pinkish flowers.*

Common Scurvy-grass

Cochlearia offinalis (Brassicaceae)

GROWS *on coastal rocks, salt marshes, sea walls, and motorway verges.*

This variable plant has a succulent nature and often prostrate habit, typical of many coastal plants. The long-stalked basal leaves are rounded, while the upper leaves clasp the stem and may be lobed. The four-parted white flowers are in tight clusters above stems that lengthen as the fruit develop.

tight flower clusters

round, fleshy leaves

BIENNIAL/PERENNIAL

heart-shaped base

round seed pod

PLANT HEIGHT *10–40cm.*
FLOWER SIZE *8–10mm wide.*
FLOWERING TIME *April–August.*
LEAVES *Mostly basal, rounded and fleshy.*
FRUIT *Spherical siliculas, with cork-like texture.*
SIMILAR SPECIES *Danish Scurvy-grass (C. danica), which has lilac flowers.*

Shepherd's Purse

Capsella bursa-pastoris (Brassicaceae)

This familiar, ubiquitous plant is variable in size, with tiny, four-petalled white flowers. Below them, rows of heart-shaped seed cases develop along the stem, resembling an old-fashioned leather purse. The leaves are mostly basal in a loose rosette. If Shepherd's Purse is fed to chickens, the egg yolks become darker.

rows of seed cases

tiny white flowers above seeds

FLOURISHES even in poor soil, in fields, gardens, cultivated or waste ground, along walls, and in pavement cracks.

ANNUAL/BIENNIAL

lance-shaped leaf

upper leaves clasp stem

heart-shaped fruit

PLANT HEIGHT *8–50cm.*
FLOWER SIZE *2–3mm wide.*
FLOWERING TIME *Year round.*
LEAVES *Basal leaves pinnately lobed; stem leaves alternate, lance-shaped, toothed.*
FRUIT *Heart-shaped capsules in racemes.*
SIMILAR SPECIES *Field Penny-cress (below); Field Pepperwort (p.50) has oval fruit.*

Field Penny-cress

Thlaspi arvense (Brassicaceae)

The seed pods of this cabbage family member form papery discs with broad, rounded wings that resemble notched coins. When the sun catches the papery discs, they appear to glow yellow. The white flowers are at the top of the branched stems.

FOUND in disturbed areas such as margins of arable land where the soil is rich, and in wasteland.

toothed leaves

stem elongates in fruit

coin-like fruit

tiny flowers in tight clusters

ANNUAL

PLANT HEIGHT *20–60cm.*
FLOWER SIZE *4–6mm wide.*
FLOWERING TIME *May–July.*
LEAVES *Alternate, narrow and roughly toothed.*
FRUIT *Papery, disc-like wings in clusters.*
SIMILAR SPECIES *Shepherd's Purse (above), which has heart-shaped seed capsules.*

Field Pepperwort

Lepidium campestre (Brassicaceae)

This widespread weed of cultivated land is more noticeable when the fruit appear, forming long columns of seed pods (siliculas). The stems of the plant, on which the seed pods are held horizontally, elongate as the fruit develops. Each fruit is flat on one side, curved on the other, and faintly winged with a notch at the tip. The tiny, four-petalled white flowers are in tight clusters at the tops of the stems. The upper leaves, clasping the stem, are narrow and toothed, while the lower leaves are oval.

INHABITS *cultivated, waste and disturbed ground, dry, open places, and roadsides.*

tight flower cluster

narrow upper leaves clasp stem

ANNUAL/BIENNIAL

small white flowers

notched fruit

PLANT HEIGHT *30–60cm.*
FLOWER SIZE *2mm wide.*
FLOWERING TIME *May–August.*
LEAVES *Alternate, narrow, toothed upper leaves; basal leaves wither by flowering time.*
FRUIT *Oval silicula, 5–6mm long.*
SIMILAR SPECIES *Shepherd's Purse (p.49), which has heart-shaped fruit.*

Hoary Cress

Cardaria draba (Brassicaceae)

Long associated with coastal areas, often in dry, stony places, this plant is now common along salted roadways. It is easily spotted by the foaming mass of tiny creamy white flowers on its many-branched stems, forming attractive drifts. Each flower has four petals, and develops into a rounded fruit. The toothed, greyish leaves are oblong.

GROWS *in drifts along roadsides, trackways, and on cultivated and disturbed ground, by the coast.*

flowers in clusters

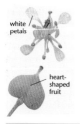

white petals

heart-shaped fruit

unstalked stem leaves
PERENNIAL

PLANT HEIGHT *30–80cm.*
FLOWER SIZE *5–6mm wide.*
FLOWERING TIME *May–June.*
LEAVES *Alternate, oval and coarsely toothed; basal leaves may be untoothed.*
FRUIT *Heart-shaped silicula, 3–4mm long.*
SIMILAR SPECIES *Sea Kale (right), which has similar characteristics but is more robust.*

Sea Kale

Crambe maritima (Brassicaceae)

The great clumps of grey-green, waxy leaves of this plant are difficult to miss in the barren expanse of a shingle beach or coastal sands. They are succulent, lobed, and with wavy margins, like those of a cabbage. The young leaves are furled, with crisped edges, and may be strongly tinged red. Large, domed clusters of four-petalled white flowers are produced in profusion, and by late summer the plant carries hundreds of ball-shaped fruit that look like marbles on the bare branches of the flower stalks.

FORMS *clumps, often close to the shoreline, on shingle beaches and coastal sands, sometimes on cliffs and sea walls.*

plant forms large clumps

dense clusters of white flowers

PERENNIAL

NOTE

The young, cabbage-like leaves of this plant used to be blanched by piling shingle on top, then cooked and eaten as a vegetable.

thick, fleshy leaves

spherical fruit

thick, branched stem

PLANT HEIGHT *30–80cm.*
FLOWER SIZE *1–1.5cm wide.*
FLOWERING TIME *June–August.*
LEAVES *Mostly basal, lobed with wavy margins; lower leaves unstalked; grey-green.*
FRUIT *Fleshy, rounded siliculas, 8–14mm long.*
SIMILAR SPECIES *Hoary Cress (left), which is less robust; Wild Cabbage (p.112), which has larger and yellow flowers.*

Round-leaved Sundew

Drosera rotundifolia (Droseraceae)

This plant is usually seen nestling in moss, and its curiously adapted leaves are unmistakable. They are clothed in long, red glandular hairs, each tipped with a drop of sticky liquid. These ensnare an insect hoping to find nectar, whereupon the leaf rolls up and digests the insect inside. The small white flowers are borne in a loose spike at the top of a leafless stalk, high above the leaves.

GROWS *among sphagnum moss and other plants, on bare peat in acid bogs, in moist conditions.*

rounded leaf blade

white flower

PERENNIAL

leaves with sticky red hairs

PLANT HEIGHT *5–15cm.*
FLOWER SIZE *5mm wide.*
FLOWERING TIME *June–August.*
LEAVES *Basal, rounded, with glandular hairs.*
FRUIT *Small, many-seeded capsule.*
SIMILAR SPECIES *Great Sundew* (D. longifolia), *which has narrow, oblong leaves covered in sticky glands.*

White Stonecrop

Sedum album (Crassulaceae)

The fleshy, cylindrical leaves of this plant, like little waxy fingers, help it to conserve moisture in the dry conditions in which it lives. The leafy stems are branched at the top, where they bear a mass of starry white flowers. English Stonecrop is smaller, with white flowers that are distinctly red-tinged.

OCCURS *on rocks, walls, and dunes, in shingle or on gravel paths, in very dry, exposed places.*

broad, terminal cluster of flowers

PERENNIAL

5-petalled flowers

succulent leaves

leaves often red-tinged

prominent stamens

PLANT HEIGHT *8–20cm.*
FLOWER SIZE *6–9mm wide.*
FLOWERING TIME *June–August.*
LEAVES *Alternate, small, cylindrical, and succulent.*
FRUIT *Cluster of small follicles.*
SIMILAR SPECIES *Biting Stonecrop (p.115), English Stonecrop* (S. anglicum).

Rue-leaved Saxifrage

Saxifraga tridactylites (Saxifragaceae)

This is a diminutive plant but one that is clearly visible in the dry, bare places it inhabits. It is red-tinged, or entirely red in colour, with tiny but characteristic three- or five-lobed leaves, the lower ones often withered. The minute five-petalled white flowers are on long stalks, and each sits in a red calyx, which inflates as the fruit is formed.

INHABITS *dry, rocky and bare places such as old walls, sandy heaths, dunes, and field margins, usually on chalky soil.*

tiny white flowers

reddish stems

ANNUAL

flower stalks longer than flowers

lobed lower leaves

PLANT HEIGHT *4–15cm.*
FLOWER SIZE *3–5mm wide.*
FLOWERING TIME *June–September.*
LEAVES *Alternate, fleshy, three- or five-lobed, reddish.*
FRUIT *Two-parted capsule inside the calyx.*
SIMILAR SPECIES *None; this plant is unique with its reddish foliage.*

Meadow Saxifrage

Saxifraga granulata (Saxifragaceae)

The white flowers of this delicate plant stand out among the grasses of old meadows. The flowers are borne in loosely branched clusters of up to 12, on a single, leafless stem arising from a basal rosette of leaves. Bulbils usually form just below the soil surface, at the base of the lowest leaves.

FOUND *in meadows, pastures, on road verges and rocky places; on chalky soil.*

bluntly lobed leaves

5-petalled flowers

PERENNIAL

rounded petals

PLANT HEIGHT *20–50cm.*
FLOWER SIZE *1.5–3cm wide.*
FLOWERING TIME *April–June.*
LEAVES *Mostly basal rosettes, rounded or kidney-shaped and bluntly toothed.*
FRUIT *Small, two-parted capsule.*
SIMILAR SPECIES *Grass of Parnassus (p.54), which has stalked, heart-shaped leaves.*

Grass of Parnassus

Parnassia palustris (Parnassiaceae)

FAVOURS *damp, grassy places, marshes, fens, and meadows; on neutral or chalky soils, also in mountains.*

The solitary flowers of this meadow plant have five white petals with greenish veins and a characteristic and unusual arrangement of branched staminodes surrounding the true stamens. Most of the leaves are basal and heart-shaped, on long stalks, but there is also a single leaf that clasps the stem. The fruit is a single capsule which contains many seeds.

5-petalled white flower

heart-shaped leaf

feathery yellow staminodes

PERENNIAL

long stalk

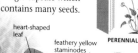

PLANT HEIGHT *10–30cm.*
FLOWER SIZE *1.5–3cm wide.*
FLOWERING TIME *June–September.*
LEAVES *Basal, heart-shaped, with a single clasping stem leaf.*
FRUIT *Capsule that splits into four.*
SIMILAR SPECIES *Meadow Saxifrage (p.53), which has lobed, toothed leaves.*

Mountain Avens

Dryas octopetala (Rosaceae)

FOUND *in rock crevices and on ledges, cliffs, mountain heaths, and sand dunes; on neutral or chalky soils.*

A plant of often inaccessible places, Mountain Avens has flowers that identify it as a rose family member, with eight white petals and many yellow stamens, each flower on a single stem. The leathery leaves, shaped like miniature oak leaves, are distinctive.

bluntly toothed leaf

numerous stamens

glossy green leaves

PERENNIAL

silvery underside

feathery fruit

PLANT HEIGHT *10–25cm.*
FLOWER SIZE *2–4cm wide.*
FLOWERING TIME *May–July.*
LEAVES *Alternate, oblong; glossy above, silvery below.*
FRUIT *Collection of achenes.*
SIMILAR SPECIES *Cloudberry (p.58), which has berry-like orange fruit.*

Baneberry

Actaea spicata (Ranunculaceae)

This rare plant is an exceptional member of the buttercup family, sharing features with other families. The leaves are large, divided into groups of three leaflets. The flowers have 4–6 small petals, and numerous stamens, which give them a feathery look. The fruit, unusually for this family, is a highly poisonous berry, which ripens from green to black.

GROWS on limestone, in woods or woodland edges, or in fissures in limestone pavements.

PERENNIAL

feathery white flowers

coarsely toothed leaves

shiny black berry

PLANT HEIGHT 30–70cm.
FLOWER SIZE 1–2cm wide.
FLOWERING TIME May–July.
LEAVES Mostly basal, pinnate.
FRUIT Berry, 1–1.3cm long, in spikes.
SIMILAR SPECIES Common Meadow-rue (p.103), which is taller with creamy flowers and much smaller leaves.

Dropwort

Filipendula vulgaris (Rosaceae)

This plant is most easily identified by the small, round, pink-flushed flower buds, which look like beads, borne at the tops of the long, upright stems. The flowers each have six white petals and numerous long stamens; when they open they give the plant a fluffy appearance. The leaves are finely divided into many pairs of leaflets.

THRIVES in meadows and dry grassland, and on roadsides, especially on chalky soil. Prefers open, sunny situations.

pink-flushed buds

long flower stalks

PERENNIAL

fluffy white flowers

feathery leaves

tiny leaflets

numerous stamens

PLANT HEIGHT 15–50cm.
FLOWER SIZE 0.8–1.6cm wide.
FLOWERING TIME May–August.
LEAVES Alternate, most appearing basal, finely divided, and feathery.
FRUIT Head of achenes, with 1–2 seeds.
SIMILAR SPECIES Meadowsweet (p.56), which is larger overall, with larger leaflets.

Meadowsweet

Filipendula ulmaria (Rosaceae)

This member of the rose family is most attractive when its creamy white flowerheads are seen in great masses along a river bank. The fragrant flowers, each with many stamens, open from the spherical buds at the top of branched stems, which stand tall above other vegetation. The seeds are coiled together like tiny snail shells. The deep green foliage has a rough texture similar to that of elm leaves.

FLOURISHES *in wet meadows, fens, and tall herb communities, and along river banks, stream margins, and damp road verges.*

spherical flower buds

PERENNIAL

tall, rigid stems

flowers in loose clusters

toothed leaflets

deep green leaves

spirally twisted seeds

NOTE

This fragrant herb was once strewn on the floors of houses to impart its scent; it was also used to flavour mead or honey wine.

PLANT HEIGHT 60–120cm.
FLOWER SIZE 4–8mm wide.
FLOWERING TIME June–August.
LEAVES Alternate, pinnately divided, small leaflets between bigger ones.
FRUIT Small collection of achenes, individual fruits tightly coiled.
SIMILAR SPECIES Dropwort (p.55), which has long fern-like leaves;
Common Meadow-rue (p.103), which has three-lobed leaves and
flowers with tiny petals.

Bramble

Rubus fruticosus (Rosaceae)

Also known as Blackberry, this species is divided by some botanists into hundreds of microspecies, but they all look very similar. The tenacious scrambling stems are covered with vicious thorns and, arching down to the ground, take root to form new plants. Rose-like flowers, present throughout summer, may be any shade from white to deep pink or purple. The edible fruit is a cluster of segments called drupelets that ripen from green to red to blue-black and may be seen at the same time as the flowers.

THRIVES in almost any habitat on many types of soil, but favours woodland, hedges, and scrub, where it may form thickets.

PERENNIAL

5-petalled flowers

prickly, arching stems

3 leaflets

numerous stamens

toothed margin

cluster of drupelets

NOTE

Crawling under a Bramble bush was once thought to be an effective charm against rheumatism and boils.

PLANT HEIGHT *0.5–2.5m.*
FLOWER SIZE *2–3cm wide.*
FLOWERING TIME *May–September.*
LEAVES *Alternate; divided into three toothed leaflets with prickly surface.*
FRUIT *Cluster of segments or drupelets.*
SIMILAR SPECIES *Cloudberry (p.58) has no prickles; Raspberry (p.58) has tiny petals, five-lobed leaves, and red fruit; Field Rose (p.59) and Dog Rose (p.203), which have larger, neater flowers and scarlet hips.*

Cloudberry

Rubus chamaemorus (Rosaceae)

A low, creeping plant of northern areas, Cloudberry forms extensive patches. It has rounded, wrinkled leaves that are shallowly lobed and coarsely toothed, and bears solitary white flowers, males and females on separate plants. The fruit, a cluster of drupelets, ripens from red to bright orange.

FORMS *patches on upland bogs, damp moors, and tundra; prefers acid, peaty soil, up to 1,400m.*

rose-like white flower

wrinkled leaf surface

shallow lobes

PERENNIAL

smooth stem without prickles

bright orange fruit

PLANT HEIGHT *10–20cm.*
FLOWER SIZE *1.5–2cm wide.*
FLOWERING TIME *June–August.*
LEAVES *Alternate, rounded, lobed, toothed.*
FRUIT *Collection of up to 20 drupelets.*
SIMILAR SPECIES *Mountain Avens (p.54), which has different leaves and fruit; Bramble (p.57), which is a prickly plant.*

Raspberry

Rubus idaeus (Rosaceae)

Clusters of nodding flowers are borne on this tall, bushy plant, each flower having five tiny white petals, which are bent backwards and are smaller than the green sepals between them. The leaves, on prickly stems, are divided into finely toothed leaflets, pale green above with whitish down beneath. The slightly hairy fruit is a cluster of bright red drupelets.

PREFERS *shady areas in woodland and scrub, and on heaths, wasteland, and embankments.*

PERENNIAL

pale green leaves

nodding white flowers

green sepals

cluster of red drupelets

oval leaflets

PLANT HEIGHT *80–150cm.*
FLOWER SIZE *9–11mm wide.*
FLOWERING TIME *May–August.*
LEAVES *Alternate, pinnately divided into 5–7 leaflets.*
FRUIT *Collection of red drupelets.*
SIMILAR SPECIES *Bramble (p.57), which has larger prickles and flowers, and black fruit.*

Field Rose

Rosa arvensis (Rosaceae)

This climbing, straggling rose has white flowers, with the styles forming short columns, protruding about 5mm. Its leaves, borne on sparsely prickled stems, are divided into two or three pairs of small, neat, oval leaflets. The fruit is an oval, bright red hip, emerging from the flower sepals which fall off when the fruit ripens.

CLAMBERS *over other vegetation in scrub, hedgerows, and woodland margins. May form low bushes.*

styles form column

PERENNIAL

white petals

finely toothed margins

oval, smooth hip

PLANT HEIGHT *Up to 3m if climbing on other shrubs, otherwise 1m.*
FLOWER SIZE *3–5cm wide.*
FLOWERING TIME *June–August.*
LEAVES *Alternate, pinnately divided.*
FRUIT *Smooth, bright red hip, without sepals.*
SIMILAR SPECIES *Bramble (p.57); Dog Rose (p.203), which has flowers with short styles.*

Wild Strawberry

Fragaria vesca (Rosaceae)

The fruit of this plant has an excellent flavour, but is much smaller than that of the cultivated variety. The plant creeps by runners, which root to form new plants. Its conspicuous flowers have five rounded white petals, backed with ten green sepals. The leaves have three coarsely toothed leaflets, like a giant clover leaf.

CREEPS *along the ground in woods, scrub, rocky places, and hedgerows, and along walls; on chalky soil.*

PERENNIAL

yellow stamens

veined leaf

green sepals

fleshy red fruit

PLANT HEIGHT *10–25cm.*
FLOWER SIZE *1.2–1.8cm wide.*
FLOWERING TIME *April–July.*
LEAVES *Mostly basal, with three leaflets.*
FRUIT *Strawberry with seeds on the outside.*
SIMILAR SPECIES *Barren Strawberry (Potentilla sterilis), which has a smaller terminal tooth to each leaflet.*

Wild Liquorice

Astragalus glycyphyllos (Fabaceae)

STRAGGLES *among vegetation on road verges, and in open woodland, scrub, and other rough places; prefers chalky soil.*

This straggling plant is not the source of the liquorice used in medicine and confectionery, which comes from *Glycyrrhiza glabra*, but its leaves are similar to those of true liquorice. They are pinnately divided with oval leaflets, including a terminal leaflet rather than a tendril. The tight cluster of peaflowers on a long stalk is greenish cream with green streaks on the upper or standard petal.

long flower stalk

cluster of creamy flowers

blunt, oval leaflets

PERENNIAL

green streaks on standard petal

PLANT HEIGHT *40–100cm.*
FLOWER SIZE *1–1.5cm long.*
FLOWERING TIME *June–August.*
LEAVES *Alternate; pinnately divided with terminal leaflet.*
FRUIT *Curved pod, 3–4cm long.*
SIMILAR SPECIES *Goat's-rue (p.200), which has similar leaves but pink flowers.*

White Clover

Trifolium repens (Fabaceae)

A familiar grassland plant, White Clover spreads by means of rooting runners. Its three-parted leaves usually have a white band on each leaflet. Rounded heads of white or cream peaflowers may become pinkish brown as they mature, the lower flowers drooping like a wide skirt. The flowers are sweet-scented and a rich source of nectar.

PROLIFERATES *in pastures, commons, lawns, roadsides, heaths, and other grassy places.*

rounded, cream to white flowerhead

3 oval leaflets

V-shaped, whitish band on leaflet

drooping lower flowers

ball-shaped flower cluster

PERENNIAL

PLANT HEIGHT *5–20cm.*
FLOWER SIZE *7–10mm long.*
FLOWERING TIME *June–September.*
LEAVES *Alternate with three oval leaflets.*
FRUIT *Narrow pod with 3–4 seeds.*
SIMILAR SPECIES *Red Clover (p.172), which has darker red flowers; Strawberry Clover (p.202), which has smaller flowerheads.*

Bird's-foot

Ornithopus perpusillus (Fabaceae)

A diminutive member of the pea family, with a prostrate habit, this plant is worth looking at close up. It bears 3–8 tiny peaflowers, which are predominantly white, each with a yellow blotch and delicate pink veins. The leaves are ladder-like and pinnately divided, with many pairs of leaflets, ending in a terminal leaflet. The curved, segmented seed pods resemble the claws of a bird's foot.

GROWS *in patches in open places such as sandy grassland and heaths, or among short turf; prefers acid soil.*

ANNUAL

terminal leaflet

tiny, pink-veined peaflowers

ladder-like leaf

PLANT HEIGHT *5–30cm.*
FLOWER SIZE *3–5mm wide.*
FLOWERING TIME *May–August.*
LEAVES *Alternate, pinnate with 5–12 pairs of leaflets and terminal leaflet.*
FRUIT *Many-seeded pod.*
SIMILAR SPECIES *Horseshoe Vetch (p.125), which has bright yellow flowers.*

Wood Sorrel

Oxalis acetosella (Oxalidaceae)

This dainty, creeping plant has bell-like white flowers veined pink or white. Its leaves are distinctive, divided into three drooping, folded, heart-shaped leaflets, which close up in strong sunlight and at night. Bright green above and purplish beneath, they contain a mild acid which gives them a sharp, lemony flavour.

FORMS *patches in scrub, woodland, hedgerows, and rocky places, in shade; on humus-rich soils.*

bell-like flowers

PERENNIAL

leaf folded in centre

solitary flowers

drooping leaflets

5-petalled flower

PLANT HEIGHT *4–10cm.*
FLOWER SIZE *0.8–1.5cm wide.*
FLOWERING TIME *April–June.*
LEAVES *Basal, with three leaflets.*
FRUIT *Capsule 3–4mm long, that explodes, expelling seeds over a distance.*
SIMILAR SPECIES *Wood Anemone (p.44) has six-petalled flowers and divided leaves.*

Field Pansy

Viola arvensis (Violaceae)

This small plant has long and toothed leaves. More obvious are the deeply pinnately divided stipules at the base of the leaf stalks, like little ladders. The flowers are variable, cream to white with a small or large yellow blotch on the lower petal, and varying degrees of purple streaks. They open fully only in strong sunshine, and are otherwise hidden within the long green sepals.

FOUND *in arable fields, or bare ground, spreading over an entire field; on chalky or neutral soils.*

ANNUAL

shallowly toothed margin

oblong leaf

5 petals

yellow blotch

solitary flower

long green sepals

pinnately divided stipules

PLANT HEIGHT *8–20cm.*
FLOWER SIZE *4–8mm wide.*
FLOWERING TIME *May–October.*
LEAVES *Alternate, oblong, toothed.*
FRUIT *Rounded, green-yellow capsule.*
SIMILAR SPECIES *Eyebright (p.84) has jagged leaves; Wild Pansy (p.257) has larger flowers; other Viola flowers may be white.*

Enchanter's-nightshade

Circaea lutetiana (Onagraceae)

The tiny white flowers of this plant are easily spotted in the gloom of its preferred habitat. The petals are deeply notched; the sepals and anthers are rosy-pink. Several flowers are arranged loosely along the leafless, upright stems, often above rows of drooping club-shaped, bristly fruits which attach themselves to clothing. The leaves are elliptical, with a barely toothed margin, and are noticeably veined.

OCCUPIES *dark and shaded corners of woodland, gardens, and pathways, under hedges or bushes.*

leafless stem

PERENNIAL

white flowers

rosy-pink anthers

pink sepals

elliptical leaf

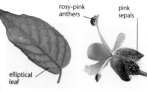

PLANT HEIGHT *20–60cm.*
FLOWER SIZE *4–7mm wide.*
FLOWERING TIME *June–August.*
LEAVES *Opposite, elliptical.*
FRUIT *Semi-pendent achene with bristles.*
SIMILAR SPECIES *Alpine Enchanter's-nightshade (C. alpina), which grows in upland sites.*

Dwarf Cornel

Cornus suecica (Cornaceae)

A low creeping plant of northern areas, Dwarf Cornel has a small umbel of tiny dark purple flowers, which is surrounded by four large oval white bracts, giving the appearance of a single flower. In autumn, these develop into clusters of shiny bright red berries, which may be abundant in the far north. The elliptical leaves are in opposite pairs, without teeth and with distinct veins.

FORMS *patches or carpets on moors, heaths, mountains, and tundra, becoming more abundant in the Arctic. Prefers acid soil.*

4 white bracts surround flowers

untoothed leaves

dark purple flowers

shiny red berries

PLANT HEIGHT *15–25cm.*
FLOWER SIZE *2cm wide, including bracts.*
FLOWERING TIME *July–September.*
LEAVES *Opposite, elliptical, untoothed, distinctly veined.*
FRUIT *Red berry, 5mm wide.*
SIMILAR SPECIES *Unmistakable, especially within its habitat.*

PERENNIAL

Sanicle

Sanicula europaea (Apiaceae)

This plant bears small umbels of white flowers at the end of the long, branched stalks. The outer flowers of each umbel are male and have protruding stamens. Mostly basal, the leaves are broadly rounded but with three or five deep-cut lobes, each with a few bristly teeth.

INHABITS *shady places in ancient deciduous woodland, edges of old fields, and meadows.*

small white umbels

deeply lobed leaf

coarsely toothed margin

long, branched stalks

protruding stamens

PERENNIAL

PLANT HEIGHT *20–50cm.*
FLOWER SIZE *Umbels 5–10mm wide.*
FLOWERING TIME *May–July.*
LEAVES *Basal, three- or five-lobed, toothed.*
FRUIT *Oval, bristly mericarp, 4–5mm long.*
SIMILAR SPECIES *Upright Hedge-parsley (p.65) has larger umbels and finely divided leaves; Pignut (p.68) has thread-like leaves.*

Cow Parsley

Anthriscus sylvestris (Apiaceae)

One of the first members of the carrot family to bloom in spring, Cow Parsley is also one of the most familiar, often forming crowds of frothy white flowerheads along roadsides. Occasional plants may flower as early as February, but the spectacular display does not begin until April – still earlier than any similar species. The deeply divided leaves may appear during winter. They are slightly hairy, and each has a small sheath at the base of the leaf stalk. The ridged and hollow stems are unspotted.

GROWS in masses along roadsides, woodland margins, and hedgerows, and in meadows and pastures. Prefers moist soil.

BIENNIAL/ PERENNIAL

white flowers in frothy heads

NOTE

Mildly poisonous, this plant is closely related to the herb, Garden Chervil (A. cerefolium).

broad umbels with 4–15 spokes

toothed leaf segments

sheath at base of leaf stalk

beak-like tip

2-parted fruit

PLANT HEIGHT 60–150cm.
FLOWER SIZE Umbels 6–12mm wide.
FLOWERING TIME April–June.
LEAVES Alternate, deeply divided with toothed segments; hairy surface.
FRUIT Two-parted, narrow mericarp, 7–10mm long.
SIMILAR SPECIES Upright Hedge-parsley (right); Fool's Parsley (right), which has long bracteoles; Sweet Cicely (p.67), which is more robust, with fern-like leaves and very large fruit; Garden Chervil (A. cerefolium).

Upright Hedge-parsley

Torilis japonica (Apiaceae)

This plant resembles a smaller version of Cow Parsley (left), but appears much later in the year. The umbels of tiny white, pink, or pale purplish flowers are relatively small and spaced out on widely branching slender stems, showing up clearly against the dark background of hedges. The leaves are like small, neat fern fronds.

small, neat umbels

FOUND on the edges of hedgerows and grassy woodland, and on roadsides, with supporting vegetation and partial shade.

small, fern-like leaves

coarsely toothed leaflets

slender, branched stems

tiny flowers

flowers may be pink in bud

ANNUAL/BIENNIAL

PLANT HEIGHT 50–120cm.
FLOWER SIZE Umbels 3–4cm wide.
FLOWERING TIME July–September.
LEAVES Alternate and pinnately divided.
FRUIT Egg-shaped mericarp, 3–4mm long, and covered in tiny spines.
SIMILAR SPECIES Cow Parsley (left), Sanicle (p.63); Sweet Cicely (p.67).

Fool's Parsley

Aethusa cynapium (Apiaceae)

The most distinguishing feature of this delicate plant is the long bracteoles that hang beneath the flowers; these form smaller umbels than in the similar Wild Carrot (p.66). The stems are ridged and leaves are finely divided. Fool's Parsley is poisonous so care should be taken if found growing near salad vegetables.

INHABITS cultivated land at edges of crops, wasteland, gardens, and roadsides.

flowers in umbels

finely divided leaves

ANNUAL

long, pendent bracteoles

PLANT HEIGHT 50–90cm.
FLOWER SIZE 3–6cm wide.
FLOWERING TIME June–October.
LEAVES Alternate, finely divided.
FRUIT Egg-shaped, ridged mericarp, 3–4mm long, divided into two parts.
SIMILAR SPECIES Cow Parsley (left); Wild Carrot (p.66); Sweet Cicely (p.67).

Wild Carrot

Daucus carota (Apiaceae)

This is one of the easiest members of the carrot family to identify. The umbels of flowers are domed and often pink at first and then flatten out, turning white. Very close examination often reveals a purple flower in the centre of the mass of flowers in each umbel. There is a spreading ruff of bracts beneath the umbel, which turns brown and contracts as the fruit develops. The fruit and the bracts that enclose it resemble a tight bird's nest. The leaves are pinnately divided with many narrow segments.

INHABITS *grassy and waste places, roadsides, dry cliffs, and field margins. Prefers dry, open situations, often near the coast.*

lace-like umbels fan out

outer florets larger than inner ones

BIENNIAL

long flower stems

NOTE

An ancestor of the cultivated carrot, Wild Carrot has many applications. Among these is the use of the seeds in liqueurs, in perfumery, and also as a cure for hangovers.

finely divided leaves

dense fruit clusters

PLANT HEIGHT *30–100cm.*
FLOWER SIZE *Umbels 5–10cm wide.*
FLOWERING TIME *June–August.*
LEAVES *Alternate, finely divided.*
FRUIT *Two-parted mericarp, 2–4mm long, in a cluster that contracts to look like a bird's nest.*
SIMILAR SPECIES *Fool's Parsley (p.65) has smaller umbels and long bracteoles instead of bracts; Labrador Tea (p.74); Yarrow (p.88).*

Sweet Cicely

Myrrhis odorata (Apiaceae)

A member of the carrot family, Sweet Cicely is highly aromatic and has often been used for flavouring food. The hollow, unspotted stems smell strongly of aniseed when crushed. The plant often grows tall and bushy, and has large, finely divided, fern-like leaves. The white flowers each have five petals, and are borne in tightly packed umbels, the petals on the outer flowers being uneven. However, it is the two-parted fruit that is the plant's most distinctive feature. Strongly ridged and beaked at the tip, it is very long and slender, and also tastes of aniseed.

GROWS *in semi-shade in damp meadows, woodland margins, pastures, and streamsides, and on roadsides, mainly in mountains.*

PERENNIAL

NOTE

The seeds of this plant were once used to polish and scent wooden floors; a decoction made from the roots was used to treat dog and snake bites.

pale green leaves

densely packed flower umbels

finely divided leaves

long, narrow fruit

ridged surface

PLANT HEIGHT *0.8–1.8m.*
FLOWER SIZE *Umbels 5cm wide.*
FLOWERING TIME *May–July.*
LEAVES *Alternate, finely pinnate and fern-like; pale green, occasionally with white spots.*
FRUIT *Two-parted, elliptical, ridged mericarp, 2.5cm long.*
SIMILAR SPECIES *Cow Parsley (p.64) is less robust and has small fruit; Hemlock (p.71) has finer leaves and red-spotted stems.*

Pignut

Conopodium majus (Apiaceae)

A small, delicate plant of grassland and woods, Pignut has feathery leaves, the upper ones almost hair-like, the lowest leaves having withered by flowering time. It bears white flowers in loose umbels, each with spokes that have tiny bracts beneath. The plant has small, edible brown tubers with a pleasant nutty taste, which used to be gathered in quantity by children.

INHABITS *meadows, woodland edges and clearings, road verges, and hedgerows; rarely on chalky soil.*

white flowers in loose umbels

PERENNIAL

finely pinnate leaves

slender, erect stems

6–12 spokes

PLANT HEIGHT *20–50cm.*
FLOWER SIZE *Umbels 3–7cm wide.*
FLOWERING TIME *May–July.*
LEAVES *Alternate, finely divided and feathery; hair-like upper leaves.*
FRUIT *Ridged mericarp, 3–4mm long.*
SIMILAR SPECIES *Burnet-saxifrage (below), Sanicle (p.63), Fennel (p.131).*

Burnet-saxifrage

Pimpinella saxifraga (Apiaceae)

Flowering later in the year than Pignut (above), this plant has more compact umbels of 10–20 spokes. The lower leaves, divided into oval, veined leaflets, are like those of Salad Burnet (p.171). The word "saxifraga" means "stone-breaker", as this plant was once thought to dissolve stones in the kidneys or bladder.

THRIVES *in dry, grassy places with little or no shade, also in rocky places, on chalky soil. Usually spreads out in loose colonies.*

10–20 spokes with no bracts

slender, upright stems

finely divided leaves

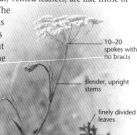

PERENNIAL

compact umbels

PLANT HEIGHT *30–90cm.*
FLOWER SIZE *Umbels 4–8cm wide.*
FLOWERING TIME *July–September.*
LEAVES *Alternate; pinnate basal leaves with narrow leaflets, feathery.*
FRUIT *Ridged mericarp, 2–3mm long.*
SIMILAR SPECIES *Pignut (above) has more feathery leaves and flowers earlier in the year.*

Ground-elder

Aegopodium podagraria (Apiaceae)

An invasive plant that creeps to cover large areas by means of its underground stolons, Ground-elder may be a persistent weed in gardens. The soft leaves resemble those of the elder tree. They were once cooked and eaten as spinach, so it has been spread throughout Europe. The delicate white flowerheads show up well in shade.

FORMS *colonies on shaded wasteland and roadsides, in open woodland, and close to human habitation.*

small, delicate flowers

branched umbels

PERENNIAL

broad, toothed leaflets

flowers in umbels

PLANT HEIGHT *30–80cm.*
FLOWER SIZE *Flowerhead 4–7cm wide.*
FLOWERING TIME *May–July.*
LEAVES *Basal and alternate, divided into three broad, toothed leaflets.*
FRUIT *Mericarp, oval and finely ridged.*
SIMILAR SPECIES *Cow Parsley (p.64), which has more finely divided leaves.*

Hemlock Water-dropwort

Oenanthe crocata (Apiaceae)

This robust member of the carrot family is one of the most poisonous plants in Europe, responsible for the deaths of many cattle. It has large white flowerheads and triangular leaves divided into leaflets of the same shape. Its damp habitat is a key to identification.

FLOURISHES *in damp sites by fresh water, in ditches, and along rivers and streams.*

large white umbels

toothed leaflets

fruithead

PERENNIAL

stout, rigid stem

PLANT HEIGHT *60–150cm.*
FLOWER SIZE *Umbels 5–10cm wide.*
FLOWERING TIME *June–July.*
LEAVES *Alternate, pinnate.*
FRUIT *Cylindrical fruithead, 4–6mm long.*
SIMILAR SPECIES *Fine-leaved Water-dropwort (p.70), which has finer leaves, Wild Angelica (p.72), which has purple stems.*

Fine-leaved Water-dropwort

Oenanthe aquatica (Apiaceae)

GROWS *in shallow, freshwater habitats such as ditches and river and stream margins; often on floodplains.*

The leaves of this plant are very finely divided, resembling the filigree foliage of a fern or of Hemlock (right). It always grows in shallow water, with its thread-like leaves under the surface. The hollow, plain green stems are thick and grooved, especially at the base. The flowerheads appear rather small for what is often quite a large plant.

feathery leaves

petals of equal size

stout stem

flowers in small white umbels

PLANT HEIGHT *1–1.5m.*
FLOWER SIZE *Umbels 3–5cm wide.*
FLOWERING TIME *June–September.*
LEAVES *Alternate, finely pinnate.*
FRUIT *Oblong mericarp, 3–4mm long, with very short styles.*
SIMILAR SPECIES *Hemlock Water-dropwort (p.69); Hemlock (right).*

PERENNIAL

Fool's-water-cress

Apium nodiflorum (Apiaceae)

This water-loving member of the carrot family is unusual in that its flowers arise midway along the stems, opposite leaf junctions, rather than at the end. There are 3–12 widely separated spokes to each umbel, the tiny flowers in small clusters. The leaves are divided into oval leaflets in a ladder-like fashion.

SPRAWLS *along ditches, slow streams, marshes, and lake and river margins. May clamber on long stems among other vegetation.*

alternate leaves

off-white flowers in rounded clusters

PERENNIAL

toothed leaflets

small umbels

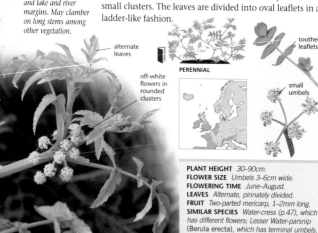

PLANT HEIGHT *30–90cm.*
FLOWER SIZE *Umbels 3–6cm wide.*
FLOWERING TIME *June–August.*
LEAVES *Alternate, pinnately divided.*
FRUIT *Two-parted mericarp, 1–2mm long.*
SIMILAR SPECIES *Water-cress (p.47), which has different flowers; Lesser Water-parsnip (Berula erecta), which has terminal umbels.*

Hemlock

Conium maculatum (Apiaceae)

All parts of the Hemlock plant are poisonous, but the seeds
contain the greatest amount of coniine, just a few drops of
which are fatal. Fortunately, it is one of the easiest of the
carrot family to identify. Hemlock is extremely tall and
robust, and its leaves are finely divided like those
of a fern – the lower ones large and
triangular in outline. The ridged,
hollow stems are clearly
spotted and blotched with
purple, and the white
flower umbels are small
with tiny bracts beneath.

FOUND *at the margins
of damp places such as
ditches, rivers, and
streams; also grows
on wasteland
and roadsides.*

purple-spotted
stems

BIENNIAL/ANNUAL

small, white
umbels

NOTE
*The juice of this
poisonous plant
was administered
to criminals as
capital punishment,
and it was the fatal
poison that Socrates
was forced to drink.*

fern-like leaves

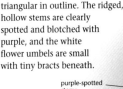

oval
fruit

PLANT HEIGHT *1–2m.*
FLOWER SIZE *Umbels 2–5cm wide.*
FLOWERING TIME *June–July.*
LEAVES *Alternate; finely pinnate, lower ones large and triangular,
upper ones smaller.*
FRUIT *Two-parted mericarp, 2.5–3.5mm long, with wavy ridges.*
SIMILAR SPECIES *Fine-leaved Water-dropwort (left) has no purple spots
on stems; Sweet Cicely (p.67); Hogweed (p.72) has coarser leaves.*

Wild Angelica

Angelica sylvestris (Apiaceae)

The stout purplish stems and round, pink- to brown-tinged flowerheads make this tall member of the carrot family easy to identify. The neatly divided leaves are quite different from those of Hogweed (below) with which it may grow. Wild Angelica is often seen towering above other vegetation.

GROWS *among tall herb communities, in damp meadows and wet woodland; also along river banks.*

PERENNIAL

neat leaf segments

inflated sheath base of upper leaves

purple stems

large, rounded flowerheads

PLANT HEIGHT 1–2m.
FLOWER SIZE Umbels 8–20cm wide.
FLOWERING TIME July–September.
LEAVES Alternate, pinnately divided into neat, oval segments.
FRUIT Two-parted mericarp, 4–5mm long.
SIMILAR SPECIES Hogweed (below), Giant Hogweed (right).

Hogweed

Heracleum sphondylium (Apiaceae)

This familiar, coarse weed lacks the grace of its relatives in the carrot family. The unpleasant-smelling flowerheads are dirty white, broad, and flat-topped, the outer petals of each umbel having clearly larger petals. Each leaf has an inflated sheath where it joins the stem.

DOMINATES *rough areas such as hedgerows, roadsides, woodland margins, and embankments.*

grey-white flowers

coarsely divided leaves

large, flat umbels

BIENNIAL

flattened fruit

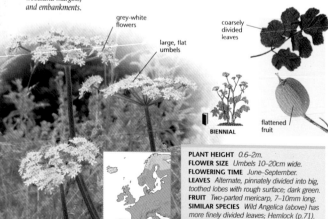

PLANT HEIGHT 0.6–2m.
FLOWER SIZE Umbels 10–20cm wide.
FLOWERING TIME June–September.
LEAVES Alternate, pinnately divided into big, toothed lobes with rough surface; dark green.
FRUIT Two-parted mericarp, 7–10mm long.
SIMILAR SPECIES Wild Angelica (above) has more finely divided leaves; Hemlock (p.71).

Giant Hogweed

Heracleum mantegazzianum (Apiaceae)

Exceptionally large specimens of Hogweed (left) are sometimes misidentified as this plant, but once Giant Hogweed itself is seen, it is unmistakable. Everything about it is bigger, even in shorter specimens. The umbels, made up of large flowers, are much bigger than dinner plates. The purple-spotted stems may be 10cm wide, and the rough leaves up to a metre long. The whole plant may be twice as tall as a human. Introduced from southeast Europe, it has now become a pest in some areas.

FLOURISHES *on damp ground along river banks or roadside ditches. May dominate areas where it has become established.*

BIENNIAL/PERENNIAL

NOTE

The sap causes severe blisters on the skin when exposed to sunlight. It is especially harmful to children who use the stems for blow-pipes or other games.

large, domed or flat umbels

sharply jagged edges

fruiting head with over 50 rays

PLANT HEIGHT *1.5–5m.*
FLOWER SIZE *Umbels up to 50cm wide.*
FLOWERING TIME *June–July.*
LEAVES *Alternate, deeply lobed with sharply jagged margins; to 1m long.*
FRUIT *Oval, broadly winged fruithead, 0.9–1cm long.*
SIMILAR SPECIES *Wild Angelica (left), which has more finely divided leaves; Hogweed (left), which is smaller and has less jagged leaves.*

Common Wintergreen

Pyrola minor (Pyrolaceae)

FOUND in damp places, woodland, moors, marshes, and mountains.

The tiny, bell-like flowers of this plant resemble those of Lily-of-the-Valley (p.92) but are arranged on all sides of the straight, upright stem. They have five petals that are white or tinged with pink, and an enclosed, straight style. The oval leaves are mostly in loose rosettes. Wintergreen oil, used medicinally and to flavour chewing gum, is extracted from the leaves.

bell-like flowers

oval leaves

PERENNIAL

finely toothed margin

PLANT HEIGHT *10–25cm.*
FLOWER SIZE *6mm wide.*
FLOWERING TIME *June–August.*
LEAVES *Mostly basal in loose rosette.*
FRUIT *Round capsule, splitting into five segments.*
SIMILAR SPECIES *Lily-of-the-Valley (p.92), which has flowers only on one side.*

Labrador Tea

Ledum palustre (Ericaceae)

INHABITS damp places in woodland, bogs, heaths, and alongside ditches and streams; prefers acid soil.

This plant forms a compact bush with upright stems, each topped with an umbel of many strongly scented, creamy white flowers; it looks like a small rhododendron shrub, to which it is related. Each flower has five well-separated petals and protruding white stamens. The alternate, rather densely packed leathery leaves are linear with in-rolled edges, and are rust-coloured and felty beneath.

dense flower umbels

narrow leaves

prominent stamens

pendent fruit capsules

PERENNIAL

PLANT HEIGHT *Up to 1m.*
FLOWER SIZE *1–1.5cm wide.*
FLOWERING TIME *May–June.*
LEAVES *Alternate, linear with in-rolled edges.*
FRUIT *Capsule in five parts, 3–6mm long.*
SIMILAR SPECIES *Wild Carrot (p.66) and other members of the carrot family, which do not have leathery leaves.*

Cowberry

Vaccinium vitis-idaea (Ericaceae)

This small, neat shrubby plant is a member of the heather family. The five-petalled, bell-shaped flowers are in tight clusters. They are white with a pinkish tinge and the pointed tip of each petal is turned slightly outwards. The leathery leaves have downturned margins. The berries have a bitter taste.

GROWS *in coniferous woodland, moors, heaths, tundra, and mountains, on acid soil; forms colonies.*

PERENNIAL

oblong leaves

notched leaf tip

upturned petal tip

round red berries

PLANT HEIGHT	*30–70cm.*
FLOWER SIZE	*5–8mm wide.*
FLOWERING TIME	*May–August.*
LEAVES	*Alternate, oblong.*
FRUIT	*Rounded red berry, 5–10mm wide.*
SIMILAR SPECIES	*Bilberry (p.173) has black berries; Bog Rosemary (p.213); Bearberry (p.214) has darker pink flowers.*

Chickweed Wintergreen

Trientalis europaea (Primulaceae)

The starry white flowers of this plant brighten its coniferous woodland habitat, forming carpets in spring. The flowers are usually solitary, but are sometimes in pairs, on long stalks. The large, oblong leaves are in whorls beneath the flowers, and below them on the single, slender stem are a few tiny leaves.

OCCURS *in coniferous woodland, moors, and heaths, on acid soil.*

5–9 pointed petals

whorl of leaves

unbranched stem

PERENNIAL

untoothed leaf margin

yellow anthers

PLANT HEIGHT	*10–25cm.*
FLOWER SIZE	*1.2–1.8cm wide.*
FLOWERING TIME	*May–July.*
LEAVES	*Whorled, oblong.*
FRUIT	*Capsule splitting into five parts.*
SIMILAR SPECIES	*Wood Anemone (p.44), Meadow Saxifrage (p.53), and Grass of Parnassus (p.54): all have different leaves.*

Bogbean

Menyanthes trifoliata (Menyanthaceae)

This plant is unmistakable when seen en masse, with its white blossoms dotted over the surface of acid bog pools. The flowers appear in a loose cluster on a single stem. Rosy-pink in bud, the fully open flowers are white, each petal with an extraordinary fringe of long white hairs that give the flower a fluffy appearance. Rising up out of the water, the rather fleshy, trifoliate leaves have elliptical leaflets and are reminiscent of those of a garden bean.

RISES *up out of the water in pools of bogs, fens, mountains, and lake margins; often forming large colonies.*

NOTE

Bogbean was once valued as a cure for scurvy, with the leaves dried and made into tea, and was also used as a substitute for hops in beer-making.

pink buds

flowers in loose clusters

PERENNIAL

trifoliate leaves

fleshy, elliptical leaflets

petals fringed with white hairs

PLANT HEIGHT *10–35cm.*
FLOWER SIZE *1.4–1.6cm wide.*
FLOWERING TIME *April–June.*
LEAVES *Basal, in three elliptical leaflets rising above water surface, fleshy and bean-like.*
FRUIT *Egg-shaped capsule that splits into two halves when ripe.*
SIMILAR SPECIES *Water Violet (p.215), which has no aerial leaves and has pinkish lilac flowers.*

Swallow-wort

Vincetoxicum hirundinaria (Asclepiadaceae)

The only common member of the milkweed
family in Europe, this is a fairly tall plant,
with long, glossy leaves that sometimes
have a heart-shaped base. Clustered
in whorls at the base of the leaves,
the starry flowers are whitish
or greenish yellow, with five
fused petals. The entire plant
is very poisonous.

flowers in
clustered
whorls

PREFERS *rocky places
such as open woods,
grassland, scrub,
roadsides, woodland
glades, and rides; on
chalky soil.*

erect stem

PERENNIAL

opposite
leaves

lance-shaped
leaf

greenish yellow
flowers

PLANT HEIGHT *40–80cm.*
FLOWER SIZE *5–10mm wide.*
FLOWERING TIME *May–September.*
LEAVES *Opposite, lance-shaped, untoothed.*
FRUIT *Elongated, forked pods up to 5cm
long with silky seeds.*
SIMILAR SPECIES *Great Yellow Gentian
(p.136), which has larger yellow flowers.*

Squinancywort

Asperula cynanchica (Rubiaceae)

This small, ground-hugging plant forms masses of pink
blooms. The tiny flowers, at the ends of slender, many-
branched stems, are white or pink, with four petals fused
at the base to form a tube. Like other members of the
bedstraw family, the leaves are in whorls, but they are
very small and narrow.

FORMS *cushions of
flowers on short, dry
chalk grassland or
sand dunes.*

pink or white
flowers

small
linear
leaves

branched
flower stems

four petals

PERENNIAL

PLANT HEIGHT *5–30cm.*
FLOWER SIZE *3mm wide.*
FLOWERING TIME *June–September.*
LEAVES *Whorled, linear or lance-shaped.*
FRUIT *Tiny, two-parted mericarp, finely warty.*
SIMILAR SPECIES *Field Madder (p.218) and
other bedstraws, which generally have
broader leaves.*

Sweet Woodruff

Galium odoratum (Rubiaceae)

GROWS *in the shade of deciduous woodland and hedgerows, sometimes forming extensive patches, usually on chalky soil.*

This neat, attractive plant has whorls of 6–9 elliptical leaves up the stem, each with tiny prickles along the margin. The white flowers form small, branched clusters, set off by the leaf whorl beneath them. The leaves contain an aromatic substance called coumarin, which is used to flavour liqueurs.

PERENNIAL

4-petalled flowers

6–9 elliptical leaves

small flower clusters

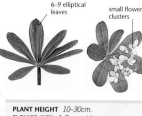

PLANT HEIGHT *10–30cm.*
FLOWER SIZE *4–7mm wide.*
FLOWERING TIME *May–June.*
LEAVES *Whorls, elliptical.*
FRUIT *Nutlet, 2–3mm wide, with bristles.*
SIMILAR SPECIES *Cleavers (p.37), which is a scrambling plant; Hedge Bedstraw (below) which has smaller leaves.*

Hedge Bedstraw

Galium mollugo (Rubiaceae)

Masses of creamy white flowers are produced by this scrambling plant along hedgerows and roadsides. Each tiny flower has four petals in the form of a cross, and is borne in loose, many-branched clusters. The leaves are small with rough prickly margins, and the stem is smooth and square. Hedge Bedstraw does not grow on acid soil, unlike the similar Heath Bedstraw.

CLAMBERS *over hedgerows, scrub, dry grassland, meadows, and along roadsides.*

many-branched flower clusters

whorls of 6–8 leaves

pairs of fused nutlets

creamy white flowers

PERENNIAL

PLANT HEIGHT *40–150cm.*
FLOWER SIZE *2–3mm wide.*
FLOWERING TIME *June–September.*
LEAVES *Whorls, oblong.*
FRUIT *Fused nutlets, black when ripe.*
SIMILAR SPECIES *Sweet Woodruff (above); Lady's Bedstraw (p.137) has yellow flowers; Heath Bedstraw (G. saxatile) is shorter.*

Hedge Bindweed

Calystegia sepium (Convolvulaceae)

This familiar weed may completely cover hedges and fences with its white flowers in late summer, often becoming a serious garden pest. The tough, sinuous stems twist and wind themselves around other plant stems or any other object in their path, and produce heart-shaped leaves at intervals. The trumpet-shaped, bold white flower unfurls like an umbrella, and has two green sepals at the base, partially hidden by two bracts which do not quite overlap.

CLIMBS *over hedges, other tall plants, scrub, woodland margins, fences, and poles. Prefers damp soil.*

PERENNIAL

trumpet-shaped white flowers

NOTE

The flowers have no scent but are rich in nectar, and are attractive to long-tongued moths, such as the Convolvulus Hawk-moth, at night.

heart-shaped leaf

bracts do not overlap

PLANT HEIGHT *1–3m.*
FLOWER SIZE *3–3.5cm wide.*
FLOWERING TIME *July–September.*
LEAVES *Alternate, arrow- or heart-shaped.*
FRUIT *Rounded green capsule.*
SIMILAR SPECIES *Black Bryony (p.28), which has smaller flowers; Field Bindweed (p.218), which usually has pink flowers; Large Bindweed (C. sylvatica), which has larger flowers and bracts that do overlap.*

Common Comfrey

Symphytum officinale (Boraginaceae)

This robust and bushy, damp-loving plant has bristly, spear-shaped leaves that are generally stalkless, the leaf base continuing down the stem to the next leaf joint, forming a pair of wings. The tubular or bell-shaped flowers appear in a coiled spray like a scorpion's tail, opening in sequence, and are creamy white, pink, or violet. Common Comfrey was once grown in cottage gardens for its efficacy in helping to heal wounds and mend broken bones.

FLOURISHES *in damp places such as river and stream margins, marshes, fens, wet woodland, and damp meadows.*

PERENNIAL

spear-shaped leaves

untoothed leaf margin

bushy habit

tubular flowers

stalkless leaf

flowers may be pink

coiled spray

NOTE

Steeped in water and left to decay, comfrey leaves make an excellent liquid garden manure.

PLANT HEIGHT *80–150cm.*
FLOWER SIZE *1.2–1.8cm long.*
FLOWERING TIME *May–July.*
LEAVES *Alternate and basal; stalkless, untoothed, coarsely hairy, running down the stem to the next leaf joint.*
FRUIT *Four shiny nutlets.*
SIMILAR SPECIES *Russian Comfrey* (S. x uplandicum), *which has shorter wings down the stem and blue flowers.*

Common Gromwell

Lithospermum officinale (Boraginaceae)

This tufted, rather erect plant is more noticeable for its mass of lance-shaped leaves than for its tiny white or creamy yellow flowers; these are borne in spiralled clusters that are tucked tightly into the stem. The fruit consists of hard, shiny white nutlets, which look like little beads of porcelain and persist even after the foliage dies down.

GROWS *in semi-shaded woodland margins, hedgerows, and scrub, always on chalky soil.*

PERENNIAL

5-petalled flower

flowers tucked into stem

narrow leaf

very leafy stems

PLANT HEIGHT *40–80cm.*
FLOWER SIZE *3–6mm long.*
FLOWERING TIME *May–August.*
LEAVES *Alternate, lance-shaped, untoothed.*
FRUIT *Four shiny, white or greyish nutlets.*
SIMILAR SPECIES *Corn Gromwell (L. arvense), which is less leafy and grows in arable fields.*

White Dead-nettle

Lamium album (Lamiaceae)

The leaves of this plant resemble those of common nettles, but do not have stinging hairs. Like other members of the mint family, this plant has a square stem and leaves on opposite sides. Two-lipped white flowers emerge in tight whorls, and bloom for many months.

INHABITS *grassy roadsides, wasteland, and hedgerows; on rich soil, particularly where disturbed.*

coarsely toothed leaf margin

large, pure white flowers

alternate leaves

hairy upper lip

black anthers

PERENNIAL

PLANT HEIGHT *20–50cm.*
FLOWER SIZE *1.8–2.5cm long.*
FLOWERING TIME *April–November.*
LEAVES *Opposite; oval to heart-shaped, stalked, with toothed margins.*
FRUIT *Four small nutlets.*
SIMILAR SPECIES *None with such large white flowers.*

Balm

Melissa officinalis (Lamiaceae)

A native of southern Europe, Balm has long been grown in gardens in northern Europe, frequently escaping into the countryside. The leaves are small and diamond-shaped with coarse, rounded teeth, but the most distinctive feature is the strong scent of lemon when they are crushed. The small two-lipped flowers, in loose whorls at the base of the leaves, are mostly white, with a pinkish tinge.

FORMS *tufts on wasteland, dry banks, scrub, and along hedgerows, often near human habitation.*

rounded teeth

opposite leaves

small white flowers

pink tinge

2-lipped flower

PERENNIAL

PLANT HEIGHT	*40–70cm.*
FLOWER SIZE	*8–15mm long.*
FLOWERING TIME	*July–September.*
LEAVES	*Opposite, diamond-shaped, slightly pointed with rounded teeth.*
FRUIT	*Four nutlets.*
SIMILAR SPECIES	*White Dead-nettle (p.81), which has larger flowers.*

Gipsywort

Lycopus europaeus (Lamiaceae)

Instantly recognizable in its habitat, this plant has very distinctive leaves. They are oval to elliptical, with large, jagged, forward-pointing teeth, and are arranged in opposite pairs at well-spaced intervals along the stem. The whorls of tiny white flowers, patterned with minute purple dots, are clustered very tightly on the stem, and each has a rather spiny calyx of sepals.

THRIVES *in wet areas such as pond margins, boggy woodland, and edges of reedbeds, often growing among taller vegetation.*

jagged teeth

tiny dots on petals

evenly spaced leaves

tight whorl of flowers

spiny calyx

PERENNIAL

PLANT HEIGHT	*30–80cm.*
FLOWER SIZE	*3–4mm long.*
FLOWERING TIME	*July–September.*
LEAVES	*Opposite, oval to elliptical.*
FRUIT	*Four nutlets.*
SIMILAR SPECIES	*Corn Mint (Mentha arvensis), which has pinker flowers, more rounded leaves, and a sickly smell.*

Black Nightshade

Solanum nigrum (Solanaceae)

This common bushy weed has similar
flowers to those of the potato plant, with
which it often grows. Each consists of
a yellow cone of anthers surrounded
by five white petals. These later form
clusters of poisonous, round berries,
which ripen from green to black.
The stems are blackish, and the
variable leaves are slightly
toothed or lobed.

pointed,
oval
leaves

INHABITS *wasteland,
bare soil, and rich
cultivated ground,
often with crops.*

starry, white and
yellow flowers

ANNUAL

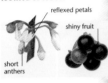

reflexed petals

shiny fruit

short
anthers

PLANT HEIGHT *10–50cm.*
FLOWER SIZE *1–1.4cm wide.*
FLOWERING TIME *July–October.*
LEAVES *Alternate, oval to broadly triangular.*
FRUIT *Clusters of round berries, ripening
from green to black.*
SIMILAR SPECIES *Bittersweet (p.271); Hairy
Nightshade (S. luteum) has orange fruit.*

Thorn-apple

Datura stramonium (Solanaceae)

A poisonous plant, Thorn-apple has jaggedly toothed, oval
leaves with an unpleasant smell. The long white flowers,
similar to Hedge Bindweed (p.79), may be flushed with
purple and are generally produced
singly. The egg-shaped green fruit
splits open to reveal the highly
toxic black seeds. The plant
may be absent in some years
and prolific in others.

trumpet-
shaped
flower

GROWS *on wasteland,
cultivated or disturbed
sites, and in farmyards
and field margins;
on rich soil.*

ANNUAL

bushy habit

sharp-
toothed
margin

fruit covered
with spines

PLANT HEIGHT *70–150cm.*
FLOWER SIZE *5–10cm long.*
FLOWERING TIME *July–October.*
LEAVES *Alternate, oval, jaggedly toothed.*
FRUIT *Egg-shaped, spiny green capsule.*
SIMILAR SPECIES *Hedge Bindweed (p.79),
which is a climbing plant and has arrow-
shaped leaves.*

Eyebright

Euphrasia species (Scrophulariaceae)

FOUND *in grassy sites, heaths, sand dunes, and on woodland edges, usually in small patches.*

There are about 30 *Euphrasia* species in Europe, but they are extremely difficult to tell apart. All have the same basic structure of small, two-lipped flowers, the lower lip being three-lobed. The flowers are usually white or lilac with a yellow blotch and purple streaks. The leaves, sometimes purple-flushed, are small and stalkless, with jagged teeth.

The plant is semi-parasitic on the grasses with which it grows.

flowers in short spikes

ANNUAL

toothed leaf margin

3-lobed lower lip

2-lipped white flowers

branched stem

purple veins

PLANT HEIGHT 5–25cm.
FLOWER SIZE 5–7mm long.
FLOWERING TIME June–September.
LEAVES Opposite, with jagged toothed margins, stalkless.
FRUIT Capsule, splitting lengthwise.
SIMILAR SPECIES Field Pansy (p.62), which has oblong, shallowly toothed leaves.

Honeysuckle

Lonicera periclymenum (Caprifoliaceae)

CLIMBS *over hedges, fences, or high up a tree to form a "bush" midway; trails on ground in woodland.*

The delightful fragrance of Honeysuckle flowers, most noticeable on warm summer evenings, is designed to attract pollinating moths. The plant trails over the ground or climbs high into trees, bearing oblong leaves. In clusters of up to 12, the two-lipped flowers may be white or cream to dark peach, darkening as they mature, followed by a cluster of berries.

whorl of flowers

PERENNIAL

protruding stamens

bright red berries

long flower tube

PLANT HEIGHT 1–6m
FLOWER SIZE 3.5–5cm long.
FLOWERING TIME June–October.
LEAVES Opposite, oblong to elliptical, untoothed.
FRUIT Red berries.
SIMILAR SPECIES Fly Honeysuckle (L. xylosteum), which has flowers in pairs.

Dwarf Elder

Sambucus ebulus (Caprifoliaceae)

A strong-smelling plant, often growing in a large patch, Dwarf Elder is hard to miss. It resembles the elder tree, but does not have woody stems. It has branched clusters of white flowers with purple stamens, which later produce poisonous purple-black berries on reddened stems. The leaves are divided into narrow, finely toothed leaflets.

FORMS *large patches or colonies on disturbed ground, roadsides, woodland margins, and hedgerows. Dislikes acid soil.*

many clusters of white flowers

large, neat leaves

PERENNIAL

5-petalled flower

purple-black berries

PLANT HEIGHT *80–150cm.*
FLOWER SIZE *Clusters 7–14cm wide.*
FLOWERING TIME *July–August.*
LEAVES *Opposite, pinnate, finely toothed.*
FRUIT *Small, fleshy berries.*
SIMILAR SPECIES *Common Valerian (p.223), which is less leafy and does not have berries.*

Small Teasel

Dipsacus pilosus (Dipsacaceae)

Just as tall and robust as Teasel (p.278), this plant has much smaller, almost spherical flowerheads with a ruff of small spines beneath them. The individual flowers are white, with prominent purple stamens. The leaves are more oval than those of Teasel, without spines under the midrib, and often have a pair of leaflets at their base. The whole plant is prickly, including the stems.

GROWS *in damp places with partial shade such as stream- and riversides, open woodland, and scrub.*

BIENNIAL

spherical white flowerhead

prickly leaf

protruding purple stamens

PLANT HEIGHT *1–2m.*
FLOWER SIZE *Flowerhead 1.5–2cm wide.*
FLOWERING TIME *August–September.*
LEAVES *Opposite, oval to elliptical, hairy; often with a pair of basal leaflets.*
FRUIT *Small achene.*
SIMILAR SPECIES *Teasel (p.278), which is taller and has violet flowerheads.*

Spiked Rampion

Phyteuma spicatum (Campanulaceae)

With its tall spikes of massed, creamy white flowers, this is a distinctive and unusual member of the bellflower family. Each floret is curved and greenish at first, but later splits towards the base to reveal the long stigmas. The lower leaves are oval, with heart-shaped bases and long stalks; the upper leaves are narrower and unstalked.

GROWS *among grasses and other vegetation in woodland edges and glades, in meadows, and on roadsides; prefers semi-shade.*

bottle-brush flowerhead

PERENNIAL

long stigma

oval lower leaf

PLANT HEIGHT *50–80cm.*
FLOWER SIZE *Flower spikes 5–10cm long.*
FLOWERING TIME *May–July.*
LEAVES *Basal, oval, bluntly toothed, with a heart-shaped base, unstalked stem leaves.*
FRUIT *Many-seeded capsule.*
SIMILAR SPECIES *Ribwort Plantain (p.39), which has white anthers and narrow leaves.*

Daisy

Bellis perennis (Asteraceae)

A familiar plant, Daisy is easily recognized. The small, central yellow disc of the solitary flower is surrounded by numerous white rays which are tinged pink on the undersides, visible when the flower closes in the evening or when in bud. The hairy leaves are often bluntly toothed, and crowded into a tight rosette.

ASSOCIATED *with old grassland, this plant is now ubiquitous on railway embankments, lawns, roadsides, and short turf by the sea.*

spoon-shaped leaf

solitary flower

PERENNIAL

central yellow disc florets

white rays tinged pink below

PLANT HEIGHT *5–10cm.*
FLOWER SIZE *Flowerhead 1.5–2.5cm wide.*
FLOWERING TIME *Year round.*
LEAVES *Basal, spoon-shaped with short stalk.*
FRUIT *Simple achene, with no feathery attachment.*
SIMILAR SPECIES *Oxeye Daisy (p.89) has larger flowers, but can be very short.*

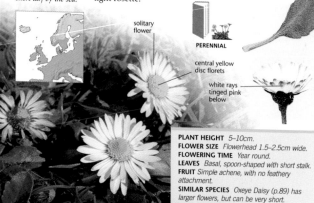

Edelweiss

Leontopodium alpinum (Asteraceae)

This plant has adapted to conditions at high altitudes by developing a covering of thick, woolly, grey-white hairs, particularly on the ruff of bracts that surrounds the small yellow disc of flowers. The silkily hairy basal leaves are oblong and form a rosette, while the alternate stem leaves are smaller and narrower. Edelweiss is a protected plant in many areas.

INHABITS *grassy or rocky mountains, cliffs, screes, and limestone, at 1,700–3,400m.*

small yellow flowerhead

narrow grey-green leaves

PERENNIAL

white bracts

alternate stem leaves

PLANT HEIGHT *5–20cm.*
FLOWER SIZE *Flowerhead 4–6mm wide.*
FLOWERING TIME *July–September.*
LEAVES *Basal rosette, alternate stem leaves, ruff of leaf-like bracts.*
FRUIT *Tiny achene, with small, hairy pappus.*
SIMILAR SPECIES *Marsh Cudweed (p.147), which lacks the flat ruff of woolly bracts.*

Sneezewort

Achillea ptarmica (Asteraceae)

Closely related to Yarrow (p.88), Sneezewort inhabits damp sites and often grows among taller vegetation. It has daisy-like flowerheads, each with a distinct, pale greenish white disc surrounded by white rays, and borne in loose clusters. The scentless leaves are small, narrow, and undivided, but finely toothed.

FOUND *in damp, grassy places, marshes, and meadows, on heavy, acid soil.*

white flowerheads

linear, deep green leaves

PERENNIAL

disc of tubular florets

PLANT HEIGHT *20–50cm.*
FLOWER SIZE *Flowerhead 1.2–1.8cm wide.*
FLOWERING TIME *July–September.*
LEAVES *Alternate, lance-shaped to linear.*
FRUIT *Achene, no pappus, 1.2–1.8cm wide.*
SIMILAR SPECIES *Yarrow (p.88), which has smaller flowerheads and feathery leaves with a pungent aroma.*

Yarrow

Achillea millefolium (Asteraceae)

This plant may form large drifts of white flowers among the dry grasses of late summer. The erect stems are very tough and hairy. Numerous small flowers are borne in flat-topped clusters, and are usually white but may be tinged with pink. The yellow anthers soon turn brown, making the flowers look rather dirty. The dark green leaves are very finely divided and have a strong and pungent aroma. In the past, they were traditionally used to flavour liqueurs.

FORMS *patches in dry grassland and meadows, and on embankments and roadsides; commonly found in untended lawns and wasteland.*

PERENNIAL

flat-topped flowerheads

hairy, erect stems

stiff, green leaves

fine leaf segments

flowers may be tinged pink

NOTE

Yarrow is drought resistant and may look green and fresh even in dried-up grassland in the heat of summer.

PLANT HEIGHT *40–80cm.*
FLOWER SIZE *4–6mm wide.*
FLOWERING TIME *July–October.*
LEAVES *Alternate, feathery, divided into many fine segments; aromatic when crushed.*
FRUIT *Achenes with no pappus.*
SIMILAR SPECIES *Wild Carrot (p.66), which has umbels of numerous flowers; Sneezewort (p.87), which has narrow, toothed leaves.*

Oxeye Daisy

Leucanthemum vulgare (Asteraceae)

Although very variable in height, there is no mistaking the
Oxeye Daisy for the common Daisy (p.86), as its
flowerheads are much larger. These comprise a bright
yellow disc surrounded by a ring of pure white ray florets
and they are borne singly on branched or unbranched
stems. The leaves are bright green and spoon-shaped,
becoming small and clasping the stem towards the top of
the plant. Oxeye Daisy is being used increasingly in
wildflower seed mixes, particularly on the embankments of
new motorways, although the seed used is often
not native to the region.

GROWS *profusely in
grassy meadows and
on wasteland; also
along embankments
and road verges.*

PERENNIAL

large flowerhead

prominent yellow
central disc

rigid, upright
stem

small leaves on
upper stem

NOTE

*The bracts beneath
the flowerhead
contain an acrid
juice distasteful to
insects, which
deters them from
biting through to
the nectaries.*

coarsely
toothed
margin

spoon-
shaped
leaf

broad,
spreading
ray florets

PLANT HEIGHT *20–70cm.*
FLOWER SIZE *Flowerhead 2.5–5cm wide.*
FLOWERING TIME *May–September.*
LEAVES *Alternate and basal; spoon-shaped.*
FRUIT *Small single-seeded achenes.*
SIMILAR SPECIES *Daisy (p.86), which has smaller flowers;
Scentless Mayweed (p.90), which has finer leaves; Corn Marigold
(p.149); Shasta Daisy (L. x superbum), which has larger flowers.*

Scentless Mayweed

Tripleurospermum inodorum (Asteraceae)

This attractive plant forms bushy masses, and bears larger flowers than other mayweeds, each with a solid, dome-shaped, central yellow disc. The leaves are fleshy, very finely divided and feathery, and have no scent. In Scented Mayweed, the disc is hollow and the plant has a looser habit and a chamomile scent.

PROLIFERATES *on disturbed soil of arable fields, and on wasteland, roadsides, bare ground, and neglected farmland.*

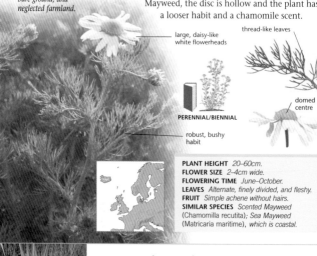

large, daisy-like white flowerheads

thread-like leaves

domed centre

PERENNIAL/BIENNIAL

robust, bushy habit

PLANT HEIGHT *20–60cm.*
FLOWER SIZE *2–4cm wide.*
FLOWERING TIME *June–October.*
LEAVES *Alternate, finely divided, and fleshy.*
FRUIT *Simple achene without hairs.*
SIMILAR SPECIES *Scented Mayweed* (Chamomilla recutita); *Sea Mayweed* (Matricaria maritime), *which is coastal.*

Arrowhead

Sagittaria sagittifolia (Alismataceae)

A semi-aquatic plant, Arrowhead has large, arrow-shaped leaves that rise up on long stalks out of the water. It also has smaller, elliptical leaves that float on the surface, and these are the first to appear in spring. The three-petalled flowers, in whorls of three, are white with dark purple centres; male flowers sit above the females.

INHABITS *margins of shallow, freshwater lakes, slow-moving rivers and streams, and ditches.*

long-lobed leaf

PERENNIAL

white flowers with purple anthers

unbranched stem

3 petals

PLANT HEIGHT *60–100cm.*
FLOWER SIZE *2–2.5cm wide.*
FLOWERING TIME *July–August.*
LEAVES *Basal, arrow-shaped; smaller, elliptical leaves on water surface.*
FRUIT *Round, knobbly, bur-like achene.*
SIMILAR SPECIES *Water-plantain (right), which has smaller flowers.*

Water-plantain

Alisma plantago-aquatica (Alismataceae)

This plant forms a large tuft of spear-shaped leaves at the edges of standing water, and these are often more obvious than the small flowers borne on the tall, widely branching stems. Each flower has three white petals, which may have a pinkish tinge, and numerous yellow anthers. Each flower lasts for a day and only opens in the afternoon.

FOUND *in ponds, streams, lakes, marshes, and rivers, in the water or in mud at the water's edge.*

PERENNIAL

untoothed margin

long-stalked flowers

white or pinkish petals

flowers in whorls

PLANT HEIGHT *30–100cm.*
FLOWER SIZE *6–10mm wide.*
FLOWERING TIME *June–August.*
LEAVES *Basal and elliptical to oval, long-stalked, with a pointed tip.*
FRUIT *Tight cluster of in-curved achenes.*
SIMILAR SPECIES *Arrowhead (left); Flowering Rush (p.230).*

Frogbit

Hydrocharis morsus-ranae (Hydrocharitaceae)

Floating on the water surface, this pretty plant looks like a miniature water-lily. Each leaf is rounded, with a heart-shaped base, often with a bronze tinge. The flowers have three white petals and a yellow centre and the male and female flowers are borne on separate plants. Frogbit spreads by means of long runners under the water, rooting at intervals.

GROWS *in unpolluted, slow-moving water of ditches, ponds, lakes, and canals.*

PERENNIAL

rounded leaves

curved veins on leaf

wrinkled petals

white flowers with yellow centres

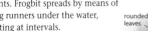

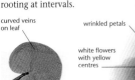

PLANT HEIGHT *Water surface.*
FLOWER SIZE *1.8–2cm wide.*
FLOWERING TIME *June–August.*
LEAVES *In whorls from runners, rounded with heart-shaped base; often tinged bronze.*
FRUIT *Small capsule.*
SIMILAR SPECIES *Marsh Pennywort (p.25), which has similar leaves, but is not aquatic.*

St Bernard's Lily

Anthericum liliago (Liliaceae)

This attractive plant is easily recognized by its delicate, six-petalled, glistening white flowers borne in racemes up the stem. On close inspection, the large yellow anthers are prominent, and the style in the centre is curved upwards. The basal leaves are linear and grass-like, each tapering to a fine point.

PREFERS *well-drained sites such as grassy slopes, mountainsides, and meadows, on lime-rich soil.*

PERENNIAL

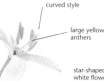

curved style

large yellow anthers

grass-like leaf

star-shaped white flowers

PLANT HEIGHT *30–70cm.*
FLOWER SIZE *2–3.5cm wide.*
FLOWERING TIME *May–July.*
LEAVES *Basal, linear.*
FRUIT *Three-parted, many-seeded capsule.*
SIMILAR SPECIES *Star-of-Bethlehem (p.96), which has larger flowers; A. ramosum has a straight, not curved, style.*

Lily-of-the-Valley

Convallaria majalis (Liliaceae)

Although the leaves of this plant are simple in shape, they are distinctive when seen in pairs along the woodland floor. The small, fragrant white flowers are like little bells, borne in a loose raceme on one side of the stalk, and develop into poisonous red berries. The plant spreads by means of underground runners.

FORMS *patches in dry woodland, mountain meadows, and on limestone pavements. Grown in gardens and escapes from cultivation.*

PERENNIAL

bell-shaped flowers

leaves in pairs

elliptical leaves

one-sided raceme of flowers

deep green leaves

pendent red berries

PLANT HEIGHT *15–25cm.*
FLOWER SIZE *5–8mm long.*
FLOWERING TIME *May–June.*
LEAVES *Basal in pairs, elliptical and untoothed.*
FRUIT *Pendent, poisonous red berries.*
SIMILAR SPECIES *Ramsons (right); Common Wintergreen (p.74); May Lily (p.96).*

Ramsons

Allium ursinum (Liliaceae)

Woodland floors can be entirely carpeted with this vigorous plant in spring, to the exclusion of all other plants, and the scent of garlic may be overpowering when a colony of Ramsons is in full bloom. There are two or three bright green leaves, each broadly elliptical and rising directly from the bulb below the ground. They have a mild taste of garlic and may be used in salads. Each cluster of up to 25 six-petalled, starry flowers is enclosed within two papery spathes before it opens out.

GROWS *in extensive colonies in deciduous woodland, scrub, coppices, shaded banks, and hedgerows. Prefers damp sites on rich soil.*

PERENNIAL

umbels of 6-petalled white flowers

widely spreading petals

NOTE

The juice from the onion-like bulb has been used to treat rheumatic pain and as a slimming aid.

pointed tip

bright green leaf

2 spathes enclose buds

broadly elliptical leaves

PLANT HEIGHT *30–45cm.*
FLOWER SIZE *1.2–2cm wide.*
FLOWERING TIME *April–June.*
LEAVES *Basal, growing directly from the underground bulb; broadly elliptical; bright green.*
FRUIT *Small, three-parted capsule, containing numerous black seeds.*
SIMILAR SPECIES *Lily-of-the-Valley (left), which has diminutive flowers borne in racemes.*

Solomon's-seal

Polygonatum multiflorum (Liliaceae)

This plant has leaves arranged alternately, in two rows on either side of the long, arching, round stems. Each leaf is oval and pointed, with distinct parallel veins, and the margin is untoothed. Hanging in small clusters of 1–6 from the leaf axils, the nodding, unscented, green-tipped white flowers are like elongated bells. The fruit persists on the plant into autumn.

GROWS *in shady places in ancient woodland and along hedgerows, on chalky soil.*

PERENNIAL

alternate leaves
in two rows

narrow, bell-shaped
flowers

round
black
berries

long
stem

PLANT HEIGHT *40–70cm.*
FLOWER SIZE *1–2cm long.*
FLOWERING TIME *May–June.*
LEAVES *Alternate, oval, pointed.*
FRUIT *Black berry with bluish bloom, 1cm wide.*
SIMILAR SPECIES *Angular Solomon's-seal (P. odoratum) has larger, scented flowers.*

Bog Arum

Calla palustris (Araceae)

This aquatic plant is recognized by the broad, pure white bract (spathe) that sits behind the short column of true flowers (spadix), without hiding it. The tiny flowers themselves are yellow-green, later forming a spike of bright red berries. The long-stalked leaves are oval, with heart-shaped bases.

FOUND *in marshes, swamps, and margins of lakes and ponds, often seen growing among sphagnum or other mosses.*

bright red
berries

PERENNIAL

shiny, bright
green leaves

broad, pure
white spathe

PLANT HEIGHT *Up to 30cm.*
FLOWER SIZE *Spadix 2–3cm long.*
FLOWERING TIME *June–August.*
LEAVES *Basal, oval, up to 12cm long.*
FRUIT *Red berries, 5mm wide, in a clustered spike.*
SIMILAR SPECIES *Lords and Ladies (p.32), which is larger, with a green spathe.*

Summer Snowflake

Leucojum aestivum (Amaryllidaceae)

The daffodil-like leaves of Summer Snowflake are tall, strap-shaped, and dark green. The flower stalk (scape) unfurls to reveal 3–6 bell-shaped flowers, each having six white petals with a green spot at the tip. Spring Snowflake is similar but has solitary or paired flowers that open in early spring.

INHABITS *moist places close to rivers and streams, marshes, wet meadows, and damp woodland. Grown in gardens and frequently naturalized.*

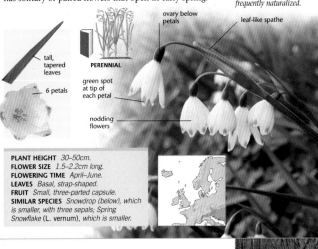

ovary below petals

leaf-like spathe

tall, tapered leaves

PERENNIAL

green spot at tip of each petal

6 petals

nodding flowers

PLANT HEIGHT *30–50cm.*
FLOWER SIZE *1.5–2.2cm long.*
FLOWERING TIME *April–June.*
LEAVES *Basal, strap-shaped.*
FRUIT *Small, three-parted capsule.*
SIMILAR SPECIES *Snowdrop (below), which is smaller, with three sepals; Spring Snowflake (L. vernum), which is smaller.*

Snowdrop

Galanthus nivalis (Amaryllidaceae)

Among the earliest of plants to flower, the Snowdrop first pushes its two slender grey-green leaves up through the bare earth, and these are closely followed by the flower stalks. Each bears a solitary white flower with three spreading sepals, and three much shorter notched petals streaked green on the inside. Leaves continue to grow from the bulbs after flowering.

FORMS *patches in scrub, woodland, and shady meadows, and on banks. Cultivated and naturalized.*

nodding flower

PERENNIAL

3 white sepals

3 shorter petals

double flower

green streaks

strap-shaped leaves

clump-forming habit

PLANT HEIGHT *10–20cm.*
FLOWER SIZE *1.5–2cm long.*
FLOWERING TIME *January–March.*
LEAVES *Basal, strap-shaped.*
FRUIT *Small, three-parted capsule.*
SIMILAR SPECIES *Summer Snowflake (above); Spring Snowflake (Leucojum vernum), which has six green-tipped petals.*

May Lily

Maianthemum bifolium (Liliaceae)

A delicately flowered woodland plant, May Lily is recognizable by its two alternate, broad, heart-shaped leaves halfway up the single, unbranched stem, although only one leaf is produced in the first year. The white flowers are loosely clustered into spikes. Each flower has four pointed petals and four prominent stamens, and later develops into a red berry.

FORMS *carpets in coniferous as well as deciduous woodland; prefers humus-rich soil.*

PERENNIAL

spike of up to 20 flowers

heart-shaped leaves

shiny red berry

PLANT HEIGHT *15–20cm.*
FLOWER SIZE *2–5mm wide.*
FLOWERING TIME *May–June.*
LEAVES *Alternate, heart-shaped, usually two, halfway up stem.*
FRUIT *Red berry, 5mm wide.*
SIMILAR SPECIES *Lily-of-the-Valley (p.92), which has bell-shaped flowers.*

Star-of-Bethlehem

Ornithogalum umbellatum (Liliaceae)

This plant has loose clusters of starry white flowers. The petals have a green stripe on the outside that is clearly visible, except in sunshine when the flowers open fully. Each flower, with its six prominent anthers, appears flat-topped, like an umbel. The leaves have a pale central stripe.

INHABITS *grassy places, woodland glades, meadows, roadsides, scrub, and wasteland.*

yellow anthers

long, narrow leaves

grass-like leaf

6-petalled flower

PERENNIAL

green stripe on petal

PLANT HEIGHT *15–30cm.*
FLOWER SIZE *3–4cm wide.*
FLOWERING TIME *April–June.*
LEAVES *Basal, linear, with pale stripe, limp and floppy.*
FRUIT *Three-parted capsule with numerous seeds.*
SIMILAR SPECIES *St Bernard's Lily (p.92).*

Marsh Helleborine

Epipactis palustris (Orchidaceae)

The subtle colouring of this orchid's flowers is best
appreciated when seen close-up. Each flower has three
white petals, flushed and striped with pink. The lower
petal of each flower has a yellow blotch and a frilly
margin; it is longer than the other petals, and shaped with
a constricted waist. The three erect, spreading sepals are
green but often tinted strongly with red. The 3–8 alternate
leaves are spear- or lance-shaped and
decrease in size up the stem. This plant
is declining, especially inland, due
to the destruction of its habitat
by land drainage and water
pollution, but it may respond
well to conservation attempts.

GROWS *in colonies in
wet places such as
marshes, fens, and
dune slacks. Prefers
chalky soil.*

PERENNIAL

frilly-edged
petals

flowers in
loose spike

NOTE

*Like many orchids,
this helleborine has
a complex life-cycle
and takes many
years to reach
flowering maturity.
Many orchids
require particular
help from soil fungi
in order to thrive.*

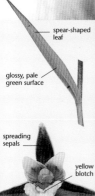

spear-shaped
leaf

glossy, pale
green surface

spreading
sepals

yellow
blotch

PLANT HEIGHT *30–50cm.*
FLOWER SIZE *Lower lip 1–2cm long.*
FLOWERING TIME *July–August.*
LEAVES *Alternate, spear- or lance-shaped.*
FRUIT *Three-parted, pendent capsule.*
SIMILAR SPECIES *Red Helleborine (p.184), which has dark
pink flowers; Broad-leaved Helleborine (p.234), which has much
broader leaves.*

Lesser Butterfly Orchid

Platanthera bifolia (Orchidaceae)

GROWS *in various habitats such as bogs, heaths, pastures, woodland margins and clearings; on a variety of soils.*

This attractive orchid has just two oblong, shiny leaves arising from the base. It produces a stout spike, with a few scale-like leaves, bearing vanilla-scented, creamy or greenish white flowers. The outer sepals are thinly triangular, but most noticeable is the very long, thin, unlobed lower lip, increasingly green towards the tip, with a very long, slender spur behind. The two small yellow anthers are parallel to each other. The Greater Butterfly Orchid is larger, more strongly vanilla-scented, and has anthers that diverge.

butterfly-like flower

slender unlobed lip

PERENNIAL

narrow basal leaf

small anthers

NOTE

Many orchids, such as Lesser Butterfly Orchid, have a vanilla-like fragrance. The seed pod of a tropical orchid, carefully cured to intensify the flavour, is the vanilla pod used in cooking. The scent attracts night-flying moths, which pollinate the flowers.

PLANT HEIGHT *30–45cm.*
FLOWER SIZE *Lower lip 6–12mm long; spur 2.5–3cm.*
FLOWERING TIME *May–July.*
LEAVES *Basal, oblong.*
FRUIT *Capsule containing many tiny seeds.*
SIMILAR SPECIES *Greater Butterfly Orchid (P. chlorantha), which is larger in all parts and the flowers have a stronger, richer fragrance. It occurs mostly on alkaline soils.*

Narrow-leaved Helleborine

Cephalanthera longifolia (Orchidaceae)

Borne in slender, loose racemes, the large, pure white flowers of this orchid show up brightly in the dim light of woodland shade. Both the sepals and petals are fairly long and pointed, although the lower lip is shorter and bears orange markings. The alternate leaves are long, narrow, and taper towards the tip.

FOUND in woodland, often of beech, and other shady sites. Prefers chalky soil.

flowers borne in spikes

short flower stalk

tapered leaf

orange inside lip

PERENNIAL

PLANT HEIGHT 40–60cm.
FLOWER SIZE Lower lip 1–1.6cm long.
FLOWERING TIME May–June.
LEAVES Alternate; lance-shaped to linear, and tapered; dark green.
FRUIT Capsule containing many tiny seeds.
SIMILAR SPECIES White Helleborine (C. damasonium), which has broader leaves.

Autumn Lady's-tresses

Spiranthes spiralis (Orchidaceae)

This small orchid is difficult to spot even in short grassland, but once seen is easily recognized. Numerous tiny flowers, each with a frilly-margined lower lip, are borne in a spiral up the spike. The greyish green leaves, in a basal rosette, wither by flowering time, but the following year's rosette is often present next to the flowering spike.

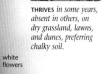

THRIVES in some years, absent in others, on dry grassland, lawns, and dunes, preferring chalky soil.

white flowers

flower spike

oval, fleshy leaf

yellowish lower lip

PERENNIAL

PLANT HEIGHT 8–15cm.
FLOWER SIZE 4–6mm long.
FLOWERING TIME August–September.
LEAVES Basal rosette, scale leaves on stem.
FRUIT Capsule containing many tiny seeds.
SIMILAR SPECIES Creeping Lady's-tresses (Goodyera repens), which has fewer flowers in a less obvious spiral.

Yellow-Brown

Flowers with yellow petals, such as the Fringed Water-lily below, seem to be particularly attractive to pollinating insects, including flies, beetles, butterflies, and bees. Studies have also shown that many bees are able to detect ultraviolet light and that yellow flowers, such as Tutsan, are among those that reflect it. Some plants even exhibit darker lines in this part of the spectrum that guide bees to the pollen at the centre of the flower. Brown flowers are much less conspicuous, relying on scent to attract insects or, as in the case of Reed Mace, wind pollination.

HENBANE   LADY'S SLIPPER   COMMON BIRD'S-FOOT   TUTSAN
                                              TREFOIL

Yellow Water-lily

Nuphar lutea (Nymphaeaceae)

This robust, aquatic plant has the largest leaves of any water-lily in the region, and can cover large expanses of water. The solitary, spherical, deep yellow flowers are small in comparison, and are always held slightly above the water on thick stalks. Each flower has five or six large, overlapping, concave sepals and several smaller, narrower yellow petals, which never open fully to reveal the numerous curved stamens. They go on to form green fruit, shaped like a flask, each with a flat cap marked by prominent stigma rays. The leaves are of two kinds. The thick, leathery floating leaves are oval, deeply cleft, and more pointed than those of other water-lilies, while the submerged leaves are thin and translucent, rounded, and short-stalked. Both arise from thick, woody rhizomes buried in underwater mud.

GROWS *abundantly in freshwater lakes, ponds, dykes, and slow-moving streams and rivers, often in water up to 5m in depth.*

flask-shaped green seed capsule

curved stamens

PERENNIAL

NOTE

The flowers of Yellow Water-lily attract pollinating flies by producing a strong scent of stale alcohol. The green fruit capsule, coincidentally, has a shape that bears a resemblance to a brandy bottle.

flower raised above water surface

oval floating leaves

PLANT HEIGHT *Water surface.*
FLOWER SIZE *4–6cm wide.*
FLOWERING TIME *June–August.*
LEAVES *Basal, arising from rhizomes; floating leaves oval, thick and leathery, submerged leaves rounded, thin, and translucent.*
FRUIT *Flask-shaped fruit capsule.*
SIMILAR SPECIES *White Water-lily (p.43) has larger flowers; Fringed Water-lily (p.135) has smaller leaves and fringed petals that open fully.*

Marsh Marigold

Caltha palustris (Ranunculaceae)

THRIVES *in damp places in the open or in shade, forming clumps and small colonies in marshes, bogs, stream margins, and wet woodland.*

The bright golden yellow flowers of this huge buttercup are a striking and unmistakable feature of damp places in early spring. Each flower is composed of five brightly coloured sepals, opening at daybreak to expose up to a hundred stamens. The glossy green leaves are heart-shaped with toothed margins, mostly arising from the base but occasionally rooting at the nodes to form a new clump. The stem leaves are smaller and almost stalkless. In common with many other members of the buttercup family, the whole plant is poisonous.

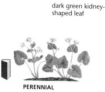

PERENNIAL

dark green kidney-shaped leaf

long leaf stalk

large, bright yellow flowers

numerous stamens

5 yellow sepals

NOTE

The scientific name – Caltha palustris – of Marsh Marigold comes from the Greek calathos, which means "cup-shaped", referring to the appearance of the flowers. Palustris is from the Latin palus, which means "marsh". Double-flowered forms of this plant are often grown in gardens.

PLANT HEIGHT *30–60cm.*
FLOWER SIZE *2.5–5cm wide.*
FLOWERING TIME *March–June.*
LEAVES *Mostly basal, heart- or kidney-shaped, with finely toothed margins; glossy green; stem leaves almost stalkless.*
FRUIT *Cluster of pod-like follicles, each containing several seeds.*
SIMILAR SPECIES *Globeflower (right), which has spherical flowers and divided leaves. Other buttercups have smaller flowers.*

Globeflower

Trollius europaeus (Ranunculaceae)

A member of the buttercup family, Globeflower owes its distinctive spherical shape to the incurved form of its many lemon-yellow sepals. The whole plant is robust, the flower stems rising above the basal leaves, which are lobed into five or seven coarsely toothed segments. Smaller in size, the stem leaves may be stalkless. The whole plant is poisonous.

FORMS *colonies in damp open grassland, often among rocks or close to streams.*

palmately divided leaves

single flower on long stalk

rounded flowers

PERENNIAL

curved sepals

PLANT HEIGHT *40–70cm.*
FLOWER SIZE *3–5cm wide.*
FLOWERING TIME *May–August.*
LEAVES *Mostly basal, palmately lobed, coarsely toothed; smaller stem leaves.*
FRUIT *Many-seeded follicles.*
SIMILAR SPECIES *Marsh Marigold (left) has open flowers and kidney-shaped leaves.*

Common Meadow-rue

Thalictrum flavum (Ranunculaceae)

The flowers of this plant appear to consist almost entirely of numerous creamy yellow stamens, although there are four tiny sepals. The leaves are divided into distinctive, dark greyish green leaflets, each one usually bearing three points. The leaves are difficult to spot among vegetation but the tall, bright flowerheads are very noticeable.

FOUND *in damp meadows, fens, and flooded areas, usually among other tall vegetation in lowland.*

fluffy flowerhead

flowers on tall stems

PERENNIAL

3-pointed leaflets

long stamens

PLANT HEIGHT *0.6–1.5m.*
FLOWER SIZE *1–1.5cm wide.*
FLOWERING TIME *June–August.*
LEAVES *Alternate, pinnately divided.*
FRUIT *Achenes twisted together.*
SIMILAR SPECIES *Baneberry (p.55) is smaller; Meadowsweet (p.56) has coarser leaves; Great Meadow-rue (p.199).*

Creeping Buttercup

Ranunculus repens (Ranunculaceae)

The creeping surface runners of this plant enable it to rapidly colonize entire fields, which may appear entirely yellow in early summer. The flowers have five bright yellow petals. The leaves are triangular in outline and divided into three coarsely toothed lobes; the middle lobe usually has a short stalk.

THRIVES *in meadows, and other grassy places; on damp soil, forming large colonies.*

numerous stamens

bright yellow flowers

triangular leaf

rounded fruit cluster

PERENNIAL

PLANT HEIGHT *10–50cm.*
FLOWER SIZE *1.5–2.5cm wide.*
FLOWERING TIME *May–September.*
LEAVES *Basal, alternate, three toothed lobes.*
FRUIT *Spherical cluster of hooked achenes.*
SIMILAR SPECIES *Lesser Celandine (right); Meadow Buttercup (R. acris) has finer leaves and no runners.*

Celery-leaved Buttercup

Ranunculus sceleratus (Ranunculaceae)

The small flowers of this plant are distinctive, as the oblong fruiting head of green achenes is already formed when the well-separated yellow petals open. The entire plant has a succulent appearance, with thick, grooved stems often growing out of water. Its lower leaves have rounded lobes with rounded teeth, while the upper leaves are much narrower and untoothed.

INHABITS *marshes, ditches, pond and lake margins, wet tracks, and woodland rides.*

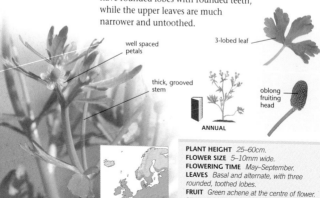

well spaced petals

3-lobed leaf

thick, grooved stem

oblong fruiting head

ANNUAL

PLANT HEIGHT *25–60cm.*
FLOWER SIZE *5–10mm wide.*
FLOWERING TIME *May–September.*
LEAVES *Basal and alternate, with three rounded, toothed lobes.*
FRUIT *Green achene at the centre of flower.*
SIMILAR SPECIES *Lesser Spearwort (right), which has yellow centres to flowers.*

Lesser Spearwort

Ranunculus flammula (Ranunculaceae)

This common buttercup has narrow, spear-shaped leaves in twos or threes. The long-stemmed basal leaves may be broader. Its flowers are in loosely branched clusters, and its stems, which run along the ground and root at intervals, are often reddish.

loose clusters of flowers

FORMS *colonies in wet meadows, marshes, or pond margins, often in mountainous areas in the south of its range.*

PERENNIAL

reddish stems

untoothed leaf

5 petals

PLANT HEIGHT *10–50cm.*
FLOWER SIZE *1–2cm wide.*
FLOWERING TIME *May–September.*
LEAVES *Alternate, spear-shaped, untoothed.*
FRUIT *Spherical achene.*
SIMILAR SPECIES *Celery-leaved Buttercup (left); Greater Spearwort (p.106), which has larger flowers and fleshier leaves and stems.*

Lesser Celandine

Ranunculus ficaria (Ranunculaceae)

This is the first of the buttercups to appear in spring, and its flowers are easy to recognize with their three green sepals and up to 12 golden yellow petals, which open fully only in bright sunshine. Sometimes, the petals fade to white as they age. The leaves are heart-shaped, deeply cleft, and with blunt tips. Dark glossy green, they are often mottled with purplish or pale markings.

GROWS *in moderately damp, open places, preferring the partial shade of deciduous woodland and hedgerows.*

PERENNIAL

blunt leaf tip

glossy surface

green fruiting head

8–12 narrow petals

PLANT HEIGHT *7–20cm.*
FLOWER SIZE *2–3cm wide.*
FLOWERING TIME *March–May.*
LEAVES *Mostly basal, heart-shaped.*
FRUIT *Rounded head of achenes.*
SIMILAR SPECIES *Creeping Buttercup (left) and other members of the buttercup family, which have divided leaves.*

Greater Spearwort

Ranunculus lingua (Ranunculaceae)

Although this member of the buttercup family shares many characteristics with Lesser Spearwort (p.105), it is quite distinct. Its tall stems are erect and fleshy, and the spear-shaped grey-green leaves, much broader than those of its relative, are often thick and leathery. The flowers have five broad, rather rounded yellow petals and are strikingly large. Greater Spearwort has a fairly localized distribution, often growing among taller plants emerging from shallow water. Its attractive appearance makes it a favourite plant for use in garden ponds.

INHABITS *streams, ditches, marshes, fens, and pond margins. Often in shallow water among taller plants, on neutral or chalky soils.*

PERENNIAL

NOTE

Many buttercups contain an acrid sap which is a skin irritant. At one time it was used by beggars to keep sores open in order to gain sympathy.

large flowers

thick, fleshy stems

spear-shaped grey-green leaf

5-petalled flower

PLANT HEIGHT *80–150cm.*
FLOWER SIZE *3–5cm wide.*
FLOWERING TIME *June–September.*
LEAVES *Alternate, broadly lance-shaped, untoothed, leathery; grey-green.*
FRUIT *Spherical cluster of achenes.*
SIMILAR SPECIES *Lesser Spearwort (p.105), which is smaller in all respects and less robust, with reddish stems.*

Welsh Poppy

Meconopsis cambrica (Papaveraceae)

The four rounded, tissue-thin petals of this plant's poppy-like flowers open orange-yellow but soon fade to bright lemon-yellow. Each bloom is borne on a slender stem with two hairy sepals that fall when the flower opens, and goes on to form a ribbed fruit capsule. The leaves are often pale yellow-green and pinnately divided into five toothed lobes.

FOUND *in moist, semi-shaded, rocky places, old walls, and upland woods. Commonly cultivated in gardens, from which it frequently escapes.*

BIENNIAL/PERENNIAL

numerous stamens

pale green leaves

four orange-yellow petals

PLANT HEIGHT *40–60cm.*
FLOWER SIZE *4–8cm wide.*
FLOWERING TIME *June–August.*
LEAVES *Alternate, pinnately divided; pale yellow-green.*
FRUIT *Erect capsule with many seeds.*
SIMILAR SPECIES *Greater Celandine (p.108), which has similar leaves but smaller flowers.*

Yellow Horned Poppy

Glaucium flavum (Papaveraceae)

This distinctive and colourful beach flower is easily recognized by its fleshy, grey-green leaves, which are pinnately divided into coarse, toothed segments with an undulating surface. The large, bright yellow flowers have four tissue-like petals and the very unusual fruit is a narrow, elongated capsule.

OCCURS *on shingle or sandy beaches, dunes, sea-cliffs, and very occasionally on waste ground inland.*

overlapping petals

grey-green leaves

large yellow flowers

long, slender capsule

PLANT HEIGHT *50–90cm.*
FLOWER SIZE *6–9cm wide.*
LEAVES *Alternate, pinnately divided.*
FRUIT *Elongated capsule, up to 30cm long.*
FLOWERING TIME *June–September.*
SIMILAR SPECIES *None (its large flowers and coastal habitat prevent confusion with other species).*

BIENNIAL/PERENNIAL

Greater Celandine

Chelidonium majus (Papaveraceae)

An unusual member of the poppy family, this plant has small flowers with four well-separated yellow petals, numerous yellow stamens, and a prominent style in the centre. The same plant may produce flowers for several months and flowering is said to coincide with the presence of swallows in Europe (*chelidon* is Greek for swallow). The leaves are pale green, with very rounded lobes. Ants are attracted to the oily seeds and often unwittingly carry them off stuck to their bodies.

GROWS *in semi-shaded places such as hedgerows, alongside walls, rocky places, and wasteland, often close to habitation.*

NOTE

The brittle stems exude a caustic orange sap, which has been used historically to treat warts and, even less wisely, sore eyes. Do not attempt.

PERENNIAL

4 separated petals

numerous stamens

slender fruit capsule

pinnate leaves

PLANT HEIGHT *40–90cm.*
FLOWER SIZE *1.5–2.5cm long.*
FLOWERING TIME *April–October.*
LEAVES *Alternate; pinnate with rounded lobes.*
FRUIT *Linear-oblong, hairless capsule, splitting to release seeds.*
SIMILAR SPECIES *Welsh Poppy (p.107), which has larger flowers; yellow members of the cabbage family have fewer stamens and different leaf shapes.*

Climbing Corydalis

Ceratocapnos claviculata (Fumariaceae)

This delicate, climbing plant is easily missed as it scrambles over other vegetation. Borne on thin, twining red stems, the small, almost lace-like leaves are divided into three or more oval leaflets and end in branched tendrils. The tiny, two-lipped flowers, have a complex tubular shape.

CLIMBS *over other vegetation or on the ground in the shade, on acid or peaty soils.*

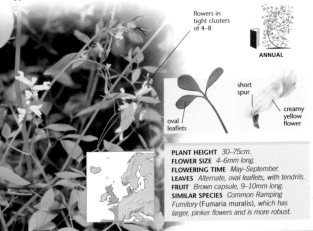

flowers in tight clusters of 4–8

ANNUAL

oval leaflets

short spur

creamy yellow flower

PLANT HEIGHT *30–75cm.*
FLOWER SIZE *4–6mm long.*
FLOWERING TIME *May–September.*
LEAVES *Alternate, oval leaflets, with tendrils.*
FRUIT *Brown capsule, 9–10mm long.*
SIMILAR SPECIES *Common Ramping Fumitory (Fumaria muralis), which has larger, pinker flowers and is more robust.*

Yellow Corydalis

Pseudofumaria lutea (Fumariaceae)

Although originally from the Alps, this plant is now naturalized throughout much of Europe. The golden yellow flowers with two outer lips are borne in one-sided spikes, and the whole plant may continue to flower for many months. The delicate leaves are pinnately divided, each leaflet with three rounded lobes.

CLINGS *to limestone rocks in native habitat. Also found on moist, shady old walls in towns and gardens.*

pinnate leaves

up to 16 flowers in spike

bright yellow flowers

PERENNIAL

pendent capsule

PLANT HEIGHT *15–30cm.*
FLOWER SIZE *1.2–2cm long.*
FLOWERING TIME *May–October.*
LEAVES *Alternate, pinnately divided, leaflets with three lobes.*
FRUIT *Pendent capsule, 1–1.2cm long, containing black seeds.*
SIMILAR SPECIES *None.*

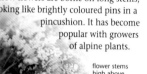

Yellow Whitlow-grass

Draba aizoides (Brassicaceae)

FORMS *tight cushions on mountain rocks, cliffs, and screes, and sometimes old walls. Prefers chalky soil.*

This attractive member of the cabbage family forms tufts of linear, deep green leaves, each in a tight rosette and edged with stiff bristles. The clusters of four-petalled yellow flowers are borne on long stems, looking like brightly coloured pins in a pincushion. It has become popular with growers of alpine plants.

PERENNIAL

tapered seed pod

flower stems high above leaf rosettes

dense clusters of flowers

4 yellow petals

PLANT HEIGHT *5–15cm.*
FLOWER SIZE *5–7mm wide.*
FLOWERING TIME *March–May.*
LEAVES *Basal, linear to lance-shaped.*
FRUIT *Silicula, oval to elliptical.*
SIMILAR SPECIES *Alpine Whitlow-grass (D. alpina) of Norway and Iceland, which has broader leaves.*

Hedge Mustard

Sisymbrium officinale (Brassicaceae)

A common and coarse-looking weed of wasteland, Hedge Mustard is notable for its clusters of tiny yellow flowers at the end of long, branched stems that elongate further as the fruit develop. The fruit is pressed close to the stem. The lower leaves are divided into jagged lobes, the points of which turn back towards the stem; the upper leaves are narrower.

PROLIFERATES *on bare ground, wasteland, in margins of arable fields, and on roadsides, often with poppies.*

ANNUAL/BIENNIAL

clusters of yellow flowers

jagged leaves

triangular leaf lobe

unnotched petals

slender seed pods

PLANT HEIGHT *40–90cm.*
FLOWER SIZE *3–4mm wide.*
FLOWERING TIME *May–September.*
LEAVES *Alternate; pinnately divided, stalked lower leaves, narrow, stalkless upper leaves.*
FRUIT *Siliqua, 1–2cm long.*
SIMILAR SPECIES *Wintercress (right), which has larger flowers.*

Wallflower

Erysimum cheiri (Brassicaceae)

Originally from southeast Europe, the Wallflower is now frequently used as a garden plant in many other regions. It has tufts of narrowly lance-shaped, hairy leaves on branched stems that often become woody near the bases. The large and fragrant flowers range from orange-yellow to golden brown. Some garden escapes have white or purple flowers.

CLINGS to cliffs, old walls, monuments, and rocky places, often close to the sea.

golden yellow flowers

4-petalled flowers

narrow, hairy leaves

long, slender seed pod

PERENNIAL

PLANT HEIGHT *30–60cm.*
FLOWER SIZE *2–2.5cm wide.*
FLOWERING TIME *March–June.*
LEAVES *Alternate, lance-shaped, hairy, with a short stalk.*
FRUIT *Siliqua, 7.5cm long.*
SIMILAR SPECIES *Wild Cabbage (p.112), which has a woody stem and larger leaves.*

Wintercress

Barbarea vulgaris (Brassicaceae)

The four-petalled yellow flowers of Wintercress brighten the banks of streams and damp ditches in spring. They are clustered at the top of the stems, which elongate as the long seed pods develop beneath. The lower leaves, which are a rich source of vitamin C, have a large terminal lobe each, while the unlobed upper leaves clasp the stem.

GROWS close to ditches, ponds, and streams, alongside roads, and in wet places in disturbed soil.

pinnately lobed lower leaves

branched stems

small yellow flowers

BIENNIAL/PERENNIAL

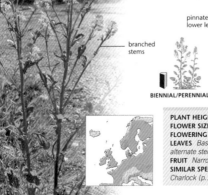

PLANT HEIGHT *30–90cm.*
FLOWER SIZE *7–9mm wide.*
FLOWERING TIME *May–August.*
LEAVES *Basal leaves, lobed and stalked; alternate stem leaves, unstalked, toothed.*
FRUIT *Narrow siliqua, 1.5–3cm long.*
SIMILAR SPECIES *Hedge Mustard (left); Charlock (p.113), which has broader leaves.*

Wild Cabbage

Brassica oleracea (Brassicaceae)

GROWS *at the top of sea-cliffs and rocky maritime places, particularly on thin, chalky soil.*

BIENNIAL/PERENNIAL

A large number of cultivated vegetables are derived from this rather rare, robust, and hairless plant of coastal cliffs. Wild Cabbage leaves are indeed cabbage-like – thick, fleshy, and grey-green in colour, with a thick midrib, the basal leaves somewhat pinnate with small lobes. The stout woody stem base bears the scars of former leaf attachments, and the large four-petalled yellow flowers are borne in long branched spikes. Shaped like a long, cylindrical pod, the fruit is rather fleshy.

prominent upright
flower stems

long-branched
flower spikes

4-petalled
flowers

thick,
fleshy leaf

PLANT HEIGHT *60–120cm.*
FLOWER SIZE *3–4cm wide.*
FLOWERING TIME *May–September.*
LEAVES *Basal leaves fleshy and lobed, upper leaves unlobed and clasping the stem; grey-green.*
FRUIT *Long, fleshy siliqua, 5–7cm long.*
SIMILAR SPECIES *Rape (right) has less fleshy leaves; Sea Kale (p.51) has white flowers; Wallflower (p.111) has smaller leaves.*

Rape

Brassica napus (Brassicaceae)

Frequently grown as a crop for its oil, this is a tall plant. Its large yellow flowers are usually overtopped slightly by unopened buds, with long seed pods on the elongated stems beneath. The leaves are greyish green with very wavy margins and a pale midrib, the lower ones stalked and lobed, the upper unstalked and clasping the stem.

NATURALIZES *on cultivated land, field margins, roadsides, bare and waste ground, usually close to farmland.*

4-petalled yellow flowers

elongated stems

rounded lobes

slender seed pod

ANNUAL/BIENNIAL

PLANT HEIGHT *50–150cm.*
FLOWER SIZE *1.5–2.5cm wide.*
FLOWERING TIME *May–Aug.*
LEAVES *Basal leaves stalked and lobed, stem leaves alternate and unstalked.*
FRUIT *Cylindrical siliqua, 5–10cm long.*
SIMILAR SPECIES *Wild Cabbage (left); Charlock (below) has less lobed leaves.*

Charlock

Sinapis arvensis (Brassicaceae)

One of the commonest yellow crucifers, which used to be a serious arable pest, this plant is rather bristly, with coarsely toothed, lyre-shaped basal leaves that have a wrinkled surface. Its upper leaves are narrower, without lobes, and do not clasp the stem. The flowers have four yellow petals, widely separated to reveal the narrow sepals underneath.

APPEARS *on disturbed ground, roadsides and rubbish tips, often on chalky soil.*

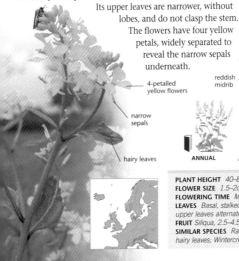

4-petalled yellow flowers

narrow sepals

hairy leaves

reddish midrib

beaked seed pod

ANNUAL

PLANT HEIGHT *40–80cm.*
FLOWER SIZE *1.5–2cm wide.*
FLOWERING TIME *May–October.*
LEAVES *Basal, stalked, coarsely toothed; upper leaves alternate, unstalked, unlobed.*
FRUIT *Siliqua, 2.5–4.5cm long.*
SIMILAR SPECIES *Rape (above) has less hairy leaves; Wintercress (p.111).*

Woad

Isatis tinctoria (Brassicaceae)

APPEARS *in dry and rocky places, on cultivated and waste ground, on dry soil.*

This robust plant was once cultivated for the blue dye that its greyish leaves yield. The stiff, sparsely leaved stems branch towards the top where they form large heads of four-petalled yellow flowers. The fruit, which look like a row of tear-drops, ripen from green to brown.

dense, yellow flowerheads

lance-shaped leaf

BIENNIAL

pendent row of fruit

PLANT HEIGHT *80–150cm.*
FLOWER SIZE *3–4mm wide.*
FLOWERING TIME *July–August.*
LEAVES *Alternate, lance-shaped, untoothed, clasping the stem; some stalked basal leaves.*
FRUIT *Pendent silicula, 1.2–2.5cm long.*
SIMILAR SPECIES *Warty Cabbage (Bunias orientalis), which has deeply lobed leaves.*

Weld

Reseda luteola (Resedaceae)

GROWS *on roadsides, field margins, waste or arable land, or grassy places, on chalky soil.*

An easy plant to identify even at a distance, Weld has tall, thin flowering spikes. These are often branched towards the top, and are clothed in hundreds of tiny flowers with deeply cut petals, held very close to the stem. The untoothed leaves, simple but with wavy edges, form a rosette in the first year.

flowers in tall spikes

upright stem

BIENNIAL

linear leaf

yellow-green flowers

small fruit capsule

PLANT HEIGHT *80–150cm.*
FLOWER SIZE *4–5mm wide.*
FLOWERING TIME *June–September.*
LEAVES *Basal rosette and alternate, lance-shaped, with wavy edges.*
FRUIT *Open-ended capsule, 3–4mm long.*
SIMILAR SPECIES *Wild Mignonette (right) has pinnately divided leaves; Agrimony (p.118).*

Wild Mignonette

Reseda lutea (Resedaceae)

The attractive yellow flowers of this plant have short stalks and deeply notched petals, giving the flowering spike a "fluffy" look, accentuated by its branched, bushy habit. The rough, dark green leaves are pinnately divided into long thin lobes, each with a wavy margin, folding around the midrib. The fruit is an elongated capsule.

OCCURS *on roadsides, embankments, field margins, and dry grassland.*

BIENNIAL/PERENNIAL

flowers in loose spikes

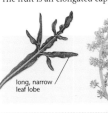

long, narrow leaf lobe

tiny flowers

PLANT HEIGHT *40–80cm.*
FLOWER SIZE *7–9mm wide.*
FLOWERING TIME *May–September.*
LEAVES *Alternate, pinnately and thinly lobed.*
FRUIT *Open-ended, elongated capsule, 7–12mm long.*
SIMILAR SPECIES *Weld (left), which is taller and more upright, with unlobed leaves.*

Biting Stonecrop

Sedum acre (Crassulaceae)

The brilliant yellow flowers of this mat-forming, creeping plant, each with five petals and ten stamens, make a bold impact when seen in its dry, bare habitat. The short, blunt leaves, adapted to hold moisture, are succulent and overlap each other close to the tip, often turning partially or wholly red.

FORMS *mats in dry, stony or sandy places such as old walls, embankments, shingle beaches, and rooftops.*

star-shaped flowers

PERENNIAL

flowers in small clusters

red-tinged leaves

PLANT HEIGHT *4–10cm.*
FLOWER SIZE *1–1.2cm wide.*
FLOWERING TIME *May–July.*
LEAVES *Alternate, succulent, 3–6mm.*
FRUIT *Five follicles in star shape, 4mm long.*
SIMILAR SPECIES *Sea Sandwort (p.36) and White Stonecrop (p.52) have similar leaves; Yellow Saxifrage (p.116) is bushier.*

Roseroot

Rhodiola rosea (Crassulaceae)

Often found on cliffs, Roseroot forms mounded tufts, like giant pincushions of yellow-headed pins. The thick, erect stems arise from a common base, each with many fleshy, reddish-tinged leaves. At the apex of each stem is a cluster of rose-scented, greenish yellow flowers with four petals, many yellow stamens, and purple anthers.

FORMS *cushions on inland and coastal cliffs, mountain slopes, and rocky places.*

fruit in clusters

leaves spiral up the stem

PERENNIAL

tight terminal flower cluster

fleshy oval leaves

PLANT HEIGHT *20–35cm.*
FLOWER SIZE *5–8mm wide.*
FLOWERING TIME *May–July.*
LEAVES *Alternate, fleshy, oval, and toothed.*
FRUIT *Cluster of orange-red follicles.*
SIMILAR SPECIES *Orpine (p.170) is similar when not in flower, but without the clustered habit.*

Yellow Saxifrage

Saxifraga aizoides (Saxifragaceae)

Creating bold splashes of colour in its rocky habitat, this saxifrage has numerous hairy, slightly toothed leaves. Not all stems bear flowers but those that do, bear branched clusters of flowers, each with five bright yellow, sometimes red-spotted petals, with clearly visible sepals in between.

FOUND *in rocky places and marshes, and along mountain streams, from sea level to 3,000m.*

loose, bright yellow flower clusters

narrow, unstalked leaves

PERENNIAL

green sepals

orange anthers

PLANT HEIGHT *10–25cm.*
FLOWER SIZE *5–10mm wide.*
FLOWERING TIME *June–September.*
LEAVES *Alternate, narrowly linear, fleshy and hairy, slightly toothed.*
FRUIT *Two-parted capsule.*
SIMILAR SPECIES *Biting Stonecrop (p.115), which has smaller, succulent leaves.*

Opposite-leaved Golden-saxifrage

Chrysosplenium oppositifolium (Saxifragaceae)

Forming golden-green mats in wet woodland, this short plant hugs the ground, spreading by creeping shoots that root at intervals. It has yellow-green leaves and tiny flowers, with bright yellow stamens, in the upper leaf axils.

GROWS *on damp patches or streamsides, in wet woodland and rocks, in shady places, on slightly acid soil.*

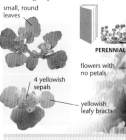

small, round leaves

PERENNIAL

flowers with no petals

4 yellowish sepals

yellowish leafy bracts

PLANT HEIGHT *5–15cm.*
FLOWER SIZE *2–3mm wide.*
FLOWERING TIME *April–July.*
LEAVES *Opposite pairs, bluntly toothed.*
FRUIT *Cup-shaped capsule.*
SIMILAR SPECIES *Alternate-leaved Golden-saxifrage (C. alternifolium), which has alternate leaves that are shinier.*

Herb Bennet

Geum urbanum (Rosaceae)

Although this leafy member of the rose family has branched flower stems, there is never a mass of flowers on display at the same time. Each five-petalled, pale yellow flower is often partnered by the fruithead, with its characteristic hooked spines. The toothed leaves are deeply lobed or divided into leaflets, the stem leaves with a pair of large leaf-like stipules at the base.

PROLIFERATES *in woodland, along hedgerows, roadsides, paths, and other shady places.*

hooked styles of fruithead

rounded petals

numerous stamens

PERENNIAL

coarsely toothed leaflets

cluster of achenes

PLANT HEIGHT *40–70cm.*
FLOWER SIZE *1–1.5cm wide.*
FLOWERING TIME *May–September.*
LEAVES *Basal with pairs of lobed leaflets; stem leaves with three lobes or leaflets.*
FRUIT *Rounded cluster of hairy achenes.*
SIMILAR SPECIES *Water Avens (p.238), which has pendent flowers.*

Agrimony

Agrimonia eupatoria (Rosaceae)

The long, narrow spires of yellow flowers are highly distinctive in this unusual member of the rose family, and particularly conspicuous as they rise above the surrounding vegetation. The leaves are divided into 3–6 toothed leaflets, with smaller leaflets in between. The hooked spines of the calyx that surrounds the fruit readily attach themselves to animal fur, and to trousers and bootlaces, helping to disperse the seeds to new locations. Fragrant Agrimony, a related plant, has scented flowers and sticky leaf undersides. It has a similar distribution but prefers acid soil.

FLOURISHES *in tall grassland, meadows, scrub, and woodland margins, and along hedgerows and road verges.*

NOTE

Extracts of this plant were used in the 15th century to help heal wounds. Modern research indicates that Agrimony does have anti-viral properties.

flowers in long, slender spikes

PERENNIAL

erect stems

divided leaves

tiny leaflets between main leaflets

5 separate petals

up to 20 stamens

PLANT HEIGHT *50–100cm.*
FLOWER SIZE *5–8mm wide.*
FLOWERING TIME *June–August.*
LEAVES *Alternate, pinnate, with 3–6 pairs of toothed leaflets, and smaller intermediate leaflets.*
FRUIT *Cup-shaped and grooved, covered with hooked bristles.*
SIMILAR SPECIES *Weld (p.114), which has smaller, yellowish green flowers; Dark Mullein (p.142), which has much larger flowers.*

Silverweed

Potentilla anserina (Rosaceae)

This creeping plant spreads by means of rooting runners. Its leaves are easily recognized by their ladder-like rows of 15–25 serrated leaflets, grey-green above and covered with fine silvery hairs below. The solitary flowers, which may not grow in some damp habitats, have rounded yellow petals, with an epicalyx behind each solitary flower.

PROLIFERATES *in open places such as farm tracks, grassy verges, waste and cultivated ground.*

bright yellow flower

sharply toothed leaflets

PERENNIAL

5–6 large petals

PLANT HEIGHT *5–20cm.*
FLOWER SIZE *1.5–2cm wide.*
FLOWERING TIME *May–August.*
LEAVES *Basal rosettes, pinnate.*
FRUIT *Tight head of achenes.*
SIMILAR SPECIES *Creeping Cinquefoil (P. reptans) has palmately lobed leaves; Tormentil (below) has four-petalled flowers.*

Tormentil

Potentilla erecta (Rosaceae)

A slender, delicate plant that trails through grassland, Tormentil has long, non-rooting flower stems held up by other vegetation. Its bright lemon-yellow flowers have four petals, notched at the tip, in the shape of a cross. The leaves are three-lobed with bluntly toothed, oval segments; there are two smaller stipules at the base.

FORMS *patches in lawns, meadows, heaths, woodland, and on roadsides, preferring acid soil.*

solitary lemon-yellow flower

slender flower stalk

3-lobed leaf

PERENNIAL

4 petals

PLANT HEIGHT *4–12cm.*
FLOWER SIZE *7–11mm wide.*
FLOWERING TIME *May–September.*
LEAVES *Alternate, three-lobed, toothed.*
FRUIT *Tiny achenes.*
SIMILAR SPECIES *Silverweed (above) has 5–6 petals; Creeping Cinquefoil (P. reptans) has five-lobed leaves.*

Broom

Cytisus scoparius (Fabaceae)

This deciduous shrub has had a long association with people, especially, as its name suggests, in the use of its branches as brooms. The many slender green branches are ridged and angled, producing surprisingly small, virtually stalkless, oval leaves which may be single or in threes. The strongly scented pealike flowers, borne in leafy spikes, are large and brilliant golden yellow, the upper and lower petals opening wide to reveal the curled stamens.

FORMS *single or clumped bushes in dry, sunny places, woodland edges, heaths, hedgerows, grassland, and coastal cliffs, on sandy soil.*

small stalkless leaflets

slender stems

wide open yellow peaflowers

oval leaf

oblong seed pod

PERENNIAL

NOTE

The branches of this shrub were used for making brooms, the buds used as capers, the leaves for flavouring beer, the fibre for making cloth, the bark for tanning leather, and the plant has had a host of medicinal uses. Its fibrous root system is excellent for stabilizing sandy banks, and it is often planted on new motorway embankments.

PLANT HEIGHT *1–2m.*
FLOWER SIZE *1.6–1.8cm long.*
FLOWERING TIME *April–June.*
LEAVES *Alternate, single or trifoliate, mostly stalkless, very small.*
FRUIT *Hairy, oblong pod, black when ripe.*
SIMILAR SPECIES *Gorse (right), which has spiny stems; Dyer's Greenweed (p.122), which is much smaller overall and has smaller flowers.*

Gorse

Ulex europaeus (Fabaceae)

Although viciously spiked on mature plants, when young the branches of Gorse are soft and palatable – so much so that, in rabbit-infested areas, this normally large shrub may grow no more than a few centimetres high. The ridged stems bear tiny, three-lobed, scale-like leaves when the plant is young, but these are soon replaced by a dense covering of grooved spines. The yellow peaflowers may be seen all through the year and are coconut-scented, with an arrangement of stamens that shoot out pollen onto visiting bees. The brown pods expel the seeds explosively when ripe, and may be heard popping open in bright sunshine.

FOUND *in grassy places such as meadows, heaths, woodland margins, or close to the sea. Usually found on light, well-drained soil.*

covering of spines

brown pod

hairy sepals

sharp spines

PERENNIAL

NOTE

Peasants with no available grazing land used to soak and pulp the spiny shoots of Gorse to provide their cattle nutritious fodder during winter.

PLANT HEIGHT *Up to 2m.*
FLOWER SIZE *1.5–2cm long.*
FLOWERING TIME *January–April, but may flower throughout the year.*
LEAVES *Tiny, three-lobed, scale-like when young, soon replaced by alternate, branched spines.*
FRUIT *Hairy brown pod, 1.2–2cm long.*
SIMILAR SPECIES *Broom (left) has smaller, oval leaves and no spines on the stems.*

Dyer's Greenweed

Genista tinctoria (Fabaceae)

OCCURS *in meadows, woodland glades, and open scrub, on roadsides and embankments; often on slightly acid soil.*

This subshrub forms small, compact bushes, resembling miniature versions of Broom (p.120). Its non-spiny branches are sparsely covered with oblong leaves, each with a pair of tiny stipules at the base. The yellow peaflowers, borne on the tops of the stems, open out wide so that the two lower wing petals droop downwards.

flowers in stalked spikes

drooping lower petals

small, simple leaves

narrow seed pod

hairless surface

PERENNIAL

PLANT HEIGHT *30–60cm.*
FLOWER SIZE *8–15mm long.*
FLOWERING TIME *May–July.*
LEAVES *Alternate, oblong, and untoothed.*
FRUIT *Pod, hairless, oblong, brown.*
SIMILAR SPECIES *Broom (p.120), which is larger; Hairy Greenweed (G. pilosa) of upland areas, which has hairy leaves and pods.*

Meadow Vetchling

Lathyrus pratensis (Fabaceae)

CLAMBERS *through meadow grasses and other vegetation, on roadsides, and in scrub and woodland.*

A member of the pea family, Meadow Vetchling clambers and twines its way through tall, grassy vegetation. Its thin stems are slightly winged, and each pair of leaflets is shaped like an arrowhead, with a twisting tendril between them, which helps to support the plant. A tight cluster of bright yellow flowers blooms at the end of a long stem.

single pair of leaflets

5–12 flowers in a cluster

yellow flowers

erect stem

tendril between leaflets

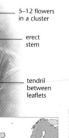

PERENNIAL

PLANT HEIGHT *50–100cm.*
FLOWER SIZE *1–1.6cm long.*
FLOWERING TIME *May–August.*
LEAVES *Alternate, pairs of arrow-shaped leaflets, with tendril between.*
FRUIT *Black pod, 2–4cm long.*
SIMILAR SPECIES *Common Bird's-foot Trefoil (p.124) has looser flowers and trifoliate leaves.*

Ribbed Melilot

Melilotus officinalis (Fabaceae)

As with many other members of the pea family, this plant has leaves divided into three leaflets. Unlike the rest, however, the margins of each oval leaflet are gently toothed as though nibbled away. The tiny peaflowers are arranged in long, branching spikes, giving the plant an untidy look; the seed pods turn brown when ripe.

GROWS *in clumps along roadsides and field edges, on waste or disturbed ground, and building sites.*

alternate leaves

flowers droop from stems

toothed margin

slender flower spikes

BIENNIAL/ PERENNIAL

PLANT HEIGHT *80–150cm.*
FLOWER SIZE *3–4mm wide.*
FLOWERING TIME *July–September.*
LEAVES *Alternate with three oval leaflets, sharply toothed.*
FRUIT *Rounded pod with transverse ridges.*
SIMILAR SPECIES *Tall Melilot (M. altissima), which has hairy black pods.*

Black Medick

Medicago lupulina (Fabaceae)

There are several small, trailing, clover-like species, but Black Medick may easily be identified by its yellow peaflowers and clusters of tiny, coiled seed pods, which become jet-black when ripe. The small yellow flowers are in a crowded, spherical cluster on a long stalk, while the trifoliate leaves have a minute terminal tooth on each leaflet.

SPRAWLS *over grassy places, wasteland, and recently cultivated or disturbed land.*

3 oval leaflets

cluster of 10–20 tiny flowers

ANNUAL

small teeth

coiled black pods

PLANT HEIGHT *10–50cm.*
FLOWER SIZE *Flowerheads 6–10mm wide.*
FLOWERING TIME *May–August.*
LEAVES *Alternate, with three oval leaflets.*
FRUIT *Black pods, 2–3mm long, in clusters.*
SIMILAR SPECIES *Lesser Trefoil (Trifolium dubium), which has tiny fruit; Spotted Medick (M. arabica), which has spotted leaves.*

Hop Trefoil

Trifolium campestre (Fabaceae)

A sprawling, clover-like plant, Hop Trefoil has erect stems bearing tight clusters of untidy peaflowers, which ripen from yellow to pale brown, looking like miniature Hop fruit. The single seed of each flower remains hidden within these persistent clusters. The leaves are trifoliate, with oval, minutely toothed leaflets, the central one with a short stalk.

FLOURISHES *in dry, grassy places and on roadsides and wasteland, in well-drained soil.*

trifoliate leaves

cluster of yellow flowers

erect flower stalks

flower ripens to pale brown

ANNUAL

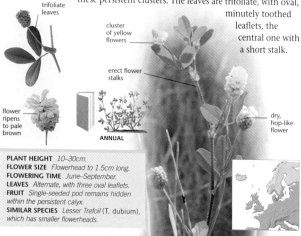

dry, hop-like flower

PLANT HEIGHT *10–30cm.*
FLOWER SIZE *Flowerhead to 1.5cm long.*
FLOWERING TIME *June–September.*
LEAVES *Alternate, with three oval leaflets.*
FRUIT *Single-seeded pod remains hidden within the persistent calyx.*
SIMILAR SPECIES *Lesser Trefoil (T. dubium), which has smaller flowerheads.*

Common Bird's-foot Trefoil

Lotus corniculatus (Fabaceae)

This common member of the pea family produces erect stems topped with fan-shaped clusters of brightly coloured yellow or orange peaflowers with red streaks, which are red-tipped in bud. The fruit cluster is also a fan of long, narrow pods, with a persistent calyx at the base, and resembles a bird's foot.

THRIVES *in grassy fields, pastures, and scrub, and along roadsides and embankments.*

leafy stems

cluster of 3–7 flowers

PERENNIAL

untidy pinnate leaves

red streaks

PLANT HEIGHT *5–30cm.*
FLOWER SIZE *1–1.6cm long.*
FLOWERING TIME *June–September.*
LEAVES *Alternate, pinnate with oval leaflets, lowest ones at very base of leaf stalk.*
FRUIT *Brown-black cylindrical pod.*
SIMILAR SPECIES *Kidney Vetch (right), Greater Bird's-foot Trefoil (L. uliginosus).*

Kidney Vetch

Anthyllis vulneraria (Fabaceae)

The colour of the flowers in this unusual member of the pea family varies widely from cream to red, even within the same flowerhead. Each flowerhead is surrounded at the base by thick, downy sepals, which give the plant a woolly and rather robust appearance. The leaves are pinnately divided, like a ladder, each with a large terminal leaflet.

FORMS *patches in dry grassland, on cliff-tops, and rocky ledges, often on slopes. Prefers chalky soil, especially near the sea.*

variable colours for individual flowers

large terminal leaflet

leaf-like bracts below flowerhead

PERENNIAL

whitish calyx

9PLANT HEIGHT *20–50cm.*
FLOWER SIZE *Flowerhead 2–4cm wide.*
FLOWERING TIME *June–September.*
LEAVES *Alternate, pinnately divided.*
FRUIT *Seed pod enclosed within calyx.*
SIMILAR SPECIES *Common Bird's-foot Trefoil (left) and Horseshoe Vetch (below), which have yellow peaflowers.*

Horseshoe Vetch

Hippocrepis comosa (Fabaceae)

This plant is an important foodplant for some of the Blue butterfly larvae. The yellow peaflowers with faint reddish veins are arranged like an open fan on a long flower stalk, while the fruithead is an extraordinary collection of twisted pods, each divided into several horseshoe-shaped segments.

GROWS *in patches on sunny grassland, often on slopes or cliff-tops, always on chalky soil.*

PERENNIAL

fan-shaped flower cluster

neat, pinnate leaves

crimped fruit

long flower stalk

PLANT HEIGHT *15–30cm.*
FLOWER SIZE *6–10mm long.*
FLOWERING TIME *May–July.*
LEAVES *Alternate, 4–7 pairs of oval leaflets.*
FRUIT *Pod divided into wavy, horseshoe-shaped segments that separate when ripe.*
SIMILAR SPECIES *Common Bird's-foot Trefoil (left), Kidney Vetch (above).*

Tutsan

Hypericum androsaemum (Clusiaceae)

GROWS *in shady corners of deciduous woodland or by walls and hedgerows; also grown in gardens from where it escapes.*

This small shrub of shady corners has clusters of five-petalled, bright yellow flowers, each studded with a pincushion of long, straight stamens. The leaves are large and oblong and feel rather soft. The fruit are inedible egg-shaped berries which ripen from red to black, to which the reflexed sepals remain attached for some time.

large, opposite leaves

pin-like stamens

PERENNIAL

reflexed sepals

shiny berries

oblong leaf

PLANT HEIGHT *50–80cm.*
FLOWER SIZE *1.8–2.2cm wide.*
FLOWERING TIME *June–August.*
LEAVES *Opposite, oval and unstalked.*
FRUIT *Oval berries, 7–10mm long.*
SIMILAR SPECIES *Rose of Sharon (H. calycinum), a garden plant that naturalizes, has larger flowers and is leafier.*

Marsh St John's-wort

Hypericum elodes (Clusiaceae)

FORMS *creeping mats in wet areas of acid bogs, heaths, marshes, and in ponds.*

A lover of damp habitats, this St John's-wort forms extensive mats of greyish green leaves. These are small, oval, and stalkless, and are covered in fine down, as are the upright stems. The yellow flowers form terminal clusters, but there is usually only one flower open at a time, and the petals unfurl fully only in strong sunlight.

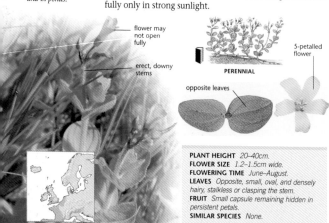

flower may not open fully

erect, downy stems

PERENNIAL

5-petalled flower

opposite leaves

PLANT HEIGHT *20–40cm.*
FLOWER SIZE *1.2–1.5cm wide.*
FLOWERING TIME *June–August.*
LEAVES *Opposite, small, oval, and densely hairy, stalkless or clasping the stem.*
FRUIT *Small capsule remaining hidden in persistent petals.*
SIMILAR SPECIES *None.*

Perforate St John's-wort

Hypericum perforatum (Clusiaceae)

There are many similar St John's-worts, but this one may be identified by its round stems, which have two opposite ridges or wings that are more easily felt than seen. The plant has an upright branched habit. Its oval, unstalked leaves are peppered with tiny, translucent dots, which are visible only when the leaf is held up to the light. They also have a few tiny black glands on the underside, as do the margins of the petals. The flowers are yellow, with five petals and numerous stamens, and are borne in clusters. The fruit is a capsule, containing many seeds.

OCCURS *singly or in loose clumps in woodland margins, hedgerows, grassy places, on roadsides and banks, in open or semi-shaded places.*

terminal flower cluster

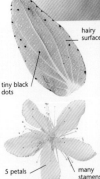

PERENNIAL

NOTE

This plant was placed over religious images as it was believed to ward off evil spirits; in Greek, "Hypericum" means "over an apparition".

hairy surface

tiny black dots

5 petals · many stamens

PLANT HEIGHT *40–80cm.*
FLOWER SIZE *1.8–2.2cm wide.*
FLOWERING TIME *May–September.*
LEAVES *Opposite, oval, and stalkless, with translucent black dots underneath.*
FRUIT *Small, many-seeded capsule.*
SIMILAR SPECIES *Imperforate St John's-wort (H. maculatum), which has square stems and no translucent leaf dots.*

Yellow Wood Violet

Viola biflora (Violaceae)

This violet is easily recognized by its yellow flowers with dark brownish streaks, which usually have four petals pointing upwards and one down. The flowers are solitary or in pairs. Most of the leaves are in basal tufts and are distinctly rounded or kidney-shaped, although there are a few stem leaves.

GROWS *in small clumps in damp, shady woodland and rocky places, mainly in mountainous areas.*

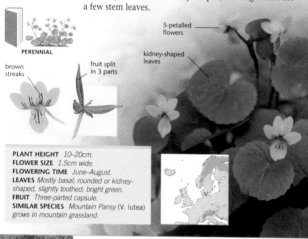

PERENNIAL

brown streaks

fruit split in 3 parts

5-petalled flowers

kidney-shaped leaves

PLANT HEIGHT *10–20cm.*
FLOWER SIZE *1.5cm wide.*
FLOWERING TIME *June–August.*
LEAVES *Mostly basal; rounded or kidney-shaped, slightly toothed; bright green.*
FRUIT *Three-parted capsule.*
SIMILAR SPECIES *Mountain Pansy (V. lutea) grows in mountain grassland.*

Common Rock Rose

Helianthemum nummularium (Cistaceae)

Thin, crumpled yellow petals like tissue paper distinguish this plant of grassy, rocky places. The five petals are backed by three large, striped sepals and two tiny ones. Drooping buds and developing fruit also display these characteristic stripes. The small, oblong, and rather stiff leaves are in opposite pairs, and the stems are woody.

INHABITS *dry areas, with short turf and thin soil over chalky rock, up to 2,500m.*

crumpled petals

drooping, striped bud

PERENNIAL

striped sepals

stiff, oblong leaves

PLANT HEIGHT *5–30cm.*
FLOWER SIZE *1.2–2cm wide.*
FLOWERING TIME *June–September.*
LEAVES *Opposite, narrow and oblong with a deep central vein and white hairs below.*
FRUIT *Small, many-seeded capsule.*
SIMILAR SPECIES *White Rock-rose (H. appeninum) has white flowers.*

Large-flowered Evening-primrose

Oenothera erythrosepala (Onagraceae)

As the name indicates, the flowers of the Evening-primrose open just before sunset. It takes just a few minutes for the sepals to curl back and the four pale primrose-yellow petals to unfurl into an almost luminous disc, but by noon the next day, this begins to wilt. The plant produces flowers every day for several weeks. These are pollinated by night-flying moths in their native North America, but in Europe they often self-pollinate. The sepals and stems of this species are covered in tiny hairs with red swollen bases; the leaves are lance-shaped, with crinkled margins and a pale midrib.

OCCURS on waste and disturbed ground, embankments, roadsides, rubbish tips, and sand dunes, on well-drained soil.

BIENNIAL

NOTE

Evening Primrose is an excellent source of gamma-linolenic acid, which is used for balancing hormone levels, especially in women.

tight bud cluster

very large yellow flowers

lance-shaped leaf

sepals covered with red hairs

crinkled leaf margin

PLANT HEIGHT 80–150cm.
FLOWER SIZE 5–8cm wide.
FLOWERING TIME June–September.
LEAVES Alternate, lance-shaped, with crinkled margins and a pale midrib.
FRUIT Four-valved capsule.
SIMILAR SPECIES Common Evening-primrose (O. biennis) has smaller flowers and no red hairs on sepals or stems.

Touch-me-not Balsam

Impatiens noli-tangere (Balsaminacae)

The long, slender seed pods of this plant burst open when touched, expelling their seeds over some distance. The five-petalled, red-spotted yellow flowers – suspended from a thin stalk – are hooded, with a broad lip and a bag-like, curved spur at the back. The whole plant is rather frail and soft, wilting rapidly if picked.

FORMS *patches in wet woodland, on stream and river banks, and in other damp and shady places.*

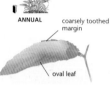

ANNUAL

coarsely toothed margin

oval leaf

yellow flowers

slender stems

PLANT HEIGHT *0.8–1.6m.*
FLOWER SIZE *2–3.5cm long, including spur.*
FLOWERING TIME *July–September.*
LEAVES *Alternate, oval with coarse teeth.*
FRUIT *Linear capsule.*
SIMILAR SPECIES *Himalayan Balsam (p.208); Small Balsam (I. parviflora), which is shorter with smaller yellow flowers.*

Wild Parsnip

Pastinaca sativa (Apiaceae)

A member of the carrot family, Wild Parsnip is the parent of cultivated parsnip, but the sap from the leaves and stems can cause intense skin irritation, especially in sunlight. Its leaves are divided into large, flat leaflets, the lower ones long-stalked, the upper ones much smaller and almost stalkless. The yellow-ochre flowers are borne in broad, flat-topped umbels.

OCCURS *in grassland on roadsides, on scrub, wasteland, and embankments, on dry, chalky soil.*

flat leaflets

coarsely toothed margin

yellow-ochre flowers

BIENNIAL

ridged stems

broad umbels

PLANT HEIGHT *60–100cm.*
FLOWER SIZE *Umbels 4–10cm wide.*
FLOWERING TIME *July–August.*
LEAVES *Alternate, pinnately divided.*
FRUIT *Two-parted mericarp, 6mm long, elliptical with ringed ridges.*
SIMILAR SPECIES *Fennel (right) has hair-like leaves; Alexanders (p.132) is more leafy.*

Fennel

Foeniculum vulgare (Apiaceae)

The stature of this tall and rather elegant plant makes it recognizable even at a distance. A member of the carrot family, it has very fine and hair-like leaves. The broad, loose umbels of flowers are bright yellow-green, remaining yellowish when in fruit; the tough, ridged stems are shiny and hollow with inflated leaf bases. Fennel has been cultivated since ancient times as a culinary and medicinal herb, and there are bronze- or purple-leaved varieties, which sometimes become naturalized. The form grown as a vegetable, with swollen leaf bases, is a variety of the same plant.

GROWS *singly or in small patches on roadsides, in rocky places, and wasteland, on chalky soil or limestone, often near the sea.*

many-branched umbels

tall, upright stems

flowers in loose cluster

PERENNIAL

NOTE

People used to chew fennel leaves on fast days to satisfy the pangs of hunger. The aromatic seeds are also used as a breath freshener after meals.

tiny yellow flower

oblong fruit

hair-like leaves

PLANT HEIGHT 1.5–2.2m.
FLOWER SIZE Umbels 4–8cm wide; flowers 2–3mm wide.
FLOWERING TIME July–October.
LEAVES Alternate, very finely divided and hair-like; grey-green or bronze-green.
FRUIT Oblong, ridged mericarp, 4–8mm long, sweet and aromatic.
SIMILAR SPECIES Pignut (p.68) is much smaller with white flowers; Wild Parsnip (left) has larger, flatter leaflets.

Alexanders

Smyrnium olusatrum (Apiaceae)

One of the earliest members of the carrot family to flower, this is a robust, clump-forming, very leafy plant. The leaves are divided into three groups of three flat leaflets, the upper ones arranged oppositely on the stem and often yellowish in colour. The five-petalled yellow or greenish yellow flowers are borne in tight, domed umbels without bracts.

FORMS *clumps or patches by the sea, along estuaries and coastal cliffs, or along salted roads inland.*

rounded flower umbels

broad, flat leaflets

long leaf stalk

yellow flowers

BIENNIAL

PLANT HEIGHT *80–150cm.*
FLOWER SIZE *Umbels 4–8cm wide.*
FLOWERING TIME *April–June.*
LEAVES *Alternate at base, opposite at top, divided into three groups of three leaflets.*
FRUIT *Oval mericarp, black when ripe.*
SIMILAR SPECIES *Wild Parsnip (p.130), which is less leafy, with flat umbels.*

Rock Samphire

Crithmum maritimum (Apiaceae)

Like many seaside plants, Rock Samphire has thickened succulent leaves that conserve moisture. The stems and leaves branch to form tight clumps and smell of polish when crushed. The tight, fairly rounded umbels are made up of small flowers that form oval, corky fruit.

OCCURS *on coastal rocks, sea-cliffs, sand, and shingle, always very close to the sea.*

finger-like leaves

greenish yellow flower umbels

PERENNIAL

tiny flowers

PLANT HEIGHT *20–50cm.*
FLOWER SIZE *Umbels 3–6cm wide.*
FLOWERING TIME *June–August.*
LEAVES *Alternate, triangular, divided into cylindrical, fleshy, upward-pointing segments.*
FRUIT *Oval mericarp, ripening yellow to purple.*
SIMILAR SPECIES *None.*

Primrose

Primula vulgaris (Primulaceae)

The pale yellow flowers of Primrose signal the arrival of spring. Each flower is on a solitary stalk and has a long, tubular calyx and broad yellow petals, often with orange markings in the centre (although other colours occur in garden cultivars). As distinctive as the flowers, the oblong, toothed leaves are in basal rosettes.

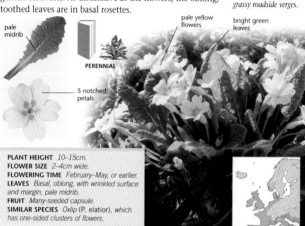

PROLIFERATES *in deciduous woodland and woodland glades, along embankments, in meadows, and grassy roadside verges.*

pale midrib

PERENNIAL

pale yellow flowers

bright green leaves

5 notched petals

PLANT HEIGHT *10–15cm.*
FLOWER SIZE *2–4cm wide.*
FLOWERING TIME *February–May, or earlier.*
LEAVES *Basal, oblong, with wrinkled surface and margin, pale midrib.*
FRUIT *Many-seeded capsule.*
SIMILAR SPECIES *Oxlip (P. elatior), which has one-sided clusters of flowers.*

Cowslip

Primula veris (Primulaceae)

Entire meadows are often coloured in spring by the abundant yellow flowers of Cowslip. Borne in tight clusters on each stem or scape, they are fragrant, with a long, yellow-green calyx and five petals that form a tube, opening slightly to reveal an orange mark on each petal. The leaves are dark green.

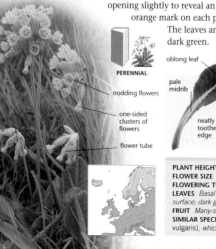

GROWS *in meadows and dry, grassy places, also on embankments, usually on chalky soil; prefers open situations.*

PERENNIAL

nodding flowers

one-sided clusters of flowers

flower tube

oblong leaf

pale midrib

neatly toothed edge

5 notched petals

PLANT HEIGHT *10–25cm.*
FLOWER SIZE *7–14mm wide.*
FLOWERING TIME *April–May.*
LEAVES *Basal rosette, oblong; with wrinkled surface; dark green.*
FRUIT *Many-seeded capsule.*
SIMILAR SPECIES *False Oxlip (P. veris x vulgaris), which has fewer one-sided umbels.*

Yellow Loosestrife

Lysimachia vulgaris (Primulaceae)

GROWS among tall vegetation in moist habitats such as streamsides, wet meadows, fens, and marshes, on neutral or chalky soils.

This tall plant punctuates the landscape of marshes and fens with its golden yellow flowers. These have five oval petals with an orange centre, and are grouped in panicles produced from the upper leaf axils. The oval to lance-shaped leaves are sometimes dotted with black or orange glands and have bluish green undersides. They are arranged in opposite pairs at the top of the stem, then in whorls of 3–4 leaves lower down. The fruit is a spherical capsule, and often occurs in the same cluster as the buds or open flowers.

PERENNIAL

tightly clustered yellow flowers

5-petalled flower

whorl of 3–4 lower leaves

spherical fruit capsule

oval leaf

NOTE

Yellow Loosestrife used to be burned in houses to clear the rooms of flies and gnats; it was also tied to cattle and horses to keep biting insects away.

PLANT HEIGHT *60–150cm.*
FLOWER SIZE *1.5–2cm wide.*
FLOWERING TIME *July–August.*
LEAVES *Opposite on upper stem, whorls of 3–4 below, oval to lance-shaped.*
FRUIT *Spherical, five-parted capsule.*
SIMILAR SPECIES *Dotted Loosestrife (L. punctata), which has narrow spikes of tightly clustered flowers.*

Creeping-Jenny

Lysimachia nummularia (Primulaceae)

This creeping plant can be easily missed among taller vegetation. Once discovered, however, there is no mistaking its cup-shaped yellow flowers nestling along the twining stem. The leaves, arranged in opposite pairs like a ladder, are rounded to oval, decreasing in size along the stem. When produced, the fruit capsule is on a long stalk.

CREEPS *along in damp habitats, in woodland, pond and stream margins, and ditches.*

oval leaves

cup-shaped flowers

smaller leaves at top of stem

broad sepals

PLANT HEIGHT *3–6cm.*
FLOWER SIZE *1.2–1.8cm wide.*
FLOWERING TIME *May–July.*
LEAVES *Opposite, rounded to oval.*
FRUIT *Five-parted capsule, rarely produced.*
SIMILAR SPECIES *Yellow Pimpernel (L. nemorum), which has less ladder-like leaves and narrow sepals.*

PERENNIAL

Fringed Water-lily

Nymphoides peltata (Menyanthaceae)

Like its close relative, the Bogbean (p.76), this aquatic plant has petals with a delicately fringed margin of tiny hairs; they may also appear creased or slightly folded. The long-stemmed, bright yellow flowers are held just above the water surface. Rounded, dark green leaves, sometimes purple blotched, have a slit to the centre where the stalk joins the leaf. They are much smaller than those of other water-lilies.

FORMS *large patches on the surface of slow-moving rivers and streams, ponds, lakes, and in ditches.*

bright yellow flower

long stem

creased petals

PERENNIAL

deep leaf cleft

5 petals

PLANT HEIGHT *Up to 10cm above water surface.*
FLOWER SIZE *3–4cm wide.*
FLOWERING TIME *June–September.*
LEAVES *Whorled, on long stems, rounded.*
FRUIT *Egg-shaped capsule.*
SIMILAR SPECIES *Yellow Water-lily (p.101), which has spherical flowers.*

Great Yellow Gentian

Gentiana lutea (Gentianaceae)

This tall, imposing plant stands out in its alpine habitat. The thick, almost fleshy, bluish green leaves are strongly veined. Arranged in opposite pairs on the stem, they are curved to form cups that seem to hold the tight clusters of brilliant yellow flowers. Each flower has five well-separated, narrow petals, with prominent stamens and a stout ovary in the centre. Grazing animals dislike the taste of this plant, so it remains untouched even in heavily grazed pasture.

FOUND *in montane meadows, pastures, woodland margins and clearings, and along roadsides, up to 2,500m.*

tight whorl of flowers above leaves

erect stem

PERENNIAL

5-petalled yellow flower

cup formed by leaves

NOTE

The roots of this plant are used to make a digestive; the bitter part is detectable on the tongue even when diluted to one part in 12,000.

PLANT HEIGHT *80–120cm.*
FLOWER SIZE *1.8–2.4cm long.*
FLOWERING TIME *June–August.*
LEAVES *Opposite, elliptical, prominently veined; lower ones stalked.*
FRUIT *Two-parted capsule.*
SIMILAR SPECIES *Swallow-wort (p.77) has smaller flowers; Spotted Gentian (G. punctata) is smaller, with bell-shaped flowers.*

Yellow-wort

Blackstonia perfoliata (Gentianaceae)

This plant has a distinctive arrangement of leaves in that each pair is fused together around the stem – the upper pairs occurring where the stems branch. Unusually for a member of the gentian family, the flowers have up to eight starry petals, which open almost flat.

GROWS *sporadically on grassland and other rocky, open places on dry, well-drained chalky soil.*

slender calyx lobes

leaves encircle stem

ANNUAL

8 starry petals

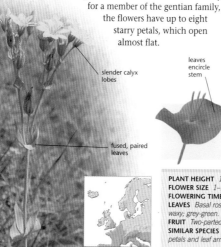

fused, paired leaves

PLANT HEIGHT	*15–40cm.*
FLOWER SIZE	*1–1.5cm wide.*
FLOWERING TIME	*June–September.*
LEAVES	*Basal rosette and opposite, oval, waxy; grey-green.*
FRUIT	*Two-parted, many-seeded capsule.*
SIMILAR SPECIES	*None; the number of petals and leaf arrangement are distinctive.*

Lady's Bedstraw

Galium verum (Rubiaceae)

The tiny flowers of Lady's Bedstraw seem, at a distance, like candyfloss. Each flower has four well-separated petals and is grouped into a branched panicle. Linear, shiny, dark green leaves are borne in many whorls along the hairy stem. The plant, which may be bushy or in spikes, is fragrant.

PERENNIAL

INHABITS *dry, open grassy places, banks, and roadsides; also sand dunes and other places near the sea.*

dense, branched panicles of flowers

whorl of tiny leaves

greenish yellow flowers

PLANT HEIGHT	*20–80cm.*
FLOWER SIZE	*2–3mm wide.*
FLOWERING TIME	*June–September.*
LEAVES	*Whorls of 8–12 small, linear leaves; dark green.*
FRUIT	*Fused black nutlets.*
SIMILAR SPECIES	*Hedge Bedstraw (p.78), which has creamy white flowers.*

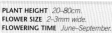

Crosswort

Cruciata laevipes (Rubiaceae)

INHABITS *road verges, meadows, pastures, hedgerows, and scrub, often close to taller, sheltering vegetation.*

This member of the bedstraw family is recognizable by its neat, tufted habit and yellowish green colour. The softly hairy leaves are arranged in whorls of four. The short-stalked, four-petalled flowers are borne in tight clusters at the base of each leaf whorl.

tiny, pale yellow flowers

flowers in clusters

erect stems

neat whorls of 4 leaves

PERENNIAL

3 main leaf veins

hairy leaves

PLANT HEIGHT *20–50cm.*
FLOWER SIZE *2–3mm wide.*
FLOWERING TIME *April–June.*
LEAVES *Whorls of four, elliptical.*
FRUIT *Rounded, smooth nutlets, black when ripe.*
SIMILAR SPECIES *None; the whorls of four leaves are distinctive.*

Wood Sage

Teucrium scorodonia (Lamiaceae)

One-sided spikes of yellow-green flowers and wrinkled leaves, similar in appearance to the leaves of the culinary sage, make this plant distinctive. Close examination of the flowers shows that they have only one lip, which is slightly lobed, so that the brown stamens are exposed. The leaves are in opposite pairs and the stems are square, as in other members of the mint family.

FORMS *tufts in dry and often sandy, open woods, grassland and hedgerows, and on heaths and dunes; prefers acid soil.*

flowers in leafless spikes

square stems

wrinkled, toothed leaf

maroon anthers

one-lipped flower

PERENNIAL

PLANT HEIGHT *30–50cm.*
FLOWER SIZE *8–9mm long.*
FLOWERING TIME *July–September.*
LEAVES *Opposite pairs, oval, toothed, with heart-shaped bases.*
FRUIT *Four nutlets within the calyx.*
SIMILAR SPECIES *None; the leafless flower spikes are distinctive within the mint family.*

Jupiter's Distaff

Salvia glutinosa (Lamiaceae)

One of the few members of the mint family that has yellow flowers, Jupiter's Distaff is easily recognized for many other reasons too. Its flowers are very large, each with a distinctly curved and hooded upper lip – similar in shape to the related Meadow Clary (p.270) – and a sticky, bright green calyx. They are borne in whorls around the upper parts of the tall stems which, along with the sepals, are covered with sticky, glandular hairs. The leaves, in opposite pairs, are very large, especially towards the base of the stem. They are arrow-shaped with coarse teeth at the margins.

OCCURS *in open woods, copses, hedgerows, shady meadows, and along roadsides, particularly in mountains up to 1,800m.*

PERENNIAL

hooded upper lip of flower

loose whorl of flowers

NOTE

Related to culinary sage, the flowers and foliage of this plant have been used to add flavour to country wines.

coarsely toothed leaf margin

PLANT HEIGHT *60–100cm.*
FLOWER SIZE *3–4cm long.*
FLOWERING TIME *June–September.*
LEAVES *Opposite pairs, arrow-shaped, with coarse teeth, stalked; bright green.*
FRUIT *Four nutlets within the calyx.*
SIMILAR SPECIES *Yellow Archangel (p.140), which is a much smaller plant and leafier towards the top.*

Yellow Archangel

Lamiastrum galeobdolon (Lamiaceae)

GROWS in shady woodland, hedgerows, and coppices, on heavy clay or chalky soil.

A plant that brightens the landscape with its striking colour in spring, Yellow Archangel has unusually large flowers for a member of the mint family. Each two-lipped flower is bright butter-yellow, with red markings on the lower lip. The paired leaves are almost triangular in outline, with coarse teeth.

PERENNIAL

2-lipped flower

jagged leaf margin

flowers in tight whorls

large, pointed leaves

red streaks on lower lip

stalked leaves

PLANT HEIGHT 20–50cm.
FLOWER SIZE 1.7–2.1cm wide.
FLOWERING TIME April–June.
LEAVES Opposite, almost triangular.
FRUIT Four nutlets at base of calyx.
SIMILAR SPECIES Yellow Rattle (p.144); Large-flowered Hemp-nettle (Galeopsis speciosa) has flowers with a violet blotch.

Henbane

Hyoscyamus niger (Solanaceae)

OCCURS on disturbed ground, field edges, farmyards, and on coastal shingles, usually on rich soil.

This poisonous, foetid-smelling plant is related to Deadly Nightshade (p.176), but looks different. The pale-veined stem leaves are unstalked and clasp the stem. Small, trumpet-shaped, five-petalled flowers are creamy yellow, with a lacy network of purple lines. The plant is very short as an annual but more vigorous as a biennial.

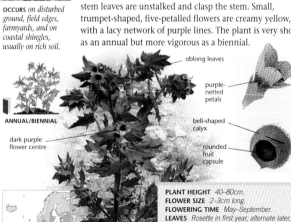

ANNUAL/BIENNIAL

oblong leaves

purple-netted petals

bell-shaped calyx

dark purple flower centre

rounded fruit capsule

PLANT HEIGHT 40–80cm.
FLOWER SIZE 2–3cm long.
FLOWERING TIME May–September.
LEAVES Rosette in first year, alternate later, soft, oblong, with coarsely jagged edges.
FRUIT Large capsule in a papery calyx.
SIMILAR SPECIES None; the purple-netted flowers make this plant unique.

Great Mullein

Verbascum thapsus (Scrophulariaceae)

Usually much taller than Dark Mullein (p.142), this plant has characteristic dense spires of bright yellow flowers. The first flowers to open are at the base of the spike, but as this elongates and branches, flowers open at intervals along it. Each flower has five spreading lobes, and stamens with white filaments. The soft, thick, felty, grey-green leaves, covered with fine, branched hairs, are easily identifiable in the plant's first year, when this biennial does not flower.

FOUND *on wasteland and banks, rough, dry grassland, along roadsides, and in stony places; often on disturbed soil.*

tall spires of
yellow flowers

NOTE

The tiny hairs, which give the leaves of this plant a velvety look, ignite easily and were once used to make lamp wicks.

BIENNIAL

grey-green
leaf

untoothed
margin

rounded
flower
lobes

PLANT HEIGHT *0.5–2m.*
FLOWER SIZE *1.2–3.5cm wide.*
FLOWERING TIME *June–August.*
LEAVES *Alternate, densely packed together, oblong to elliptical, thick and velvety.*
FRUIT *Small, many-seeded capsule.*
SIMILAR SPECIES *Dark Mullein (p.142) is a shorter plant; Small Yellow Foxglove (p.143) has small, trumpet-shaped flowers; Foxglove (p.224).*

Dark Mullein

Verbascum nigrum (Scrophulariaceae)

The upright yellow flower spikes of this robust plant make it easy to spot. Each flower has prominent purple hairs on the stamens, which contrast with the five yellow petals. Unlike Great Mullein, which has soft, velvety leaves, it has glossy, dark green leaves that are paler beneath, with gently toothed margins. The basal leaves are in tufts.

OCCURS on roadsides, embankments, dry grassland, and along hedgerows, often in semi-shade.

PERENNIAL

oval petals

purple stamens

tall, narrow flower spike

oblong leaf

PLANT HEIGHT *50–100cm.*
FLOWER SIZE *1.8–2.5cm wide.*
FLOWERING TIME *June–September.*
LEAVES *Alternate, oblong, long-stalked.*
FRUIT *Small, many-seeded capsule.*
SIMILAR SPECIES *Agrimony (p.118), which has lobed leaves; Great Mullein (p.141) is larger, with velvety leaves and white stamens.*

Common Toadflax

Linaria vulgaris (Scrophulariaceae)

The tufted spikes of Common Toadflax flower late into the autumn. Each lemon-yellow flower is composed of two closed lips, the lower with two orange bosses (palette), and a slender, tapering spur which hangs downward. Only large bees are able to push the lips apart to reach the nectar. The narrow leaves grow spirally up the stem.

GROWS in clumps on roadsides, meadows, embankments, field margins, and other open, grassy places.

PERENNIAL

2-lipped flower

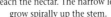

orange boss

linear leaf

alternate leaves

tapering spur

PLANT HEIGHT *30–70cm.*
FLOWER SIZE *2–3.5cm long.*
FLOWERING TIME *July–October.*
LEAVES *Alternate, linear, untoothed.*
FRUIT *Large, oval capsule, split near apex.*
SIMILAR SPECIES *Garden snapdragons (Antirrhinums), which sometimes become naturalized, and are in a range of colours.*

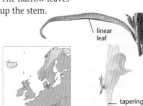

Round-leaved Fluellen

Kickxia spuria (Scrophulariaceae)

This low-growing, creeping plant has short-stalked, alternate leaves along the trailing stems. Lying close to the ground, the small, long-stalked flowers may be partially hidden by the leaves. Each flower has a three-lobed, lemon-yellow lower lip, a deep purple upper lip, and a slender curved spur at the back.

TRAILS *usually on bare ground in cultivated fields and in waste or disturbed places.*

small flowers

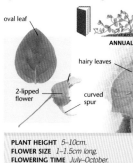

oval leaf

ANNUAL

hairy leaves

2-lipped flower

curved spur

PLANT HEIGHT *5–10cm.*
FLOWER SIZE *1–1.5cm long.*
FLOWERING TIME *July–October.*
LEAVES *Alternate, oval and hairy.*
FRUIT *Round capsule, opening near apex.*
SIMILAR SPECIES *Ivy-leaved Toadflax (p.247); Sharp-leaved Fluellen (K. elatine) has arrow-shaped leaves.*

Small Yellow Foxglove

Digitalis lutea (Scrophulariaceae)

This foxglove forms a leaf rosette in its first year, producing flowering stems with alternate leaves in subsequent years. The primrose to creamy yellow flowers are borne in neat spikes. Each flower is funnel-shaped, with faint brown markings at the mouth where the five lobes spread out slightly.

INHABITS *woodland and meadow margins, rocky places, and embankments, on chalky soil.*

flowers in spikes

BIENNIAL/ PERENNIAL

spear-shaped leaves

small, tubular flower

PLANT HEIGHT *60–100cm.*
FLOWER SIZE *1.5–2cm long.*
FLOWERING TIME *June–August.*
LEAVES *Rosette in first year, alternate afterwards, slightly toothed, hairless.*
FRUIT *Capsule, opening in three slits.*
SIMILAR SPECIES *Large Yellow Foxglove (D. grandiflora) is taller, with larger flowers.*

Common Cow-wheat

Melampyrum pratense (Scrophulariaceae)

The yellow flowers of this plant brighten shaded woodland in late summer. The two-lipped flowers are arranged in neat pairs, each one often tipped red or becoming wholly red with age. The leaves and flower bracts are in pairs and swept back away from the flowers so that they look like ranks of wings along the slender stems.

toothed bracts

leaves swept back at angles

paired flowers

FOUND in shady corners and along paths in deciduous and coniferous woodland; prefers acid soil.

ANNUAL

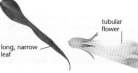

long, narrow leaf

tubular flower

PLANT HEIGHT 15–30cm.
FLOWER SIZE 1–1.8cm long.
FLOWERING TIME June–August.
LEAVES Opposite, narrowly lance-shaped, bracts with long teeth at base.
FRUIT Small capsule splitting along one side.
SIMILAR SPECIES Yellow Rattle (below), which has inflated sepals and toothed leaves.

Yellow Rattle

Rhinanthus minor (Scrophulariaceae)

This partially parasitic plant derives water and minerals from the adjoining root systems of grasses. The small, rather squat, yellow flowers have two lips, with tiny violet teeth on the upper lip. The calyx is extremely inflated and, when ripe and dry, the enclosed capsule and its seeds rattle when moved by the wind. The narrow leaves are dark green.

GROWS in open, grassy places on roadsides, banks, pastures, and meadows; prefers chalky soil.

leaves clasp stem

toothed upper lip

inflated, dry calyx

serrated leaf margins

ANNUAL

PLANT HEIGHT 20–40cm.
FLOWER SIZE 1.3–1.5cm long.
FLOWERING TIME May–August.
LEAVES Opposite, lance-shaped, unstalked.
FRUIT Round capsule, with a short beak, enclosing winged seeds.
SIMILAR SPECIES Yellow Archangel (p.140); Common Cow-wheat (above).

Greater Bladderwort

Utricularia vulgaris (Lentibulariaceae)

This extraordinary insectivorous aquatic plant has numerous thread-like leaves that float in the water. Minute sacs are attached to these, each with a microscopic "trap-door" operated by a hair-like trigger. Tiny crustacea and other pondlife that touch the trigger hairs are inadvertently sucked into the sacs as the "trap-doors" open, where they are digested by the plant. The two-lipped flowers are bright yellow, with red markings, and are borne on long stalks held above the water surface. The plant may exist for many years without flowering.

INHABITS *fresh, still water of ponds, lakes, ditches, and canals. It is intolerant of pollution.*

flowers on stalks above water surface

PERRENNIAL

bright yellow flowers

single, erect stalk

thread-like leaves

sacs to trap pondlife

two lipped flower

NOTE

This plant may suddenly come into bloom after a major disturbance in its habitat, such as cleaning out of ditches or ponds.

PLANT HEIGHT *Flowerstalk 10cm.*
FLOWER SIZE *1.2–1.8cm wide.*
FLOWERING TIME *July–August.*
LEAVES *Mass of threads.*
FRUIT *Rounded capsule.*
SIMILAR SPECIES *Lesser Bladderwort (U. minor), which has much smaller flowers. There are other* Utricularia *species that may only be identified by microscopic examination.*

Goldenrod

Solidago virgaurea (Asteraceae)

The stiff, erect stems of Goldenrod may produce a single spike of yellow flowers or many branches bearing golden bunches of flowers. Each flower is actually a mass of tiny florets, the outer ones with a single petal or ray. The leaves are narrow and slightly toothed, the lower leaves are long-stalked and broader.

INHABITS *dry, grassy places, open woods, heaths, meadows, and rocky sites.*

PERENNIAL

branched flower spikes

yellow ray florets

wavy, toothed margin

PLANT HEIGHT *10–60cm.*
FLOWER SIZE *Flowerhead 1.5–1.8cm wide.*
FLOWERING TIME *July–September.*
LEAVES *Alternate, variable but narrow.*
FRUIT *Achene with a brown pappus, forming a clock.*
SIMILAR SPECIES *Common Ragwort (p.152), which is more bushy and has divided leaves.*

Canadian Goldenrod

Solidago canadensis (Asteraceae)

Having escaped from gardens, this robust plant now forms patches or small colonies in the wild. The golden yellow flowerheads are arranged on many horizontal branches, both flowerheads and branches decreasing in size up the stem. The whole spike tends to lean over in one direction, giving the inflorescence a one-sided look. The stems are very leafy; the leaves are lance-shaped.

FORMS *patches on roadsides, railway embankments, bare ground, wasteland, and field margins.*

tall flower spike

numerous tiny flowerheads

toothed leaf margin

leafy stem

PERENNIAL

lance-shaped leaves

PLANT HEIGHT *1–2m.*
FLOWER SIZE *Flowerhead 5–6mm wide.*
FLOWERING TIME *August–October.*
LEAVES *Alternate, lance-shaped, with toothed margins.*
FRUIT *Achene with a short pappus.*
SIMILAR SPECIES *None, the tall, pyramidal one-sided spikes are characteristic.*

Marsh Cudweed

Gnaphalium uliginosum (Asteraceae)

A small, weedy plant, Marsh Cudweed is often overlooked. The stems and leaves are covered in a fine white down so that the whole plant has a pale, silvery grey appearance. The lance-shaped leaves are slightly greener on the upper surface. The tiny flowers have no rays; they are yellow only when freshly opened, and soon fade to brown.

GROWS *in damp places on bare ground or turf, in marshes, on paths, and pavement cracks.*

flowers partially concealed by leaves

ANNUAL

narrow leaves

alternate leaves

tiny flowers

silvery grey stalks

PLANT HEIGHT 5–20cm.
FLOWER SIZE *Flowerhead 3–4mm long.*
FLOWERING TIME *July–September.*
LEAVES *Alternate, lance-shaped, downy.*
FRUIT *Tiny achene.*
SIMILAR SPECIES *Common Cudweed (Filago vulgaris), which has a tighter leaf arrangement and larger flowers.*

Fleabane

Pulicaria dysenterica (Asteraceae)

This member of the daisy family may be differentiated from its relatives by the flat-topped disc in the centre of its flower, and numerous very narrow or linear rays, which are often somewhat ragged. The stems are grey with woolly hairs, and the leaves, which clasp the stem, have a finely wrinkled surface, wavy edges, and are greyish beneath.

PERENNIAL

OCCURS *in extensive colonies in damp grassland, meadows, and marshes, and by ditches and canals.*

daisy-like flowerhead

flat disc

many narrow rays

leaf clasps stem

clock of achenes

PLANT HEIGHT 40–60cm.
FLOWER SIZE 1.5–3cm wide.
FLOWERING TIME *July–September.*
LEAVES *Alternate, arrow-shaped, wrinkled surface with wavy edges, clasping the stem.*
FRUIT *Clock of hairy, brown achenes.*
SIMILAR SPECIES *Common Ragwort (p.152) is more bushy and has divided leaves.*

Nodding Bur-marigold

Bidens cernua (Asteraceae)

OCCUPIES *damp, open places such as river and lake margins, ditches, and floodplains.*

long, spear-shaped leaf

The nodding golden brown flowerheads of this plant, without rays and surrounded by a ring of long, leaf-like bracts, are rather like miniature sunflowers. Very occasionally, a few short, broad yellow rays emerge, which transform the look of the flowers. The opposite leaves have large teeth.

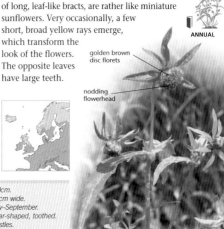

ANNUAL

golden brown disc florets

nodding flowerhead

leaf-like bracts

PLANT HEIGHT *30–60cm.*
FLOWER SIZE *1.5–2.5cm wide.*
FLOWERING TIME *July–September.*
LEAVES *Opposite, spear-shaped, toothed.*
FRUIT *Achene with bristles.*
SIMILAR SPECIES *Trifid Bur-marigold (B. tripartita), which has upright flowers, and leaves with a pair of lobes at the base.*

Tansy

Tanacetum vulgare (Asteraceae)

FORMS *small patches in waste or cultivated land, on roadsides, and riverbeds, on a variety of soils.*

This tall, aromatic plant is recognizable by its tight clusters of rayless flowerheads. These are often flat-topped on much-branched stems, and look like a collection of yellow buttons. The deeply divided leaves, with many tiny, regular teeth, are distinctive too. The whole plant is robust yet graceful, forming small patches where it grows.

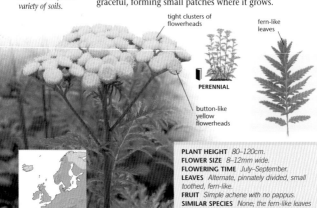

tight clusters of flowerheads

fern-like leaves

PERENNIAL

button-like yellow flowerheads

PLANT HEIGHT *80–120cm.*
FLOWER SIZE *8–12mm wide.*
FLOWERING TIME *July–September.*
LEAVES *Alternate, pinnately divided, small toothed, fern-like.*
FRUIT *Simple achene with no pappus.*
SIMILAR SPECIES *None; the fern-like leaves and button-like flowers make it distinctive.*

Corn Marigold

Chrysanthemum segetum (Asteraceae)

Although this medium to tall plant appears quite robust, it soon flops over if not supported by neighbouring vegetation in its favoured cornfield habitat. The fleshy leaves are deeply lobed and toothed; the upper leaves clasp the stem at their base. The golden yellow flowerheads, however, are the most striking feature of this plant. They have broad, overlapping rays, slightly toothed at the ends, rather like those of the Oxeye Daisy (p.89). They can appear in thousands where the plant is able to take hold.

APPEARS *among cereal crops and in fields where herbicides are not used; escapes into the wider countryside.*

daisy-like yellow flowerhead

broad ray florets

ANNUAL

NOTE

Corn Marigold used to be considered a serious pest for cereal crops, but due to modern use of herbicides, has now become much more scarce.

long flower stalk

greyish green leaves

toothed ray florets

PLANT HEIGHT *30–70cm.*
FLOWER SIZE *3–5cm wide.*
FLOWERING TIME *June–August.*
LEAVES *Alternate, oblong, clasping the stem, rather fleshy; pinnately lobed, unstalked lower leaves.*
FRUIT *Simple achene with no pappus.*
SIMILAR SPECIES *Oxeye Daisy (p.89); Yellow Chamomile (Anthemis tinctoria), which has narrow-toothed, pinnate leaves.*

Arnica

Arnica montana (Asteraceae)

One of the most beautiful members of the daisy family, Arnica enhances mountain meadows with its bright butter-yellow flowers. Borne on a solitary, long, hairy stalk, each flowerhead has a domed central disc and long, yellow rays. Most of the leaves are clustered towards the base of the plant. They are large, elliptical, and hairy on the upper surface with strongly marked veins. The flower stems generally have just a single pair of much smaller opposite leaves, about halfway up.

GROWS *in mountain pastures, meadows, and heaths in open sites, preferring neutral to acid soils, up to 2,800m.*

PERENNIAL

orange-yellow central disc

strap-like yellow rays

elliptical leaves

strongly marked veins

NOTE

A commercial preparation of Arnica is used as an effective cream to treat chilblains, sprains, bruises, and swellings.

PLANT HEIGHT *40–60cm.*
FLOWER SIZE *5–8cm wide.*
FLOWERING TIME *May–September.*
LEAVES *Mostly basal and alternate, short-stalked or unstalked, oval to elliptical; opposite stem leaves.*
FRUIT *Achene with with pappus of short hairs.*
SIMILAR SPECIES *Leopard's-bane (Doronicum pardalianches), which has loose clusters of smaller flowers, and large, heart-shaped leaves.*

Coltsfoot

Tussilago farfara (Asteraceae)

This plant flowers early and is one of the first of the daisy family to dot the February landscape with its flowerheads. Each is a small disc encircled by narrow rays, on a stem with overlapping scales like an asparagus tip. The leaves, with tiny, black-tipped teeth, grow large in summer.

FOUND in damp places, cultivated land, roadsides, spoil-heaps, gravel car-parks, embankments, and woodland edges.

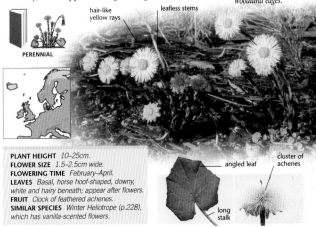

hair-like yellow rays

leafless stems

PERENNIAL

PLANT HEIGHT 10–25cm.
FLOWER SIZE 1.5–2.5cm wide.
FLOWERING TIME February–April.
LEAVES Basal, horse hoof-shaped, downy, white and hairy beneath; appear after flowers.
FRUIT Clock of feathered achenes.
SIMILAR SPECIES Winter Heliotrope (p.228), which has vanilla-scented flowers.

angled leaf

cluster of achenes

long stalk

Groundsel

Senecio vulgaris (Asteraceae)

A common, ubiquitous weed, Groundsel is found in flower at almost any time of year. It has many-branched stems topped with small yellow flowerheads, which soon become tufts of white pappus hairs, although occasionally there is a form with a few short, yellow rays. The leaves are pinnately and untidily lobed.

FLOURISHES in gardens, wasteland, cultivated land, road verges, and open habitats.

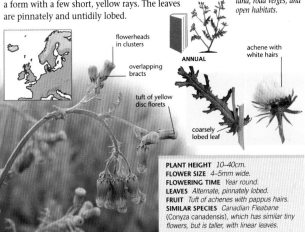

flowerheads in clusters

overlapping bracts

ANNUAL

achene with white hairs

tuft of yellow disc florets

coarsely lobed leaf

PLANT HEIGHT 10–40cm.
FLOWER SIZE 4–5mm wide.
FLOWERING TIME Year round.
LEAVES Alternate, pinnately lobed.
FRUIT Tuft of achenes with pappus hairs.
SIMILAR SPECIES Canadian Fleabane (Conyza canadensis), which has similar tiny flowers, but is taller, with linear leaves.

Common Ragwort

Senecio jacobaea (Asteraceae)

A widespread weed of cultivation, Common Ragwort forms extensive colonies. It proliferates in pastures for horses, where the seeds germinate easily in bare soil kicked up by the horses' hooves. It is poisonous to livestock, especially when dried and palatable, and has earned a bad reputation in areas where horses are kept. It produces loose clusters of bright yellow daisy-like flowerheads, each with 12–20 spreading rays above linear, black-tipped bracts. The stems are ridged and the leaves are pinnately divided.

THRIVES in disturbed soil of pastures, wasteland, rubbish tips, roadsides, and rabbit-infested areas, usually on dry soil.

BIENNIAL/PERENNIAL

long, spreading rays

flowerheads in large, flat-topped clusters

bright yellow flowerheads

branched stems

deeply lobed leaves

black-tipped bracts

NOTE

This is the sole foodplant of the Cinnabar Moth (Tyria jacobaeae) caterpillar, which absorbs its poisons as a defence against birds.

PLANT HEIGHT 80–150cm.
FLOWER SIZE Flowerhead 1.5–2.5cm wide.
FLOWERING TIME June–October.
LEAVES Alternate, deeply divided, curling up at edges.
FRUIT Achene with pappus of long white hairs.
SIMILAR SPECIES Goldenrod (p.146) has narrow leaves; Fleabane (p.147) has arrow-shaped leaves; Oxford Ragwort (S. squalidus), found on wasteland near towns has lemon-yellow flowers and tidier leaves.

Goat's-beard

Tragopogon pratensis (Asteraceae)

This stately member of the daisy family stands robust and erect. It has few branches, its stems are ridged, and the unusual leaves are linear, tapered to fine tips. In Britain and western France, there is a form whose flowerheads have very short ray florets, inside a ring of lance-like bracts that stand proud like a monarch's crown. The continental form has long ray florets, but both forms are folded tightly shut by midday. The bracts elongate and swell as the fruit develops, eventually opening out to reveal an enormous fluffy "clock".

OCCURS *among tall grasses in meadows, on road verges and embankments, and alongside paths.*

NOTE

The roots of this plant were once stored over the winter and eaten as a vegetable, and the young flowering shoots boiled and eaten as asparagus.

solitary flowerhead

single row of bracts

stem swells slightly below flowerhead

thick stem

tapered leaf

ANNUAL/ BIENNIAL/ PERENNIAL

spreading ray florets

CONTINENTAL FORM

clock-like fruithead

PLANT HEIGHT *40–75cm.*
FLOWER SIZE *Flowerhead 1.8–4cm wide, depending on length of rays.*
FLOWERING TIME *June–July.*
LEAVES *Alternate, linear to lance-shaped, grass-like.*
FRUIT *"Clock" of white feathery achenes forming a whitish ball, up to 12cm wide.*
SIMILAR SPECIES *None. Its large size and linear leaves make it distinctive.*

Cat's-ear

Hypochaeris radicata (Asteraceae)

OCCURS *in meadows, lawns, on roadsides, and other grassy places; prefers slightly acid or sandy soils.*

This plant can be difficult to distinguish from other dandelion-like plants. Its hairy leaves have very broad teeth and are in a loose, untidy rosette. The leafless flower stems are sometimes branched and have tiny, scale-like, dark-tipped bracts resembling miniature cats' ears. The outer ray florets of the yellow flowerheads are tinged green beneath.

PERENNIAL

broadly toothed margin

yellow ray florets

oblong leaf

yellow flowerhead

leafless stem

greenish tinge on underside

PLANT HEIGHT *20–60cm.*
FLOWER SIZE *Flowerhead 2–3cm wide.*
FLOWERING TIME *June–September.*
LEAVES *Basal rosette, oblong, lobed, hairy.*
FRUIT *Cluster of hairy achenes.*
SIMILAR SPECIES *Common Hawkweed (p.158) has unlobed leaves; Autumn Hawkbit (p.157) has deeper lobed leaves.*

Prickly Lettuce

Lactuca serriola (Asteraceae)

GROWS *singly or in clumps on disturbed and waste ground, and along roadsides.*

Although related, this plant has little in common with the edible garden lettuce. It has ranks of waxy, grey-green leaves up the dark stem, with stiff prickles along the midrib under each leaf. The top branches of the stem bear numerous, tiny yellow flowerheads with scaly, dark-tipped bracts beneath.

widely branched stems

tall, upright plant

leaf clasps stem vertically

prickly midrib

wavy leaf margin

tiny flowerheads

ANNUAL/BIENNIAL

PLANT HEIGHT *1–1.8m.*
FLOWER SIZE *Flowerhead 1.1–1.3cm wide.*
FLOWERING TIME *July–September.*
LEAVES *Alternate, held vertically on the stem, oblong, prickly margins and midrib.*
FRUIT *Fluffy tuft of white-haired achenes.*
SIMILAR SPECIES *Great Lettuce (L. virosa), which has horizontal stem leaves.*

Dandelion

Taraxacum officinale (Asteraceae)

Dandelions create a swathe of yellow during spring. Their flowerheads are made up of about 200 ray florets and have a ruff formed by the lower bracts. They are borne on unbranched, hollow, shiny, reddish flower stems, which exude milky-white juice if broken. The leaves have backward-pointing terminal lobes and are on winged stalks.

PROLIFERATES *in bare and grassy places, lawns, pastures, road verges, open woodland, and alongside paths.*

arrow-shaped leaf lobe

solitary flowerhead

clock of white hairs

PLANT HEIGHT *5–30cm.*
FLOWER SIZE *Flowerhead 2.5–4.5cm wide.*
FLOWERING TIME *March–October.*
LEAVES *Basal rosette, deeply lobed and toothed, pale midrib.*
FRUIT *Clock of achenes with a hairy pappus.*
SIMILAR SPECIES *Many similar Taraxacum species, all with solitary, shiny, hollow stems.*

PERENNIAL

Nipplewort

Lapsana communis (Asteraceae)

This common plant is easily recognized by its branched, slender stems bearing slim, neat buds and many small dandelion-like flowerheads. The leaves are broad, dark-tipped, slightly toothed, and are unlobed, except for the basal leaves, which are stalked and have two or more lobes.

INHABITS *semi-shaded sites alongside paths, open woodland, waste and disturbed land, old walls, and gardens.*

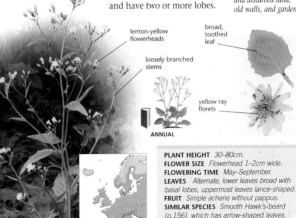

lemon-yellow flowerheads

broad, toothed leaf

loosely branched stems

yellow ray florets

ANNUAL

PLANT HEIGHT *30–80cm.*
FLOWER SIZE *Flowerhead 1–2cm wide.*
FLOWERING TIME *May–September.*
LEAVES *Alternate, lower leaves broad with basal lobes, uppermost leaves lance-shaped.*
FRUIT *Simple achene without pappus.*
SIMILAR SPECIES *Smooth Hawk's-beard (p.156), which has arrow-shaped leaves.*

Bristly Oxtongue

Picris echioides (Asteraceae)

GROWS *in rough grassy places, abandoned fields, roadsides, and wasteland.*

Easily recognized by the white pimples on the leaves, each one with a hooked bristle in the centre, this rough plant is covered with bristly hairs. The upper leaves clasp the stem and the lower ones are stalked. The flowerheads are made up of pale yellow rays, with curved bracts curling up at the base.

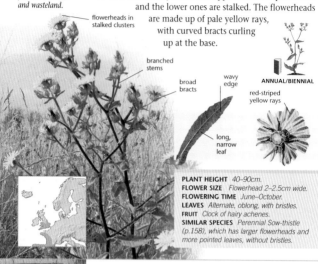

flowerheads in stalked clusters

branched stems

broad bracts

wavy edge

ANNUAL/BIENNIAL

red-striped yellow rays

long, narrow leaf

PLANT HEIGHT 40–90cm.
FLOWER SIZE *Flowerhead 2–2.5cm wide.*
FLOWERING TIME *June–October.*
LEAVES *Alternate, oblong, with bristles.*
FRUIT *Clock of hairy achenes.*
SIMILAR SPECIES *Perennial Sow-thistle (p.158), which has larger flowerheads and more pointed leaves, without bristles.*

Smooth Hawk's-beard

Crepis capillaris (Asteraceae)

FORMS *small colonies in grassy places, such as pastures, wasteland, and cultivated land.*

A dandelion-like plant with many branched flowering stems, Smooth Hawk's-beard has small flowerheads, with the outer ray florets tinged red underneath. Below the rays are two sets of green bracts, one long, and the other shorter at the base. The upper leaves clasp the stem; the lower leaves are lobed.

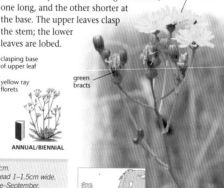

flowerheads in clusters

green bracts

clasping base of upper leaf

tapered point

yellow ray florets

ANNUAL/BIENNIAL

PLANT HEIGHT 30–80cm.
FLOWER SIZE *Flowerhead 1–1.5cm wide.*
FLOWERING TIME *June–September.*
LEAVES *Alternate, narrow upper leaves; basal rosette of lobed, toothed lower leaves.*
FRUIT *Small achene with white hairs.*
SIMILAR SPECIES *Cat's-ear (p.154), which has larger flowers and hairy leaves.*

Autumn Hawkbit

Leontodon autumnalis (Asteraceae)

This small, neat plant comes into its own in late summer, when many similar-looking species have had their main flowering period. The stems are slightly branched, with a few tiny bracts, and are topped by yellow-rayed flowerheads. The leaves are in a basal rosette and are very narrow, with long lobes that are thinner than those of Dandelion (p.155).

INHABITS *grassy places, roadsides, short-turf pasture, and rocky habitats, preferring chalky soil.*

yellow rays

PERENNIAL

tiny bracts

red stripes underneath rays

long, thin leaf

PLANT HEIGHT *5–40cm.*
FLOWER SIZE *Flowerhead 2–3cm wide.*
FLOWERING TIME *June–October.*
LEAVES *Basal rosette, hairless, lobed.*
FRUIT *Achene with pappus of white hairs.*
SIMILAR SPECIES *Cat's-ear (p.154), which has hairy leaves; Mouse-ear Hawkweed (below), which has unlobed leaves.*

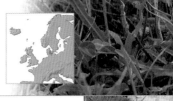

Mouse-ear Hawkweed

Pilosella officinarum (Asteraceae)

This plant spreads by overground runners or stolons that occasionally take root. The leaves, in basal rosettes, are densely white-felted beneath, with a few long, bristly white hairs on the surface. The lemon-yellow flowerheads are on leafless stalks, the rays striped red beneath.

FOUND *in dry grassy sites such as pastures, roadsides, and lawns, on acid or chalky soils.*

solitary flowerhead

PERENNIAL

oblong leaf

red-striped rays

slender runners

PLANT HEIGHT *5–20cm.*
FLOWER SIZE *Flowerhead 1.8–2.5cm wide.*
FLOWERING TIME *June–September.*
LEAVES *Basal rosette, oblong, untoothed with long hairs above, white-felted below.*
FRUIT *Small achene with brownish pappus.*
SIMILAR SPECIES *Autumn Hawkbit (above) has lobed leaves and no runners.*

Perennial Sow-thistle

Sonchus arvensis (Asteraceae)

Although superficially similar to other sow-thistles and dandelion-like plants, this bristly plant is distinctive. Its very large flowerheads, commonly seen in late summer and early autumn, sit on a base of sticky, hairy bracts. The whole plant is tall and stiff with greyish leaves, and produces milky latex when cut.

GROWS *on disturbed and cultivated ground, wasteland, abandoned fields, and along streams and rivers.*

large flowerhead

slender stems

lobed, toothed leaf

PERENNIAL

yellow ray florets

upper leaf clasps stem

PLANT HEIGHT *80–150cm.*
FLOWER SIZE *4–5cm wide.*
FLOWERING TIME *July–October.*
LEAVES *Alternate, lobed, and toothed.*
FRUIT *Achene with white pappus.*
SIMILAR SPECIES *Bristly Oxtongue (p.156) and Smooth Sow-thistle (S. oleraceus), which have smaller flowerheads.*

Common Hawkweed

Hieracium vulgatum (Asteraceae)

The hawkweeds are a complex group of species, divided further to include hundreds of "microspecies", which are difficult to differentiate. Common Hawkweed represents a group of these, recognizable by the loose rosette of mostly basal leaves that are oval to lance-shaped. They are toothed, but never lobed, and are crowded towards the base. The slender stems are branched at the top and the yellow ray florets have hairy bracts beneath them.

OCCURS *in rocky and grassy habitats, open woodland, heaths, cliff-tops, and other dry places.*

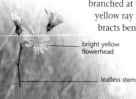

bright yellow flowerhead

leafless stem

toothed margin

ray florets

PERENNIAL

PLANT HEIGHT *30–80cm.*
FLOWER SIZE *2–3cm wide.*
FLOWERING TIME *June–September.*
LEAVES *Mostly basal, oval to lance-shaped with short stalk.*
FRUIT *Achene with brittle brown pappus.*
SIMILAR SPECIES *Cat's-ear (p.154), which has lobed leaves and a white pappus.*

Yellow Bird's-nest

Monotropa hypopitys (Monotropaceae)

This extraordinary plant is a saprophyte, drawing its nutrients from a tangled root system (said to resemble a bird's nest) that feeds on decaying vegetable matter in the soil. The leaves are scales lying close to the stem, and the flowers are a cluster of tubular bells, each with four or five petals. The stems become upright when the fruit develops.

INHABITS *dark corners of deciduous and coniferous woods of beech, pine, or hazel, or under hedgerows.*

PERENNIAL

creamy yellow plant

flowers in clusters

drooping, bell-like flowers

calyx enclosing fruit

tiny, scale-like leaf

PLANT HEIGHT *8–20cm.*
FLOWER SIZE *9–12mm long.*
FLOWERING TIME *June–August.*
LEAVES *Alternate, oval scales; yellow or ivory.*
FRUIT *Rounded capsule, held in calyx that becomes upright as it develops.*
SIMILAR SPECIES *Toothwort (p.38), which has flowers in a one-sided spike.*

Bog Asphodel

Narthecium ossifragum (Liliaceae)

This colourful plant forms large colonies within its very specific habitat. Greenish to orange stems rise from a clump of strap-shaped leaves, and buds in a neat spike open from the base upwards to produce yellow flowers, each with six furry stamens. As the fruit develops, the stems and dry sepals become fiery orange.

FOUND *only in acid bogs, moors, and heaths in damp areas, particularly on hills and mountains.*

yellow-green flower buds

orange-red fruit capsules

starry, bright yellow flower

6 petals

PERENNIAL

PLANT HEIGHT *15–40cm.*
FLOWER SIZE *1–1.6cm wide.*
FLOWERING TIME *July–September.*
LEAVES *Basal, strap-shaped, short, often orange-flushed; small, bract-like stem leaves.*
FRUIT *Narrow, oblong, three-parted capsule, orange-red.*
SIMILAR SPECIES *None.*

Wild Tulip

Tulipa sylvestris (Liliaceae)

large, bright yellow flowers

This is the only tulip native to Europe. Originally from France, it then spread throughout the region. Each solitary flower has six large petals, sometimes recurved, and flushed with green or red on the outside. The grooved leaves are grey-green on the insides.

GROWS *in meadows, grassy and rocky places, orchards, and open woodland; spreads by means of underground runners.*

narrow, untoothed leaf

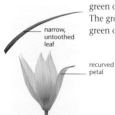

recurved petal

red-tinged outside of petals

PERENNIAL

PLANT HEIGHT *25–40cm.*
FLOWER SIZE *4–7cm long.*
FLOWERING TIME *April–May.*
LEAVES *Alternate, linear, channelled; dark green outer surface, but grey-green inside.*
FRUIT *Three-parted capsule.*
SIMILAR SPECIES *Yellow Star-of-Bethlehem (below), which has umbels of small flowers.*

Yellow Star-of-Bethlehem

Gagea lutea (Liliaceae)

Found in semi-shade, this member of the lily family produces seven flowers in an umbel, which arises from the centre of a pair of opposite leaves on the main stem. Each flower has six petals with a broad green stripe on the back and orange anthers. Below the flowers is a solitary, flat, yellowish green basal leaf.

strap-shaped basal leaf

FOUND *in damp grassland, woodland, and among scrub, on neutral to chalky soils.*

PERENNIAL

6 petals

starry, lemon-yellow flowers

PLANT HEIGHT *15–25cm.*
FLOWER SIZE *1.5–2.5cm wide.*
FLOWERING TIME *March–May.*
LEAVES *One strap-shaped basal leaf; two opposite stem leaves with hairy margins.*
FRUIT *Small capsule.*
SIMILAR SPECIES *Wild Tulip (above), which has large, solitary flowers.*

Wild Daffodil

Narcissus pseudonarcissus (Amaryllidaceae)

This tuft-forming plant has leafless stems (scapes). The solitary flowers are made up of six outer, pale primrose yellow tepals (petal-like sepals and petals), and a central trumpet (corona), which is a darker, more opaque yellow. Each flower has a green or brown papery spathe at the base. The grey-green basal leaves are flat, linear, and fleshy. The fruit capsule contains many seeds, helping extensive colonies to develop. The Wild Daffodil is smaller than the many hundreds of cultivated varieties grown in gardens, which are sometimes naturalized in the wider countryside.

FORMS *colonies in ancient deciduous woodland and meadows, on river banks, and along hedgerows.*

PERENNIAL

triangular, slightly twisted tepals

solitary flower

trumpet-shaped, deep yellow corona

papery spathe

long, narrow leaf

6 pale yellow tepals

yellow stamens

NOTE

The bulbs resemble onions but are highly poisonous, and, if eaten, can cause the fatal collapse of the nervous system.

PLANT HEIGHT *30–50cm.*
FLOWER SIZE *2.5–4cm long.*
FLOWERING TIME *March–May.*
LEAVES *Basal, linear, 6–12mm wide, 2–5 in number, fleshy; grey-green.*
FRUIT *Three-parted capsule, with many seeds.*
SIMILAR SPECIES *Many cultivated varieties of this plant, which have flowers in a wide range of sizes, colours, and shapes.*

Yellow Flag

Iris pseudacorus (Iridaceae)

THRIVES *in marshes and other wet places such as pond and river banks, swamps, margins of reedbeds, and ditches, on a range of soils.*

A marsh-loving iris, Yellow Flag often grows among other plant species with similar tall, strap-shaped leaves. It may be identified by its base, where the flat leaves grow one inside another, layered to form a chevron pattern. The leaves are sword-shaped and bright grey-green, each with a slightly raised midrib. There is no mistaking the showy, brilliant yellow iris flowers. Each is composed of three fall petals with faint brown markings, supported by a green leaf-like spathe, and three erect standard petals that are smaller, narrower, and unmarked. The large, oblong, drooping fruit capsule dries and splits to reveal neat ranks of orange-brown seeds, a little like niblets of maize.

brilliant yellow flowers

NOTE

The word "iris" comes from the name of the goddess of the rainbow in classical Greek mythology, and refers to the varied flower colours of many iris species.

PERENNIAL

pointed leaf tip

flattened, sword-like leaf

orange-brown seeds

brown fruit capsule

PLANT HEIGHT *1–1.5m.*
FLOWER SIZE *7–10cm wide.*
FLOWERING TIME *June–August.*
LEAVES *Basal, sword-shaped; bright grey-green.*
FRUIT *Three-parted capsule that splits to reveal hard, irregular orange-brown seeds.*
SIMILAR SPECIES *Sweet Flag (p.30) has tiny flowers; Branched Bur-reed (p.31); Stinking Iris (p.287), yellow form, is smaller.*

Lady's Slipper

Cypripedium calceolus (Orchidaceae)

This rare species belongs to a group more commonly found in North America, but is perhaps the most spectacular and exotic-looking of the European orchids. The four narrow, twisted petals are purplish brown, but the lower lip attracts greatest attention, being hugely inflated and pouched, bright yellow on the outside, and finely streaked and spotted with red on the inside. The brown petals are sometimes likened to loose shoelaces around the "slipper" of the yellow pouch.

OCCURS *in meadows and woodland glades; usually on mountain slopes and hilly areas, on chalky soil.*

PERENNIAL

twisted, purplish brown petals

stout, upright stem

large, pouched lower lip

NOTE

Most European orchids depend on a fungus that lives in their root systems and helps them to absorb more food from the soil.

broad, elliptical, pale green leaves

PLANT HEIGHT *25–50cm.*
FLOWER SIZE *Pouched lip 4–6cm long.*
FLOWERING TIME *May–June.*
LEAVES *Alternate, basal, usually four; broadly elliptical, strongly ribbed; pale green.*
FRUIT *Oblong capsule containing many tiny seeds.*
SIMILAR SPECIES *Calypso (Calypso bulbosa), which has a bright pink flower, also with a pouched lip; grows only in Finland and Sweden.*

Common Broomrape

Orobanche minor (Orobanchaceae)

flowers in simple spikes

Broomrapes are plants without the green pigment chlorophyll, which live parasitically on the roots of other plants, such as White Clover (p.60) and members of the daisy family, the host being the best clue to their identification. Common Broomrape is brown and dead-looking. The flowers, in spikes with tiny bracts in between, are two-lipped tubes, each with a three-lobed lower lip.

PARASITIZES *other plants in meadows, hedgerows, scrub, and grassy fields.*

PERENNIAL

pointed tip

scale-like bract

2-lipped flower

purplish yellow flowers

PLANT HEIGHT *20–50cm.*
FLOWER SIZE *1–1.8cm long.*
FLOWERING TIME *June–September.*
LEAVES *Alternate, tiny, scale-like bracts.*
FRUIT *Capsule containing small seeds.*
SIMILAR SPECIES *Toothwort (p.38); Bird's-nest Orchid (p.166) has a more complex arrangement of petals and lips.*

Mugwort

Artemisia vulgaris (Asteraceae)

A common wasteland plant with insignificant flowers, Mugwort can be distinguished from similar plants by its lower leaves. They are delicate and finely lobed, very dark green above, but bright silvery below, with distinct veins. The margins remain green, giving the leaf an "outlined" look. The flowerheads, with pale grey bracts, open golden yellow but quickly turn reddish brown.

FLOURISHES *on wasteland, disturbed ground, and rubbish tips, and in farmyards, in bare, rich soil.*

finger-like leaf lobes

numerous tiny flowerheads in clusters

reddish brown florets

erect stems

PERENNIAL

PLANT HEIGHT *80–150cm.*
FLOWER SIZE *Flowerhead 3–4mm wide.*
FLOWERING TIME *June–September.*
LEAVES *Alternate, oval in outline, lobed.*
FRUIT *Tiny, hairless achene.*
SIMILAR SPECIES *Wormwood (A. absinthium), which has yellower flowers, and more rounded leaf lobes.*

Reed Mace

Typha latifolia (Typhaceae)

This robust, often invasive plant is also known as Bulrush. It has stout stems and grows from rhizomes in shallow water or mud. Its erect, flat, sword-like leaves are difficult to distinguish from those of other similar plants, except that they are often the tallest. However, there is no mistaking the highly distinctive flowers, borne in two dense spikes, one above the other. The dark brown, felty "cigar" is actually a collection of female flowers. The yellow male flowers appear in a narrower spike immediately above this, producing copious amounts of pollen, usually before the female section is fully ripe. In winter or the following spring, the seedhead bursts, expelling thousands of light, fluffy seeds that are carried away by the wind.

PROLIFERATES *in wetland habitats such as pond and river margins, marshes, and ditches, always with its base in water.*

dense, cylindrical spikes of flowers

NOTE

The light fluffy seeds resemble cotton wool and have been used to stuff mattresses. They may also be used as a source of dry tinder in wet habitats.

PERENNIAL

tall, sword-like leaves

yellow male flowering spike

cigar-like female spike

fruiting spike

PLANT HEIGHT *1.5–2.8m.*
FLOWER SIZE *Female spike up to 15cm long.*
FLOWERING TIME *July–August.*
LEAVES *Mostly basal; flat, sword-like, and erect; up to 2cm wide; greyish green.*
FRUIT *Capsule containing light, fluffy seeds.*
SIMILAR SPECIES *Branched Bur-reed (p.31) has yellow-green flowerheads; Lesser Reed Mace (T. angustifolia) has narrower leaves.*

Carline Thistle

Carlina vulgaris (Asteraceae)

This plant appears in its first year as an easily overlooked basal rosette of leaves. However, if touched or sat upon, its spiky, needle-like spines soon make their presence felt. The flowerheads are composed of tubular, yellow-brown disc florets, surrounded by stiff, curved, straw-coloured bracts. The fruiting head persists for many months.

GROWS in meadows and dry grassland, usually among short turf on chalky or other well-drained soil.

ray-like bracts

densely leafy stems

fruiting head

feathered seeds

wavy, spiny leaf

BIENNIAL

PLANT HEIGHT 15–50cm.
FLOWER SIZE 2–4cm wide.
FLOWERING TIME July–September.
LEAVES Basal rosette at first, alternate, narrow, stiff, spiny, cottony on underside.
FRUIT Achene with pappus of yellow hairs.
SIMILAR SPECIES Stemless Carline Thistle (C. acaulis), which has all leaves in rosettes.

Bird's-nest Orchid

Neottia nidus-avis (Orchidaceae)

Lacking chlorophyll, this orchid instead derives its nutrients from a fungus within its root system that breaks down dead organic material. The whole plant is yellowish brown. There are numerous flowers, each with brown petals, a long lower lip, and small, papery bracts at the base. The leaves are reduced to papery, overlapping scales on the stem and the mass of tangled roots resembles a bird's nest.

FOUND in shady areas of deciduous woodland, particularly beech but also hazel. Blends into leaf-litter so is difficult to spot.

brown petals

lobed lower lip

many-flowered spike

yellowish brown stem

PERENNIAL

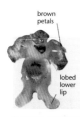

PLANT HEIGHT 20–40cm.
FLOWER SIZE Lower lip 8–12mm long.
FLOWERING TIME May–July.
LEAVES Alternate, papery scales.
FRUIT Capsule, containing many seeds.
SIMILAR SPECIES Toothwort (p.38); Common Broomrape (p.164); Ghost Orchid (Epipogium aphyllum) has very few flowers.

Red-Pink

Curiously, the colour red is invisible to most insect species, thus red flowers bloom almost exclusively in high summer, when most insects are in flight. Red flowers may contrast greatly against their background of leaves or soil, but the white element in a pink flower is much more reflective, and may also reflect ultraviolet, which is visible to bees and other insects. Pink flowers are often patterned with rings or lines, such as the pale powder-pink Musk Mallow, below. These markings serve to guide the insect to the centre of the flower.

SCARLET
PIMPERNEL

LADY ORCHID

HIMALAYAN
BALSAM

SEA
MILKWORT

Sheep's Sorrel

Rumex acetosella (Polygonaceae)

The loosely branched flowering spikes of this plant are of varying height and have many whorls of tiny greenish or reddish wind-pollinated flowers. Although male and female flowers are on separate plants, they look identical. Each oblong, stalked leaf has two lobes at the base which point forwards, so the leaf looks like an arrowhead. The leaves have a sharp, acid taste.

GROWS *abundantly in dry meadows, grassy pastures, bare places and heaths, usually on sandy, acid soil.*

arrow-shaped leaf

forward-pointing lobe

reddish flowers

tiny flowers in branched spikes

slender stems

PERENNIAL

PLANT HEIGHT *5–30cm.*
FLOWER SIZE *2mm wide.*
FLOWERING TIME *May–August.*
LEAVES *Basal, alternate, and arrow-shaped.*
FRUIT *Triangular achene, 1.5mm long.*
SIMILAR SPECIES *Common Sorrel (R. acetosa), which is larger with bigger leaves, often turning red in summer.*

Curled Dock

Rumex crispus (Polygonaceae)

This common species may be identified by its leaves. They are long-stalked and rather narrow, with distinctly wavy or crimped edges and strong midribs. The three-parted greenish flowers are arranged in dense whorls along the branched upper stems. The fruit is a rounded achene with three swollen wings or valves, without lobes or teeth.

PROLIFERATES *on cultivated and bare land, fields, rough pastures, and seashores.*

tiny flowers in whorls

curled, wavy margin

untoothed fruit valve

branched stems

narrow leaf base

PERENNIAL

PLANT HEIGHT *30–120cm.*
FLOWER SIZE *2–3mm wide.*
FLOWERING TIME *June–October.*
LEAVES *Basal, alternate, and lance-shaped.*
FRUIT *Achene, 3–5mm long.*
SIMILAR SPECIES *Broad-leaved Dock (R. obtusifolius), which has broad, heart-shaped leaves and toothed fruit valves.*

Common Poppy

Papaver rhoeas (Papaveraceae)

Poppies often appear in great profusion in fields or land that has been disturbed after a long period of neglect, as the seeds can lie dormant in the ground for many years, then germinate when brought close to the surface. The deep green leaves are deeply lobed, with toothed margins. The nodding flower buds are hairy; the flowers have four huge, overlapping scarlet petals, each with a small black blotch at the base. The stamens are also black. The smooth fruit capsule is like an oval pepper pot with holes around the rim, from which the seeds are shaken and released by the wind.

FLOURISHES *in arable fields and field margins, and disturbed and waste ground, on roadsides; often colours whole fields scarlet.*

ANNUAL

NOTE

The oil from the tiny black seeds is sold as a substitute for olive oil. As a typical drying oil (a vegetable oil that dries in normal temperature), it was also once used to mix oil paints before it was replaced with linseed oil.

brilliant red petals

black centre of flower

slender stem

pinnately divided leaves

oval fruit capsule

PLANT HEIGHT *30–60cm.*
FLOWER SIZE *7.5–10cm wide.*
FLOWERING TIME *June–September.*
LEAVES *Alternate, deeply pinnately divided, and toothed.*
FRUIT *Oval, smooth capsule with holes near the top, filled with hundreds of tiny black seeds.*
SIMILAR SPECIES *Other poppy species, which have differently shaped or prickly hairy fruit capsules.*

Pheasant's Eye

Adonis annua (Ranunculaceae)

This delightful plant is in essence a scarlet buttercup. Once a common sight in arable fields, it has become much scarcer due to modern farming practices. The 5–8 bright red petals have a black base, making the flower look like a miniature poppy. The alternate, feathery leaves are finely divided.

APPEARS in arable fields, wasteland, and recently disturbed ground, on chalky soil.

bright red petals

ANNUAL

thread-like leaves

black centre

PLANT HEIGHT *10–40cm.*
FLOWER SIZE *1.5–2.5cm wide.*
FLOWERING TIME *June–August.*
LEAVES *Alternate, feathery, divided into thread-like segments.*
FRUIT *Head of achenes.*
SIMILAR SPECIES *Common Poppy (p.169), which has larger, four-petalled flowers.*

Orpine

Sedum telephium (Crassulaceae)

An attractive member of the stonecrop family, Orpine has fairly large, succulent, pale green leaves, elliptical in shape with slightly toothed margins. The tight, domed clusters of flowers remain in bud for some weeks, but eventually open to reveal starry, five-petalled pink blooms, with purple-pink blotches on the petal tips and in the centres. The stamens are red.

OCCURS along woodland margins and road verges, and in grassy, rocky places; on light, sandy soil.

tight clusters of red-pink flowers

pale green leaf

toothed margin

PERENNIAL

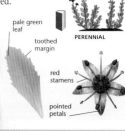

red stamens

pointed petals

leafy stems

PLANT HEIGHT *30–60cm.*
FLOWER SIZE *8–10mm wide.*
FLOWERING TIME *July–September.*
LEAVES *Alternate, elliptical, and toothed.*
FRUIT *Cluster of carpels.*
SIMILAR SPECIES *Roseroot (p.116), which has similar leaves but yellow flowers and a more bushy habit; generally grows on cliffs.*

Salad Burnet

Sanguisorba minor (Rosaceae)

The distinctive leaves of this plant are pinnately divided into pairs of tiny, oval leaflets, well separated on the leaf stalk, like a row of little bird's wings. They smell like cucumber when crushed, and may be eaten in salads. The flowerheads open first with the crimson female styles, followed by drooping male stamens with fluffy yellow anthers.

male flowers

FORMS *large colonies in dry grassland and rocky places, and on roadsides; on slopes and on chalky soil.*

rounded flowerheads

long stem

crimson female flowers

slender, pinnate leaves

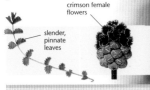

PERENNIAL

PLANT HEIGHT *20–50cm.*
FLOWER SIZE *Flowerheads 1–2cm wide.*
FLOWERING TIME *May–July.*
LEAVES *Alternate, pinnately divided with small, toothed leaflets, smelling of cucumber.*
FRUIT *One or two achenes within the calyx.*
SIMILAR SPECIES *Great Burnet (below), which is much larger and has bigger leaves.*

Great Burnet

Sanguisorba officinalis (Rosaceae)

This damp-loving plant is intolerant of grazing or drying out of its habitat. The tall, slender, branched stems bear oval flowerheads with densely packed crimson flowers, often visible above surrounding tall grasses. There are no petals, but deep red sepals and prominent stamens form the flowerheads. The alternate leaves are pinnately divided into about seven pairs of stalked and oval leaflets, dark green above but greyish beneath.

INHABITS *damp meadows and open, grassy places on chalky or rich soil.*

dark green and greyish leaves   toothed margin

oblong heads of crimson flowers

PERENNIAL

PLANT HEIGHT *40–90cm.*
FLOWER SIZE *Flowerheads 1–3cm long.*
FLOWERING TIME *June–September.*
LEAVES *Alternate, with stalked and toothed oval leaflets.*
FRUIT *Tiny achenes.*
SIMILAR SPECIES *Salad Burnet (above), which is smaller and has tiny leaflets.*

Grass Vetchling

Lathyrus nissolia (Fabaceae)

It takes sharp eyes and a little luck to find this plant, even if it is in flower. The leaves look like the grasses it grows among, each reduced to a long, flat, tapering blade. The solitary peaflowers are small, delicate, and brilliant scarlet. The long, narrow seed pod is pale brown.

GROWS *among grasses in meadows, fields and woodland margins, hedgerows, and along paths; not in dry soil.*

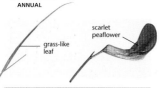

ANNUAL

tapering leaf blade

scarlet peaflower

long, slender flower stalk

grass-like leaf

PLANT HEIGHT *20–50cm.*
FLOWER SIZE *1–1.5cm long.*
FLOWERING TIME *May–July.*
LEAVES *Alternate, long, tapering, grass-like.*
FRUIT *Slender, tapering pod, 3–5cm long.*
SIMILAR SPECIES *Hairy Vetchling
(L. hirsutus), which has winged stems,
paired leaflets, and hairy seed pods.*

Red Clover

Trifolium pratense (Fabaceae)

Whole fields become crimson with the flowers of this prolific plant, which nourishes the soil with nitrogen, and is excellent fodder for livestock. The round or oblong heads of tightly clustered, pink to red flowers have a leaf directly below them. The leaves are made up of three oval leaflets, often with a V-shaped white mark. The flowers are pollinated by bumblebees.

FLOURISHES *in grassy places, old meadows, and wasteland, from lowland up to 3,000m.*

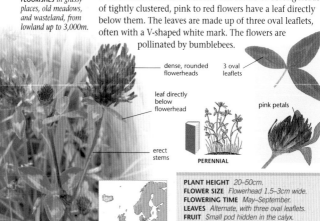

dense, rounded flowerheads

3 oval leaflets

leaf directly below flowerhead

pink petals

erect stems

PERENNIAL

PLANT HEIGHT *20–50cm.*
FLOWER SIZE *Flowerhead 1.5–3cm wide.*
FLOWERING TIME *May–September.*
LEAVES *Alternate, with three oval leaflets.*
FRUIT *Small pod hidden in the calyx.*
SIMILAR SPECIES *White Clover (p.60);
Zigzag Clover (T. medium) has stalked
flowerheads, and no leaf directly below.*

Bilberry

Vaccinium myrtillus (Ericaceae)

This compact, deciduous shrub appears in clumps. The ridged, angled stems bear soft, oval leaves with short stalks. Tiny flowers, green or flushed with red, hang in loose clusters, going on to form small black berries covered in a whitish bloom. The berries are edible, but being sparsely distributed on the plant, take time to gather.

OCCURS on moors and heaths, in deciduous or coniferous woodland, on dry, acid soils.

PERENNIAL

pale green leaves

bell-shaped flowers

bluish black berry

PLANT HEIGHT 20–50cm.
FLOWER SIZE 4–6mm wide.
FLOWERING TIME April–June.
LEAVES Alternate, oval, toothed.
FRUIT Fleshy black berry, 5–8mm wide.
SIMILAR SPECIES Cowberry (p.75); Bearberry (p.214); Bog Bilberry (V. uliginosum) has blue-green leaves.

Crowberry

Empetrum nigrum (Empetraceae)

This plant looks like a member of the heather family, but belongs to a small family distributed in the north of Europe and in South America. It is a small shrub with reddish stems and crowded, shiny green leaves, with the margins rolled under. The flowers are tiny and inconspicuous at the base of the leaves, and the fruit, which is slightly flattened, is enormous by comparison, like a miniature, shiny black bowling ball.

FORMS low mats in the damp, acid conditions of heaths, moors, bogs, and tundra; found in pine or birch woods.

round black berry

linear leaves

PERENNIAL

reddish stems

PLANT HEIGHT 15–40cm.
FLOWER SIZE 1–2mm wide, at petal base.
FLOWERING TIME May–June.
LEAVES Alternate but crowded, at all angles.
FRUIT Shiny black berry, 5–7mm wide.
SIMILAR SPECIES Cross-leaved Heath (Erica tetralix), which is similar when not in flower, but has a looser habit.

Scarlet Pimpernel

Anagallis arvensis (Primulaceae)

The brilliant red petals of this diminutive plant are easily spotted when the flowers open in bright sunshine. Occasionally, blue-flowered forms occur. The oval, shiny leaves have tiny black dots underneath, while the fruit is a tiny, rounded capsule that splits around the middle.

GROWS *on wasteland, in fields and field margins, and coastland; on dry, well-drained soil.*

opposite, oval leaves

yellow anthers

shiny leaves

ANNUAL

5-petalled flowers

toothed margin

PLANT HEIGHT *5–15cm.*
FLOWER SIZE *4–7mm wide.*
FLOWERING TIME *May–September.*
LEAVES *Opposite, oval, and unstalked.*
FRUIT *Small, rounded capsule.*
SIMILAR SPECIES *Pheasant's Eye (p.170), which has feathery leaves; Sea Milkwort (p.216), which has short-stalked flowers.*

Black Horehound

Ballota nigra (Lamiaceae)

This hairy, scruffy-looking plant has an unpleasant smell when the leaves are crushed. It has two-lipped, reddish mauve flowers, in compact whorls along the upper stem, with distinctive, sharply pointed calyces; these turn brown or black, giving the plant a dirty appearance.

FOUND *in hedgerows and woodland edges; on rich, neutral or chalky soils.*

toothed leaves

whorls of flowers

erect stems

pointed calyx

PERENNIAL

2-lipped flower

PLANT HEIGHT *50–100cm.*
FLOWER SIZE *1.2–1.5cm long.*
FLOWERING TIME *June–September.*
LEAVES *Opposite, narrow and toothed.*
FRUIT *Four nutlets at the base of the calyx.*
SIMILAR SPECIES *Red Dead-nettle (right), Common Hemp-nettle (right), Hedge Woundwort (p.246).*

Red Dead-nettle

Lamium purpureum (Lamiaceae)

One of the earliest plants to flower in the year, this plant is a member of the mint family. It does not sting as it is not related to common nettles. The smaller, upper leaves, bunched together at the top of the plant, are flushed with purple, while the two-lipped flowers are pink to red.

INVADES *cultivated, disturbed, and waste ground, roadsides, and gardens; also alongside walls.*

coarsely toothed leaves

ANNUAL

upper lip

straight tube

purple-flushed upper leaves

flowers in whorls

PLANT HEIGHT *8–25cm.*
FLOWER SIZE *1–1.8cm long.*
FLOWERING TIME *March–December.*
LEAVES *Opposite, oval, and toothed.*
FRUIT *Four tiny nutlets at the base of calyx.*
SIMILAR SPECIES *Black Horehound (left), Common Hemp-nettle (below), Wild Basil (p.222), Hedge Woundwort (p.246).*

Common Hemp-nettle

Galeopsis tetrahit (Lamiaceae)

This member of the mint family has pairs of leaves neatly arranged on opposite sides of the square, very hairy stems.
The pink flowers are in whorls around the base of the leaves; each has white and purple markings on the lower lip, and a very bristly calyx with pointed teeth.

2-lipped pink flowers

OCCURS *in woodland margins and glades, heaths, and sides of ditches and marshes.*

leafy upper stems

ANNUAL

purple markings

oval leaf

pointed calyx

PLANT HEIGHT *30–70cm.*
FLOWER SIZE *1.5–2cm long.*
FLOWERING TIME *June–September.*
LEAVES *Opposite, oval to spear-shaped.*
FRUIT *Four nutlets held within calyx.*
SIMILAR SPECIES *Black Horehound (left), Red Dead-nettle (above), Marsh Woundwort (Stachys palustris), which is less leafy.*

Deadly Nightshade

Atropa belladonna (Solanaceae)

INHABITS *semi-shaded places in old quarries, near ruins, woodland, banks, and pathways, usually among other scrubby vegetation, on chalky soil.*

A medium-sized, shrub-like plant, Deadly Nightshade looks innocuous, but is highly poisonous. Shiny black and slightly flattened, the berries look a little like cherries. They are said to taste sweet, but are deadly poisonous and can be identified by the persistent, five-sepalled calyx at the base of the fruit. The flowers are short greenish tubes flushed with brownish violet, with five spreading, triangular lobes at the mouth. Each flower is solitary in the upper leaf base. Slightly reminiscent of those of the related potato, the leaves are oval and pointed.

PERENNIAL

thick green stem

large, oval leaves

5 triangular flower lobes

bell-shaped flower

NOTE

The poisonous juice of the berry of this plant was used by women to dilate the pupils as a beauty treatment (bella donna); nowadays eye-surgeons use a refined form.

5 sepals

black ripe berry

PLANT HEIGHT *1–1.8m.*
FLOWER SIZE *2.5–3cm long.*
FLOWERING TIME *June–September.*
LEAVES *Alternate, oval, pointed and untoothed, on short stalks.*
FRUIT *Black berry, 1.5–2cm wide, with persistent five-sepalled calyx, highly poisonous.*
SIMILAR SPECIES *None; the unique combination of flower shape and black berry minimizes the chance of dangerous confusion.*

Red Valerian

Centranthus ruber (Valerianaceae)

There is no missing this distinctive plant when it is in full flower throughout most of the summer months, particularly as it clings to the walls of an ancient castle or monument. It is native to the Mediterranean and is now a popular garden plant. It has thick, erect stems, often branched at the top. The waxy leaves, in opposite pairs, clasp the stem. The numerous flowers in clusters arise from the leaf bases and are notable not only for their unequally lobed petals, but also for the very long corolla-tube with a spur at the base. The flowers are usually deep red, but pink and white forms are also common.

CLINGS to coastal rocks and cliff faces, old walls and monuments, usually near the sea, on shingle beaches and sandy places.

broad clusters of flowers

PERENNIAL

thick, erect stems

oval, grey-green leaf

long, slender flower tube

lobed, unequal petals

spur at flower base

NOTE

The leaves are used as a salad vegetable in continental Europe, and the roots are collected and sold in markets for use in soups.

PLANT HEIGHT *50–80cm.*
FLOWER SIZE *8–12mm long.*
FLOWERING TIME *July–September.*
LEAVES *Opposite, oval, fleshy, and usually untoothed, clasping the stem; grey-green.*
FRUIT *One-seeded nut with a feathery pappus.*
SIMILAR SPECIES *Common Valerian (p.223), which has pinnate leaves and prefers damp habitats.*

Ploughman's Spikenard

Inula conyza (Asteraceae)

OCCURS in open grassy and rocky places, among scrub or open woodland, preferring dry, chalky soil.

This erect and wiry-looking plant has long, slender red stems. The flowers themselves consist of a tight bunch of yellow disc florets surrounded by an eye-catching cylinder of pointed, orange-red bracts, and a few short green bracts below. The leaves are spear-shaped and toothed.

finely toothed leaf

orange-red bracts

yellow disc florets

branched flower clusters

wiry, reddish stems

PERENNIAL

PLANT HEIGHT 60–120cm.
FLOWER SIZE 9–11mm wide.
FLOWERING TIME July–September.
LEAVES Alternate, spear-shaped, toothed, upper leaves unstalked, lowermost long-stalked, with reddish veins.
FRUIT Achene with a feathery top.
SIMILAR SPECIES None.

Saw-wort

Serratula tinctoria (Asteraceae)

GROWS in rough grassland, meadows, open woodland, heaths, and bogs, on a range of soils.

Saw-wort is an exceptionally variable plant in stature, degree of branching, and leaf shape. The leaves may be deeply pinnately lobed, or spear-shaped and quite unlobed, but the margins are regularly fine-toothed. It is in effect a thistle without spines, and its chief diagnostic feature is the neat arrangement of overlapping, finely pointed, purple-tipped bracts below each small head of tubular florets.

cluster of flowerheads

finely toothed leaf

reddish purple florets

PERENNIAL

slender stems

PLANT HEIGHT 10–70cm.
FLOWER SIZE 1.5–2cm wide.
FLOWERING TIME July–August.
LEAVES Alternate, with finely serrated teeth.
FRUIT Achene with a pappus of hairs.
SIMILAR SPECIES Thistles (pp.179–181), which have spiny leaves; Common Knapweed (p.182), which has feathery bracts.

Musk Thistle

Carduus nutans (Asteraceae)

One of the most attractive thistles, Musk Thistle has large, rounded, rather regal flowerheads nodding outwards, each with a ruff of spiny bracts curving back. The flowerheads, solitary or in clusters, are made up of deep crimson-red, five-lobed, tubular florets. All the stems are covered with small wings armed with stiff spines, except for a tiny section just below each flowerhead. Narrow in outline, the deep green leaves are pinnately lobed into viciously spiny segments, and covered with a white down on the veins beneath.

INHABITS *grassy, open places, including meadows, pastures, abandoned farmland, embankments, and road verges, on rich, chalky soil.*

BIENNIAL

spine-tipped leaves

large, nodding flowerhead

spiny bracts

spiny, winged stems

NOTE

The flowers have a faint but sweet, musky scent; take care when handling the flowerheads as they are surrounded by very sharp, stiff spines.

PLANT HEIGHT *70–120cm.*
FLOWER SIZE *3–5cm wide.*
FLOWERING TIME *May–September.*
LEAVES *Alternate, narrow, pinnately divided, with sharp spines on the margins.*
FRUIT *Achene with a pappus of simple hairs.*
SIMILAR SPECIES *Spear Thistle (p.180), which has flowerheads that remain erect.*

Spear Thistle

Cirsium vulgare (Asteraceae)

PROLIFERATES on wasteland, dry, grassy sites, embankments, scrub, and roadsides on chalky soil. A persistent weed on rich, cultivated soil.

One of the most imposing and prickly of thistles, Spear Thistle has deep green leaves, which are paler beneath. They are shaped rather like a spearhead, with long, pinnate lobes, each ending in a very sharp, stiff spine. The stems are also covered in little irregular, triangular wings that are armed with spines. Part of the flowerhead is enclosed by green bracts and shaped like a vase, each bract tapering to a sharp point. The flowers themselves are reddish purple and fan out from the top, so that the whole flowerhead is shaped like a fat mushroom.

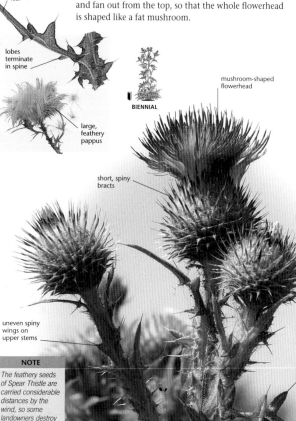

spear-shaped leaf

lobes terminate in spine

large, feathery pappus

BIENNIAL

mushroom-shaped flowerhead

short, spiny bracts

uneven spiny wings on upper stems

NOTE

The feathery seeds of Spear Thistle are carried considerable distances by the wind, so some landowners destroy the plants before they fruit.

PLANT HEIGHT *80–150cm.*
FLOWER SIZE *Flowerhead 2–4cm wide.*
FLOWERING TIME *July–October.*
LEAVES *Alternate, spear-shaped leaves with deeply cut triangular, spine-tipped lobes.*
FRUIT *Achenes with large, feathery yellowish pappus.*
SIMILAR SPECIES *Field Eryngo (p.37) has small flowerheads; Musk Thistle (p.179), which has long, spiny bracts that curve backwards.*

Marsh Thistle

Cirsium palustre (Asteraceae)

Easily identified even at a distance by its very tall, slender stature, this thistle has spiny wings along the length of its stems. The narrow leaves are pinnately lobed and, as well as being spiny, are covered in dark purplish hairs, especially when young. The small and pinkish red flowers are crowded in clusters at the top of the stems.

INHABITS *damp areas in pastures, meadows, marshy ground, and wet woods, in less disturbed places than many other thistles.*

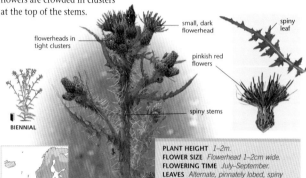

small, dark flowerhead

spiny leaf

flowerheads in tight clusters

pinkish red flowers

spiny stems

BIENNIAL

PLANT HEIGHT *1–2m.*
FLOWER SIZE *Flowerhead 1–2cm wide.*
FLOWERING TIME *July–September.*
LEAVES *Alternate, pinnately lobed, spiny margins, dark purplish hairs when young.*
FRUIT *Achene; brownish feathery pappus.*
SIMILAR SPECIES *Slender Thistle (Carduus tenuiflorus), which is shorter, with pink flowers.*

Creeping Thistle

Cirsium arvense (Asteraceae)

The stems of this spreading, persistent plant are hairy but, unlike many other thistles, have no spines or wings. Its narrow, toothed leaves, although spiny, are slightly softer too. The flowers are pale red to pink, or sometimes lilac. They are borne above narrow bracts, which are softly spiny. This untidy plant produces prodigious quantities of feathery yellow-brown seeds.

ABOUNDS *in pastures, wasteland, and farmland; may form large colonies.*

small pinkish flowerheads

spineless, hairy stems

narrow, wavy leaf

feathery pappus

PERENNIAL

PLANT HEIGHT *60–100cm.*
FLOWER SIZE *Flowerhead 1.5–2.5cm wide.*
FLOWERING TIME *June–September.*
LEAVES *Alternate, thin-spined, hairy beneath.*
FRUIT *Achene, brownish feathery pappus.*
SIMILAR SPECIES *Saw-wort (p.178), which has spineless, pinnate leaves with finely toothed margins.*

Dwarf Thistle

Cirsium acaule (Asteraceae)

This plant is stemless, making it the easiest of the thistles to identify, and the very large flowerhead is stalkless, or on a very short stalk. The leaves are in a tight rosette held flat to the ground. They have sharp spines on the margins and hairs on the surface, as a defence against being grazed.

GROWS *in the short turf of chalk grassland, in pastures, and rabbit-infested areas.*

PERENNIAL

single purple flowerhead

overlapping spineless bracts

spiny leaf margin

narrow leaf

linear florets

PLANT HEIGHT *5–12cm.*
FLOWER SIZE *Flowerhead 2.5–4cm wide.*
FLOWERING TIME *June–September.*
LEAVES *Basal rosette, pinnately lobed.*
FRUIT *Achene with a white feathery pappus.*
SIMILAR SPECIES *Stemless Carline Thistle (Carlina acaulis), which has similar leaves but very large yellowish flowers.*

Common Knapweed

Centaurea nigra (Asteraceae)

The stems of this common, colourful plant have many branches, each topped with a tight, neat head of reddish purple florets, all of equal length. Below this are overlapping dark or black bracts, each with a fringe of untidy hairs. The narrow leaves are pointed, sometimes with a few large teeth lower down.

THRIVES *in meadows, among scrub, and on road verges and embankments; absent from grazed areas.*

PERENNIAL

overlapping bracts

prominent midrib

tubular florets

PLANT HEIGHT *50–100cm.*
FLOWER SIZE *Flowerhead 2–3cm wide.*
FLOWERING TIME *June–September.*
LEAVES *Alternate, narrow, usually untoothed.*
FRUIT *Achene with short bristly hairs, enclosed by bracts.*
SIMILAR SPECIES *Brown Knapweed (C. jacea), which has spreading outer florets.*

Greater Knapweed

Centaurea scabiosa (Asteraceae)

More imposing than Common Knapweed (left), this bristly plant has stiff, slender stems. The large flowerhead has branched outer florets, which spread out in a ring. They are sterile and serve to attract bees to the flower. The bracts at the base of the flowerhead are also distinctive: green with a horseshoe-shaped fringe of black or brown hairs, and neatly overlapping like tiles on a roof. The soft, delicate, grey-green leaves are pinnately lobed, the upper leaves much smaller and unlobed. When the fruit has been dispersed, the bracts open out to form a shiny, pale brown saucer.

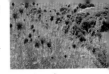

FOUND *in rough grassland and meadows, on road verges, among scrub, on embankments and cliff tops.*

PERENNIAL

large, solitary flowerhead

overlapping bracts

NOTE

The roots and seeds of this plant are known for their diuretic properties. Combined with pepper, they were once used as a remedy for loss of appetite. Do not attempt.

lobed lower leaves

spreading outer florets

inner florets

PLANT HEIGHT *80–120cm.*
FLOWER SIZE *Flowerhead 3.5–5cm wide.*
FLOWERING TIME *July–October.*
LEAVES *Alternate, pinnately divided into narrow lobes – somewhat ladder-like.*
FRUIT *Achene topped with bristly hairs.*
SIMILAR SPECIES *Cornflower (p.284); Perennial Cornflower (C. montana), which has blue florets and oblong, unlobed leaves.*

Snakeshead Fritillary

Fritillaria meleagris (Liliaceae)

FORMS *colonies in damp grassland, riverside meadows, and pastures, also frequent in gardens.*

The extraordinary pattern on the nodding flowers of this plant, neatly chequered like a chessboard, is distinctive. The six overlapping petals are usually reddish crimson but may also be white, with greenish markings. The flowerheads become upright as the papery fruit develops. The grey-green leaves are grass-like and slightly channelled.

petals may be white

3-parted papery capsule

PERENNIAL

curved stalk

crimson, chequered flowers

linear leaves

PLANT HEIGHT *25–40cm.*
FLOWER SIZE *3–4.5cm long.*
FLOWERING TIME *April–May.*
LEAVES *Alternate, linear, fleshy, channelled; grey-green.*
FRUIT *Three-valved capsule on erect stalk.*
SIMILAR SPECIES *None; the distinctive chequered flowers make this plant unique.*

Red Helleborine

Cephalanthera rubra (Orchidaceae)

FOUND *singly or in small groups in open woodland glades and rides, along shaded hedgerows; prefers semi-shade.*

The pinkish red flowers of this elegant, rather uncommon orchid, brighten the woods and copses it inhabits. The sepals and petals are alike, finely tapered to a point, the lateral sepals spreading like wings. The central lip has very fine yellow markings. The alternate, pale green leaves are narrow and tapered, each folded along its length.

flowers in loose spikes

pointed petals and sepals

leaf folded lengthwise

PERENNIAL

wing-like sepals

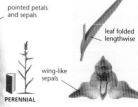

PLANT HEIGHT *40–60cm.*
FLOWER SIZE *Lower lip 1.7–2.2cm long.*
FLOWERING TIME *June–July.*
LEAVES *Alternate, long, with central fold.*
FRUIT *Capsule containing many tiny seeds.*
SIMILAR SPECIES *Dark Red Helleborine (Epipactis atrorubens) has darker, more clustered flowers and broader leaves.*

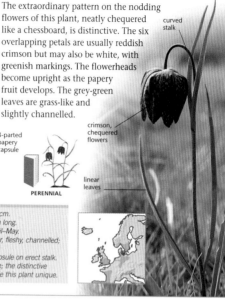

Fragrant Orchid

Gymnadenia conopsea (Orchidaceae)

This orchid's densely packed flowering spikes vary in size, but always have a delicate vanilla scent. Each pink, sometimes lilac, flower has a lower lip with three small, round lobes, wing-like sepals at either side, and a long, slender curving spur drooping down behind. The linear leaves are bright green, without any spots or markings, and are grooved along the middle.

GROWS *singly or in large, loose colonies on dry grassland and scrub, preferring slopes on chalky soil; also in undisturbed fens.*

PERENNIAL

small flowers in dense spikes

long, narrow leaf

3-lobed lower lip

long spur

erect stem

PLANT HEIGHT *20–40cm.*
FLOWER SIZE *Lower lip 4–6mm long.*
FLOWERING TIME *June–July.*
LEAVES *Alternate, simple, and linear.*
FRUIT *Capsule containing many tiny seeds*
SIMILAR SPECIES *Pyramidal Orchid (p.187), which has shorter, more conical flower spikes of a darker colour.*

Common Spotted Orchid

Dactylorhiza fuchsii (Orchidaceae)

Even before the flowering spike has developed, this orchid is identifiable by the dark, rounded blotches on its shiny, deep green leaves. Borne in spikes, the flowers have wing-like sepals set high up, and a lower lip deeply lobed into three and patterned with looping lines and dots. The colour of the petals ranges from white and pink to reddish purple, but always with the dots on the lower lip.

OCCURS *in colonies in open woods, meadows, fens, and marshes, on road verges and among scrub, on chalky soil.*

narrow leaf

rounded blotches

pattern on lip

flowers in dense spikes

solitary stem

PERENNIAL

PLANT HEIGHT *20–45cm.*
FLOWER SIZE *Lower lip 1–1.2cm long.*
FLOWERING TIME *June–July.*
LEAVES *Basal rosette at first, then alternate.*
FRUIT *Capsule containing many tiny seeds*
SIMILAR SPECIES *Heath Spotted Orchid (D. maculata), which has circular, brown leaf spots and a shallow-lobed lip.*

Broad-leaved Marsh Orchid

FORMS *loose, but sometimes extensive, colonies in damp meadows and marshes on chalky soils.*

PERENNIAL

Dactylorhiza majalis (Orchidaceae)

This orchid belongs to a group of closely related species, including Early Marsh Orchid (*D. incarnata*) and Lapland Marsh Orchid (*D. lapponica*). These are usually separated by their range, but hybridize freely where ranges overlap, making identification difficult. This plant has a leafy stem, with broad, bluish-green leaves, sometimes covered with dark brown spots. The flowers have upward-spreading sepals, and long bracts between the flowers. The lower lip of each has toothed side-lobes with dark markings, and a short, unmarked central lobe. *D. incarnata* has pale leaves without spots, while *D. lapponica* has spotted leaves.

dense flowerhead

magenta or reddish purple flowers

brick-red flower

folded lip

D. incarnata

barely lobed lip

D. lapponica

spotted leaf

D. lapponica

> **NOTE**
>
> *The Dactylorhiza species of orchid have finger-like tubers, while the Orchis species have two rounded tubers (orchis means testicle in Greek).*

PLANT HEIGHT *30–75cm.*
FLOWER SIZE *Lower lip 9–10mm long.*
FLOWERING TIME *May–July.*
LEAVES *Alternate, oval to elliptical, bluish green and deeply spotted.*
FRUIT *Capsule containing many tiny seeds.*
SIMILAR SPECIES *Common Spotted Orchid (p.185), which has narrower leaves; Northern Marsh Orchid (D. purpurella), which is shorter, with similar flowers but unspotted leaves.*

Pyramidal Orchid

Anacamptis pyramidalis (Orchidaceae)

The triangular shape of the newly formed flower spike gives this plant its name. The small, neat flowers are pale pink or, more often, deep pink, or cerise. They have no veins or spots but each has a long, slender spur at the back, from which butterflies and moths sip nectar.

PROLIFERATES *in open, grassy places, lightly grazed pastures, dunes, downland, scrub, and on roadsides. Prefers well-drained, chalky soil.*

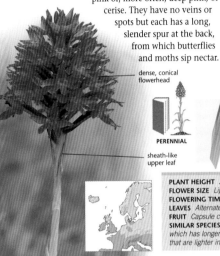

tapered point

unspotted leaf

deep pink flower

3-lobed lip

dense, conical flowerhead

PERENNIAL

sheath-like upper leaf

PLANT HEIGHT *20–40cm.*
FLOWER SIZE *Lip 6–8mm long.*
FLOWERING TIME *June–August.*
LEAVES *Alternate, lance-shaped, pale green.*
FRUIT *Capsule containing many tiny seeds.*
SIMILAR SPECIES *Fragrant Orchid (p.185), which has longer, cylindrical flower spikes that are lighter in colour.*

Lady Orchid

Orchis purpurea (Orchidaceae)

A tall, statuesque species, Lady Orchid has flowers with a dark brownish purple hood formed by the upper petals and sepals. The pale pink lower lip is said to resemble a lady, with arms on either side and a wide skirt. It is lobed with a tiny, central tooth, and spotted with purple. The broad, shiny leaves are basal, with one or two small narrow leaves on the long stem.

OCCURS *among grasses in woodland margins and glades, on road verges and hill slopes; prefers chalky soil.*

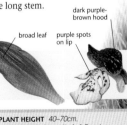

broad leaf

purple spots on lip

dark purple-brown hood

broad flower spike

PERENNIAL

solitary stem

PLANT HEIGHT *40–70cm.*
FLOWER SIZE *Lower lip 1–1.5cm long.*
FLOWERING TIME *May–June.*
LEAVES *Basal, oval to elliptical, shiny green.*
FRUIT *Capsule containing many tiny seeds.*
SIMILAR SPECIES *Burnt Orchid (O. ustulata), which is shorter, with very dark flower buds, giving it a scorched look.*

Military Orchid

Orchis militaris (Orchidaceae)

OCCURS *on chalky soil, in open grassland, embankments, fens, and woodland glades.*

The flowers of this orchid resemble a helmeted medieval soldier, as the petals form a long, pointed hood, and the lower lip is lobed into "arms and legs". Borne in a tight cluster, the flowers are pale pink with red streaks on the hood and purple spots on the "limbs". The basal leaves are oval to narrow and shiny green.

narrow, pale green leaf

hood formed by petals

reddish purple spots

flowers borne in spike

PERENNIAL

PLANT HEIGHT *30–60cm.*
FLOWER SIZE *Lower lip 1.2–1.5cm long.*
FLOWERING TIME *May–June.*
LEAVES *Mostly basal, oval to lance-shaped.*
FRUIT *Oblong capsule containing tiny seeds.*
SIMILAR SPECIES *Monkey Orchid (O. simia), which has longer "arms and legs" and a central lobe that forms a "tail".*

Early Purple Orchid

Orchis mascula (Orchidaceae)

GROWS *singly or in loose colonies in semi-shady, grassy places such as woodland, scrub, and road verges.*

Often the first orchid to appear in spring, this plant may also be identified by the long, dark purple blotches on the dark green leaves. The lower lip of the flower appears narrow, as it is folded back, and it has a pale patch with darker spots. The sepals, with a long spur behind them, are swept upwards like wings.

long, narrow spike of flowers

PERENNIAL

erect stem

long dark blotches

upward-pointing spur

PLANT HEIGHT *20–50cm.*
FLOWER SIZE *Lower lip 7–9mm long.*
FLOWERING TIME *April–May.*
LEAVES *Basal, lance-shaped.*
FRUIT *Capsule containing many tiny seeds.*
SIMILAR SPECIES *Green-winged Orchid (O. morio), which has green-tinged sepals with purple veins.*

Bee Orchid

Ophrys apifera (Orchidaceae)

The *Ophrys* species of orchids have an unusual flower shape, which mimics the form of a bee or wasp. In most species, the flower is pollinated by male insects in search of a mate, but in the Bee Orchid – unusually – the flowers are almost always self-pollinated. The stem is slender with just a few flowers, borne in a loose spike. Each flower has three prominent pink sepals, a narrow green hood, and a large lip which is bulbous, slightly velvety, and dark chocolate brown. There is a distinctive shiny patch (speculum) on the lip of the flower, with a yellow U-shaped margin and two yellow dots.

INHABITS *woodland margins, meadows, embankments, and road verges, singly or in very loose colonies; prefers chalky soil.*

PERENNIAL

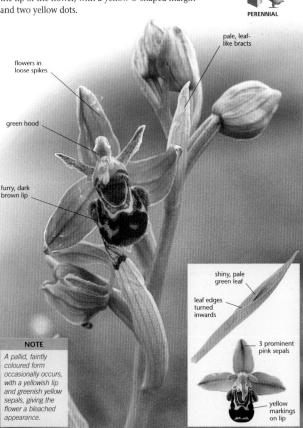

pale, leaf-like bracts

flowers in loose spikes

green hood

furry, dark brown lip

shiny, pale green leaf

leaf edges turned inwards

3 prominent pink sepals

yellow markings on lip

NOTE

A pallid, faintly coloured form occasionally occurs, with a yellowish lip and greenish yellow sepals, giving the flower a bleached appearance.

PLANT HEIGHT *25–45cm.*
FLOWER SIZE *Lower lip 1–1.3cm long.*
FLOWERING TIME *May–June.*
LEAVES *Mostly basal, forming loose rosettes, oval to lance-shaped; pale green.*
FRUIT *Capsule containing many tiny seeds.*
SIMILAR SPECIES *Fly Orchid (p.35); Late Spider Orchid (p.190), which has a broader lip with a small, central tooth.*

Late Spider Orchid

Ophrys fuciflora (Orchidaceae)

INHABITS *grassy places, such as road verges, woodland margins, meadows, pastures, and scrub, on chalky soil.*

Similar in general appearance to the Bee Orchid (p.189), the flowers of this species have a much broader lower lip, often with a small, central, forward-pointing tooth. The central area of the lip (speculum) may be in the shape of an H or X; it has a dark, metallic blue sheen and is outlined with yellow. The narrow leaves are pale green.

uppermost bract

pink sepals

dark brown lower lip

flowers in loose clusters

PERENNIAL

PLANT HEIGHT *20–40cm.*
FLOWER SIZE *Lower lip 9–13mm long.*
FLOWERING TIME *June–July.*
LEAVES *Mainly basal, lance-shaped.*
FRUIT *Capsule containing many tiny seeds.*
SIMILAR SPECIES *Bee Orchid (p.189), which has a narrower lip; Early Spider Orchid (O. sphegodes), which has green sepals.*

Hare's-foot Clover

Trifolium arvense (Fabaceae)

FORMS *mats in dry, grassy areas, scrub, and woodland margins, on sandy soil.*

The dense, fluffy flowerheads are almost like those of grass, but close examination shows that each tiny pink flower is surrounded by a calyx of long, silky hairs, which gives the flowerhead the appearance of a hare's foot. The trifoliate leaves are more slender than those of other clovers.

slender stem

cylindrical flowerheads

trifoliate leaves

ANNUAL/BIENNIAL

narrow, oblong leaflets

long, silky hairs

PLANT HEIGHT *10–25cm.*
FLOWER SIZE *3–6mm long.*
FLOWERING TIME *June–September.*
LEAVES *Trifoliate, with oval to oblong, slender leaflets, hairy and paler beneath.*
FRUIT *One-seeded pod within the calyx.*
SIMILAR SPECIES *None – the hairy calyx makes the flowerheads distinctive.*

Common Dodder

Cuscuta epithymum (Convolvulaceae)

This leafless plant obtains its nutrients by parasitizing other plants, such as heather. It is instantly recognizable by the mass of twining, hair-like, red stems, which attach themselves to the host by tiny suckers. The pale pink flowers, each with five tiny petals and protruding red stamens, appear at intervals along the stems.

TWINES *among the stems of its host plants, particularly heather, clover, and gorse; found in dry sites such as heaths.*

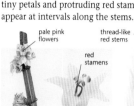

pale pink flowers

thread-like red stems

red stamens

ANNUAL

spherical clusters of flowers

PLANT HEIGHT *Up to 60cm.*
FLOWER SIZE *3–4mm wide.*
FLOWERING TIME *June–October.*
LEAVES *Tiny, inconspicuous scales.*
FRUIT *Small capsule, split transversely.*
SIMILAR SPECIES *Greater Dodder (C. europea), is larger, with thicker stems, and is parasitic on nettles and thistles.*

Amphibious Bistort

Persicaria amphibium (Polygonaceae)

This plant may be found growing in mud alongside bodies of water, but is more usually aquatic with its elliptical, pointed leaves floating on the surface of water, and dense spikes of bright pink flowers held upright on short stems just above it. The terrestrial form has hairy leaves that are more rounded at the base.

FOUND *in slow-moving water, such as lakes, ditches, dykes, and ponds, and along water edges.*

PERENNIAL

flowers in terminal spike

leaves float on surface

blunt leaf base

pointed tip

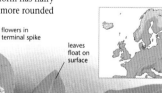

PLANT HEIGHT *Water surface, or up to 75cm on land.*
FLOWER SIZE *Flowerhead 2–6cm long.*
FLOWERING TIME *June–September.*
LEAVES *Alternate, lance-shaped.*
FRUIT *Small nut, but rarely formed.*
SIMILAR SPECIES *Bistort (p.192), which has thicker flowerheads; Redshank (p.193).*

Bistort

Persicaria bistorta (Polygonaceae)

One of the most attractive members of the dock family, this plant is recognizable by its dense, terminal clusters of pink flowers on long, slender stems, often seen en masse. Each individual flower has five petals and eight protruding stamens. The leaves are almost triangular, the lower ones large, with long, winged stalks, while the upper leaves are shorter and clasp the stem, appearing arrow-shaped. The roots of the plant are twice twisted (*bistorta* in Latin) and said to resemble two snakes, which is why Bistort was once thought to be a cure for snake bites.

FORMS *colonies or clumps in woodland and in damp, grassy places, such as old meadows and pastures. Often grown in gardens.*

NOTE

The roots contain starch and are used as a source of flour in Russia and Iceland. In Britain, the red dye made from the root was used to tan leather.

untoothed leaf margin

dense, cylindrical flowerheads

PERENNIAL

unbranched stems

small pink flowers

PLANT HEIGHT *40–100cm.*
FLOWER SIZE *Flowerhead 3–10cm long.*
FLOWERING TIME *June–October.*
LEAVES *Alternate, triangular to arrow-shaped.*
FRUIT *Small, triangular, one-seeded nut.*
SIMILAR SPECIES *Amphibious Bistort (p.191) in its terrestrial form, which has rounded leaves; Redshank (right), which has much smaller leaves and flowerheads.*

Redshank

Persicaria maculosa (Polygonaceae)

This common weed is most easily recognized by the dark patch in the centre of the leaves, although this is not always present. The leaves are otherwise rather plain, spear-shaped, untoothed, and almost stalkless. The often reddish stems bear numerous small spikes of tiny pink flowers in the leaf axils, each flower seeming to remain tightly closed.

PROLIFERATES *in arable fields, bare wasteland, and damp places such as river banks and floodplains.*

pinkish white flowerhead

branched stems

ANNUAL

dark patch

PLANT HEIGHT *30–80cm.*
FLOWER SIZE *Flowerhead 2–4cm long.*
FLOWERING TIME *June–October.*
LEAVES *Alternate, spear-shaped.*
FRUIT *Shiny black nut, 2–3mm wide.*
SIMILAR SPECIES *Bistort (left); Pale Persicaria (P. lapathifolia), which has unblotched leaves.*

Water Pepper

Persicaria hydropiper (Polygonaceae)

This plant forms extensive patches of upright stems bearing spear-shaped leaves, often with slightly wavy edges. At the base of each leaf is a small, fringed brown sheath (ochrea). The tiny, pink or greenish white flowers are arranged close to the stem in long, drooping spikes.

THRIVES *in damp meadows, pastures, and marshes; also in shallow water and semi-shaded places.*

narrow, stalkless leaves

pointed leaf

ANNUAL

flowers in slender spikes

branched stems

papery sheath

PLANT HEIGHT *30–75cm.*
FLOWER SIZE *3–4mm wide.*
FLOWERING TIME *June–September.*
LEAVES *Alternate, lance-shaped, and untoothed, with a very hot, peppery taste.*
FRUIT *Small brown nutlet.*
SIMILAR SPECIES *Redshank (above), which has slightly wider, blotched leaves.*

Greater Sand-spurrey

Spergularia media (Caryophyllaceae)

FORMS *small or extensive colonies on drier salt marshes and coastal sands, away from other plants.*

Even from a distance, the often extensive mats of this plant brighten salt marshes and coasts with their flowers. The five pink petals are whitish at the base, and interspersed with shorter green sepals. The whorled leaves are linear, fleshy, and flattened on the upper surface, rounded below, with a small sheath at the base.

petals longer than sepals

fleshy leaves

papery sheath

5-parted flower

starry petals

PERENNIAL

PLANT HEIGHT *8–20cm.*
FLOWER SIZE *7–12mm wide.*
FLOWERING TIME *May–September.*
LEAVES *Whorled, slightly fleshy.*
FRUIT *Pendent capsule, with three valves.*
SIMILAR SPECIES *Lesser Sand-spurrey (S. marina) and Sand Spurrey (S. rubra), which have petals shorter than the sepals.*

Ragged Robin

Lychnis flos-cuculi (Caryophyllaceae)

INHABITS *moist grassland, fens, wet woodland, marshes, and streamsides.*

This distinctive marsh-loving plant is easily recognized by the ragged appearance of its bright pink or red flowers. However, each of the five petals is actually rather neatly divided into four finger-like lobes. Below the petals are red-striped sepals that are fused into a tube. The opposite leaves are usually hairy; the basal leaves are almost linear, but the stem leaves are wider or spoon-shaped.

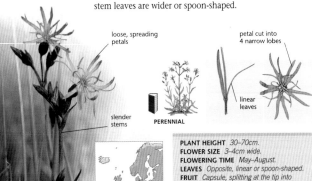

loose, spreading petals

petal cut into 4 narrow lobes

linear leaves

slender stems

PERENNIAL

PLANT HEIGHT *30–70cm.*
FLOWER SIZE *3–4cm wide.*
FLOWERING TIME *May–August.*
LEAVES *Opposite, linear or spoon-shaped.*
FRUIT *Capsule, splitting at the tip into five teeth.*
SIMILAR SPECIES *Large Pink (p.198), which has more finely divided petals.*

Alpine Catchfly

Lychnis alpina (Caryophyllaceae)

Most of the linear, slightly bluish green leaves of this plant are in tight, tufted rosettes, crowded at the base and tucked close to the ground, to minimize exposure to the harsh conditions of its mountain habitat. The flowering stems are hard to miss, however, with their tight, rounded clusters of brilliant pink flowers, each with five deeply notched petals.

FOUND *in rocky, stony, and mountainous areas, usually on soils rich in heavy metals or the mineral serpentine.*

bright pink flowers

dense, terminal flowerhead

narrow, grooved leaves

notched petal

PERENNIAL

PLANT HEIGHT *5–18cm.*
FLOWER SIZE *8–12mm wide.*
FLOWERING TIME *June–August.*
LEAVES *Basal and opposite, linear.*
FRUIT *Capsule, 4–5mm long, split at the tip into five teeth.*
SIMILAR SPECIES *Sticky Catchfly (L. viscaria), which has taller, sticky stems.*

Red Campion

Silene dioica (Caryophyllaceae)

In early spring, this plant's tufts of oblong, hairy leaves may be recognizable along woodland paths, but borne later, the profusion of bright, pinkish red flowers on the reddish stems is unmistakable. Male and female flowers are on separate plants; and the fruit capsule enlarges into a flask shape with turned back teeth.

GROWS *in field margins, woodland, and hedgerows; on roadsides and wasteland; in ditches and on rocky slopes.*

notched petals

oblong leaf

fruit splits at top

tall stem

BIENNIAL/ PERENNIAL

stalkless stem leaves

PLANT HEIGHT *50–100cm.*
FLOWER SIZE *1.8–2.5cm wide.*
FLOWERING TIME *May–August.*
LEAVES *Opposite, unstalked, hairy; oval to oblong stem leaves.*
FRUIT *Capsule with ten turned back teeth.*
SIMILAR SPECIES *Corncockle (p.196); White Campion (S. alba) has white flowers.*

Corncockle

Agrostemma githago (Caryophyllaceae)

With modern farming practices, this plant has gone from being a familiar cornfield weed to a rare wildflower, both in farmland and in the wild. However, it is still much used in wildflower seed mixes. The five broadly overlapping petals are deep pink, paler towards the centre, and open into a shallow saucer-shape. The long, hairy sepals taper to a fine point, projecting beyond the petals like a star. The hairy leaves are exceptionally long and narrow, and somewhat greyish. The large, round black seeds are finely sculpted, resembling a drill-bit.

OCCURS *sporadically in "unimproved" cornfields or other cultivated land where cereal crops grow, sometimes escaping.*

long, narrow sepals

sepals joined below

long, slender stems

ANNUAL

NOTE

The Corncockle's poisonous seeds may contaminate flour, which is why farmers have, over the years, worked to eradicate the plant.

narrow leaf

untoothed margin

pale flower centre

overlapping petals

PLANT HEIGHT *60–100cm.*
FLOWER SIZE *3–5cm wide.*
FLOWERING TIME *May–August.*
LEAVES *Opposite, linear to narrowly lance-shaped, hairy and well-spaced along the stem.*
FRUIT *Capsule, 1–2.2cm long, containing large black seeds.*
SIMILAR SPECIES *Red Campion (p.195), which has smaller flowers in clusters, with deeply cleft petals.*

Soapwort

Saponaria officinalis (Caryophyllaceae)

A robust plant found in semi-shaded places, Soapwort has fleshy, veined leaves, which were once gathered and boiled to make a soapy lather for washing. The flowers are in tight clusters, each of the petals broadening towards the tip like an aeroplane propeller, and are notable for their very long, pale green sepal tubes.

GROWS *in grassy places, woodland margins, hedgerows, and roadsides; on waste, fallow, and cultivated land.*

5 narrow, unnotched petals

oval to elliptic leaves

pale pink flowers

long sepal tube

leafy stem

PERENNIAL

PLANT HEIGHT *60–90cm.*
FLOWER SIZE *2.5–2.8cm wide.*
FLOWERING TIME *June–September.*
LEAVES *Opposite, oval to elliptic, veined.*
FRUIT *Many-seeded capsule with four teeth.*
SIMILAR SPECIES *Hybrids of Red Campion (p.195) and White Campion (Silene alba) have notched petals and striped calyces.*

Carthusian Pink

Dianthus carthusianorum (Caryophyllaceae)

Of the many species of pinks in Europe, Carthusian Pink is distinctive for its very tight clusters of flower buds surrounded by long, pointed brown bracts and its almost papery, brownish sepal tubes. The deep pink petals are broad, nearly overlapping, and have a toothed margin. As with other pinks, the leaves are narrow and grey-green.

FOUND *in dry, rocky grassland, woodland margins or clearings, and along roadsides.*

plain, deep pink petals

flowers in clusters

tapered leaves

fringed petals

PERENNIAL

PLANT HEIGHT *20–60cm.*
FLOWER SIZE *1.8–2cm wide.*
FLOWERING TIME *May–August.*
LEAVES *Opposite, linear, grey-green.*
FRUIT *Capsule with four teeth.*
SIMILAR SPECIES *Maiden Pink (p.198), which has unclustered flowers; Deptford Pink (D. armeria), which has narrower petals.*

Maiden Pink

Dianthus deltoides (Caryophyllaceae)

The deep pink petals of this plant have a row of darker spots near the base, forming a ring on the open flower. They are daintily spotted with white, like a dusting of icing sugar. The thin stems are branched, so the flowers are very loosely clustered, mingling with non-flowering shoots.

OCCURS *in dry, sandy places, such as roadsides, grassy banks, and rocky slopes; also on gravelled surfaces.*

red or purple ring

single flower on stem

PERENNIAL

grey-green leaves

toothed petals

PLANT HEIGHT *10–25cm.*
FLOWER SIZE *1.5–2cm wide.*
FLOWERING TIME *June–September.*
LEAVES *Opposite, linear to oblong.*
FRUIT *Capsule split into four teeth.*
SIMILAR SPECIES *Carthusian Pink (p.197) has unspotted flowers; Deptford Pink (D. armeria) has tightly clustered flowers.*

Large Pink

Dianthus superbus (Caryophyllaceae)

This plant has distinctive, large, pale pink or sometimes purplish petals, which are finely divided to the base, like the branches of a tree. The leaves are narrow and less grey than other pinks. The plant is tall, but straggly and branched, and easily flops over on its thin stems if not supported by other vegetation.

INHABITS *semi-shaded, dry grassland and woodland margins; sometimes riversides.*

linear leaf

finely divided petals

PERENNIAL

long calyx with short scales

PLANT HEIGHT *40–90cm.*
FLOWER SIZE *3–5cm wide.*
FLOWERING TIME *June–September.*
LEAVES *Opposite, lance-shaped.*
FRUIT *Long capsule split into four teeth.*
SIMILAR SPECIES *Ragged Robin (p.194) has neatly lobed petals; D. arenarius has white flowers.*

Great Meadow-rue

Thalictrum aquilegifolium (Ranunculaceae)

Found in hills and mountains, Great Meadow-rue is easily recognized by its flowers. Each flowerhead consists of a round, frothy mass of pink or lilac stamens, which looks like candyfloss. The greyish leaves are divided into groups of three leaflets, each with three rounded teeth at the tip, similar to those of Columbine (p.249).

GROWS *in hilly and mountain areas in meadows, woodland clearings, and scrub; sometimes cultivated.*

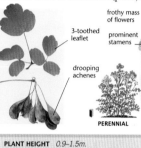

frothy mass of flowers

3-toothed leaflet

prominent stamens

drooping achenes

PERENNIAL

PLANT HEIGHT *0.9–1.5m.*
FLOWER SIZE *1–2cm wide.*
FLOWERING TIME *June–July.*
LEAVES *Alternate, pinnately divided into broad, triangular, three-toothed leaflets.*
FRUIT *Three pendent achenes.*
SIMILAR SPECIES *Common Meadow-rue (p.103), which has creamy yellow flowers.*

Cuckooflower

Cardamine pratensis (Brassicaceae)

Widespread in damp meadows and pastures, this member of the cabbage family is identifiable by its flowers, each with four broad, oval petals ranging from white to lilac or deep pink. The basal leaves have rounded lobes, similar to those of Watercress (p.47), and the stem leaves are divided into narrow, well-separated lobes that resemble a ladder.

FAVOURS *damp areas such as verges, river banks, and wet pastures.*

clusters of flowers at stem tips

PERENNIAL

yellow anthers

rounded leaflets

PLANT HEIGHT *Up to 60cm.*
FLOWER SIZE *1.2–1.8cm wide.*
FLOWERING TIME *April–June.*
LEAVES *Loose rosette of pinnately divided leaves; stem leaves with narrower leaflets.*
FRUIT *Slender pod, up to 4cm long.*
SIMILAR SPECIES *Coralroot Bittercress (C. bulbifera) has larger and elliptic leaflets.*

Sea Rocket

Cakile maritima (Brassicaceae)

In common with many coastal plants living in dry soil, the Sea Rocket has fleshy leaves that retain moisture. They are oblong, bright green, and deeply lobed into rounded "fingers". The pale pink flowers are clustered at the top of the stems, and the fleshy, bullet-shaped fruit has two shoulder-like projections at the base.

FOUND *in open, sandy areas, dunes, and shingle beaches on coastal sites.*

ANNUAL

long, rounded segments

4 petals

clusters of flowers

pale midrib

PLANT HEIGHT *Up to 30cm.*
FLOWER SIZE *6–12mm wide.*
FLOWERING TIME *June–September.*
LEAVES *Alternate, pinnately lobed, fleshy.*
FRUIT *Siliqua, 2cm long, with two segments, the lower one with two projections.*
SIMILAR SPECIES *Cuckooflower (p.199), which has less fleshy leaves.*

Goat's-rue

Galega officinalis (Fabaceae)

This robust, bushy pea family member has pink or white, but often bicoloured, flowers. Each large leaf, divided into well-separated, untoothed leaflets, ends in a terminal leaflet, and has a three-pointed green stipule at the base. A native of southern Europe, Goat's-rue is known for its fever-reducing medicinal properties.

OCCURS *on river or stream banks, in ditches, and on damp, grassy road verges.*

flowers in long-stalked spikes

large, oblong leaflets

bristly calyx

PERENNIAL

PLANT HEIGHT *80–150cm.*
FLOWER SIZE *1–1.5cm long.*
FLOWERING TIME *July–September.*
LEAVES *Alternate, pinnate.*
FRUIT *Cylindrical seed pod, 2–5cm long.*
SIMILAR SPECIES *Wild Liquorice (p.60), which has greenish flowers; Crown Vetch (right); Sainfoin (p.202) has narrower leaflets.*

Crown Vetch

Coronilla varia (Fabaceae)

Like Goat's-rue (left), this plant has flowers that may be pink, lilac, or more often bicoloured, but they are arranged in a compact ball or ring of 20 or so short-stalked flowers at the top of a long, leafless stalk. The leaves are pinnate with small, well-separated leaflets on slender leaf stalks. The narrow seed pods have 3–8 segments.

INHABITS *grassy places, particularly meadows, roadsides, wasteland, and open scrub, often on chalky soil.*

PERENNIAL

dense, rounded flowerhead

oblong leaflets

pink and white petals

leafless stalk

PLANT HEIGHT *30–100cm.*
FLOWER SIZE *1–1.5cm long.*
FLOWERING TIME *May–August.*
LEAVES *Alternate, pinnate.*
FRUIT *Slender pod, 2–6cm long.*
SIMILAR SPECIES *Goat's-rue (left), which is taller with larger flowers in spikes; Alpine Milk-vetch (Astragalus alpinus) is shorter.*

Common Restharrow

Ononis repens (Fabaceae)

The tough roots and creeping habit of this plant caused problems for farmers before the days of mechanized ploughs. It is a low, bushy plant with woody, hairy stems and rough, trifoliate leaves, each leaflet with oval stipules at the base. The flowers, larger than the leaves, consist of a huge pink standard petal, and white and pink wing and keel petals.

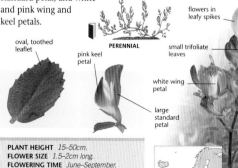

FORMS *clumps in meadows, pastures, and grassland, on chalky soil.*

PERENNIAL

oval, toothed leaflet

pink keel petal

flowers in leafy spikes

small trifoliate leaves

white wing petal

large standard petal

PLANT HEIGHT *15–50cm.*
FLOWER SIZE *1.5–2cm long.*
FLOWERING TIME *June–September.*
LEAVES *Alternate, three oval, toothed leaflets.*
FRUIT *Hairy pod, 5–8mm long, containing one or two seeds.*
SIMILAR SPECIES *Spiny Restharrow (O. spinosa), which has stiff spines.*

Strawberry Clover

Trifolium fragiferum (Fabaceae)

Similar to the pink-tinged forms of White Clover (p.60), this plant is more delicate, with smaller flowerheads. The three-parted leaves are in the characteristic cloverleaf shape, but without white marks. The hairy sepals of each flower swell up, forming the fruit. The hairs then rub off so that the fruit looks like a pinkish brown strawberry.

FORMS *loose colonies in short grassland of damp meadows and pastures, often where floods occur, or close to the sea.*

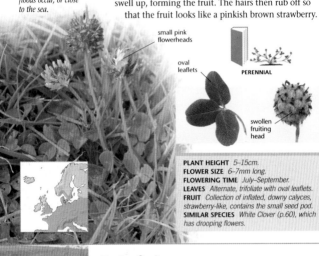

small pink flowerheads

oval leaflets

PERENNIAL

swollen fruiting head

PLANT HEIGHT *5–15cm.*
FLOWER SIZE *6–7mm long.*
FLOWERING TIME *July–September.*
LEAVES *Alternate, trifoliate with oval leaflets.*
FRUIT *Collection of inflated, downy calyces, strawberry-like, contains the small seed pod.*
SIMILAR SPECIES *White Clover (p.60), which has drooping flowers.*

Sainfoin

Onobrychis viciifolia (Fabaceae)

A tall, attractive plant, Sainfoin was once grown for cattle fodder. The long-stalked flowers are clustered in spikes, each petal striped with crimson on a pink background. The leaves are pinnately divided, with very slender, ladder-like leaflets; and the unusual, rounded seed pods have coarse, toothed ridges.

GROWS *in clumps or small colonies in short grassland and pastures, and close to cultivated land, on chalky soil.*

narrow leaflets

ridged fruit

pyramidal spikes of flowers

crimson-striped peaflowers

PERENNIAL

PLANT HEIGHT *20–70cm.*
FLOWER SIZE *1–1.4cm long.*
FLOWERING TIME *June–September.*
LEAVES *Alternate and pinnately lobed with a slender, terminal leaflet.*
FRUIT *Seed pod, 5–8mm long.*
SIMILAR SPECIES *Goat's-rue (p.200), which has broader leaflets and unstriped flowers.*

Dog Rose

Rosa canina (Rosaceae)

Perhaps one of the prettiest wildflowers to grace the countryside in early summer, the Dog Rose has long, arching, thorn-covered stems that clamber over bushes and hedges or occasionally form free-standing bushes. The stems and leaves are free from any hairs or glands, and the thorns are hooked at the end like an eagle's beak. The scentless flowers have five white petals that are usually flushed with pale pink, setting off the numerous yellow stamens. The styles form a small dome, rather than a column, in the centre of the flower.

SCRAMBLES *over hedges and bushes, along woodland margins, and in rough, scrubby, grassy places.*

PERENNIAL

pink-flushed petals

numerous yellow stamens

coarsely toothed margins

5–7 leaflets

oval red rosehip

NOTE

The hips have long been used in commercial preparations to ease coughs and sore throats; they may also be fermented to make wine.

PLANT HEIGHT *1–2.5m.*
FLOWER SIZE *4–5cm wide.*
FLOWERING TIME *June–July.*
LEAVES *Alternate, pinnately divided into 5–7 toothed leaflets, with long stipules attached to the leaf stalk.*
FRUIT *Oval to round red hips.*
SIMILAR SPECIES *Bramble (p.57); Field Rose (p.59) has flowers with styles forming a column; other Rosa species with hairy flower stalks.*

Wood Crane's-bill

Geranium sylvaticum (Geraniaceae)

The flowers of this species range from pink to violet to purple and are usually arranged in pairs. The petals are paler at the flower centre and do not overlap. The palmate leaves are divided down to the base into broad, coarsely toothed segments, and the entire plant is covered with fine hairs. The flower stalks remain erect after flowering, when the characteristic beaked fruit is formed. The beak, formed from the long styles which remain attached to the seeds, resembles the long bill of a crane or heron.

PROLIFERATES *along woodland margins, hedgerows, and streams, in mountain pastures, damp meadows, and rocky places, generally on rich soil.*

PERENNIAL

NOTE

The (male) anthers of the flower of this species ripen and wither away before the (female) stigma opens, a process called protandry. This prevents self-pollination, which would reduce the species' ability to adapt.

flowers in pairs

unstalked stem leaf

whitish flower centre

5–9 lobed leaves

barely notched petals

PLANT HEIGHT *30–70cm.*
FLOWER SIZE *2.2–2.6cm wide.*
FLOWERING TIME *June–July.*
LEAVES *Mostly basal, palmately lobed leaves.*
FRUIT *Five mericarps, joined by persistent styles into a long beak.*
SIMILAR SPECIES *Bloody Crane's-bill (right), which has more narrowly lobed leaves; Meadow Crane's-bill (p.254), which is a taller plant, with slightly larger flowers.*

Bloody Crane's-bill

Geranium sanguineum (Geraniaceae)

This crane's-bill has flowers with astonishing colours, more akin to a garden cultivar than a wild plant. They are deep purplish pink or cerise and have almost overlapping petals, with a pair of tiny bracts beneath. The distinctive, stalked leaves are almost circular in outline and are deeply divided into finger-like lobes.

PREFERS *shaded places in rocky habitats, open woodland, and glades, on well-drained soil.*

PERENNIAL

solitary flower on long stem

rounded, slightly notched petals

narrow lobes

stalked leaf

PLANT HEIGHT	10–30cm.
FLOWER SIZE	2.5–3cm wide.
FLOWERING TIME	July–August.
LEAVES	Alternate, palmately lobed.
FRUIT	Five mericarps, joined by their styles.
SIMILAR SPECIES	Wood Crane's-bill (left) and Knotted Crane's-bill (G. nodosum) have more coarsely lobed leaves.

Hedgerow Crane's-bill

Geranium pyrenaicum (Geraniaceae)

This species has long stems topped with medium-sized flowers – unlike most other pale pink crane's-bills, which have smaller flowers. The pale to mid-pink petals overlap, giving a starry effect. As with other crane's-bills, the fruit is beaked and is usually in pairs.

STRAGGLES *among tall vegetation along hedgerows and woodland margins, and in meadows.*

deeply notched petals

PERENNIAL

blunt-toothed leaf lobes

beaked fruit

flowers in pairs

PLANT HEIGHT	40–60cm.
FLOWER SIZE	1.4–1.8cm wide.
FLOWERING TIME	June–August.
LEAVES	Alternate, palmately lobed.
FRUIT	Five mericarps with a long beak, hairy, on long, downturned stalk.
SIMILAR SPECIES	Dove's-foot Crane's-bill (G. molle), which has smaller flowers.

Herb Robert

Geranium robertianum (Geraniaceae)

The often red-tinged leaves of Herb Robert help it to stand out among other vegetation. The scented leaves are characteristically deeply lobed and toothed down to the midrib. The small flowers are bright pink, fading to white at the centre, with two red stripes along their length, and bright orange anthers. As with all geraniums, the fruit bears a very long beak formed by the persistent styles attached to the seeds. As the ripe fruit dries out, they spring back, helping to disperse the seeds.

INHABITS *semi-shaded places along old walls, in woodland glades, and banks; also well-drained, rocky or gravelly sites.*

NOTE

The scent of the Herb Robert leaves recalls that of the garden geranium, which belongs to the Pelargonium genus, native to Africa.

ANNUAL/BIENNIAL

5 rounded petals

flowers in pairs

deeply lobed leaves

thin stalk

long beak on fruit

paired fruit

PLANT HEIGHT *10–50cm.*
FLOWER SIZE *1.4–1.8cm wide.*
FLOWERING TIME *May–September.*
LEAVES *Alternate, deeply palmately divided, stalked, with 3–4 lobes; often flushed red.*
FRUIT *Five mericarps, joined by their persistent styles into a long beak.*
SIMILAR SPECIES *Shiny Crane's-bill (G. lucidum), which has smaller flowers and glossy, less deeply divided leaves.*

Common Stork's-bill

Erodium cicutarium (Geraniaceae)

Stork's-bills have even longer beaks on the fruit than the related crane's-bills. An unusual characteristic is that the persistent style twists like a corkscrew as it dries, then drills the seed into the ground as it uncoils on rehydration. The leaves are pinnately, rather than palmately, divided.

FOUND *in dry, sandy places such as heathy grassland, disturbed and bare ground, often near the coast.*

fine-toothed leaflets

ANNUAL/BIENNIAL

long-beaked fruit

pink flowers

petals of unequal length

PLANT HEIGHT *10–40cm.*
FLOWER SIZE *0.8–1.8cm wide.*
FLOWERING TIME *June–September.*
LEAVES *Basal and alternate, pinnate.*
FRUIT *Five mericarps joined into a hairy beak, 1–4cm long.*
SIMILAR SPECIES *Musk Stork's-bill (E. moschatum), which has larger flowers.*

Mezereon

Daphne mezereum (Thymelaeaceae)

Although cultivated in gardens for its showy appearance, the wild form of this shrub first appears as a few meagre stems. These are transformed in early spring by the almost stalkless, bright pink flowers. The leaves appear after the flowers, in tufts at first on the stem tip.

GROWS *in woods and scrub, or in mountain pastures to 2,500m; prefers chalky soil.*

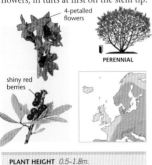

4-petalled flowers

PERENNIAL

shiny red berries

long, narrow leaves

small flower clusters

PLANT HEIGHT *0.5–1.8m.*
FLOWER SIZE *8–12mm wide.*
FLOWERING TIME *February–April.*
LEAVES *Alternate, simple, lance-shaped, untoothed; pale to bright green.*
FRUIT *Highly poisonous, glossy red berries, in tight clusters on stem.*
SIMILAR SPECIES *None.*

Himalayan Balsam

Impatiens glandulifera (Balsaminaceae)

Introduced to Europe in the 19th century from the Himalayas, this plant has now become an invasive pest along river banks in many areas. The succulent, red-tinged stems grow quickly, and bear whorls of lance-shaped, pointed leaves, each with a serrated margin and whitish midrib. At the top of the stems, numerous branches produce large, two-lipped, pendent flowers, ranging in colour from white to dark pink. Each flower has a pair of curious, almost opalescent sepals that form a sac. The long fruit capsule explodes violently when ripe, expelling the seeds some distance from the plant.

PROLIFERATES *along ditches, river banks, and streamsides, and in damp wasteland and woodland, usually in sheltered situations.*

ANNUAL

leaves in whorls

white to dark pink flowers

flowers in loosely branched clusters

NOTE

Fruit capsules that explode (catapult the seeds) are often found on plants that prefer sheltered sites, where the wind cannot aid seed dispersal.

serrated leaf margin

helmet-like upper petal

2 petals form lower lip

PLANT HEIGHT *1–2.5m.*
FLOWER SIZE *2.5–4cm long.*
FLOWERING TIME *July–October.*
LEAVES *Opposite or in whorls of 3–5, lance-shaped, finely toothed with pale midrib.*
FRUIT *Spindle-shaped capsule exploding to expel several dark seeds.*
SIMILAR SPECIES *Touch-me-not Balsam (p.130), which has yellow flowers; Orange Balsam (I. capensis), which has orange flowers.*

Musk Mallow

Malva moschata (Malvaceae)

The pale powder-pink flowers of this plant are a common sight along roadsides in late summer. They have five distinctly notched petals, with a central column of white to pink stamens, and a sweet, musky scent. The lower leaves are kidney-shaped and toothed, while the upper leaves are deeply divided into narrow segments.

FORMS *clumps along roadsides, hedgerows, and field margins, in meadows and other grassy places.*

PERENNIAL

lobed lower leaf

deeply notched petals

ring of nutlets

segmented upper leaf

PLANT HEIGHT *50–80cm.*
FLOWER SIZE *3–6cm wide.*
FLOWERING TIME *July–August.*
LEAVES *Alternate, palmately lobed, upper leaves more deeply cut into narrow segments.*
FRUIT *Nutlets, surrounded by sepals.*
SIMILAR SPECIES *Common Mallow (below), which has felty, slightly toothed leaves.*

Common Mallow

Malva sylvestris (Malvaceae)

A robust, hairy-stemmed plant frequently found in wasteland, the Common Mallow has flowers with five notched, pink to purple petals, with darker veins along their length, and a long column of pale pink stamens. Behind the petals, the calyx of sepals is backed by three narrow segments – the epicalyx. The felty leaves are rounded, with blunt-toothed margins.

GROWS *in wasteland and along field margins, hedgerows, and road verges.*

thin dark veins on petals

PERENNIAL

shallow toothed lobes

ring of nutlets

PLANT HEIGHT *50–100cm.*
FLOWER SIZE *2–5cm wide.*
FLOWERING TIME *June–September.*
LEAVES *Alternate, shallowly palmately lobed, and toothed, covered in felty hairs.*
FRUIT *Ring of nutlets within persistent calyx.*
SIMILAR SPECIES *Musk Mallow (above); Dwarf Mallow (M. neglecta), which is smaller.*

Marsh Mallow

Althaea officinalis (Malvaceae)

A tall plant found in open, mildly brackish places, the Marsh Mallow produces spires of delicately pink-flushed flowers clustered together towards the stem tops, often standing out among reeds or other tall waterside plants. The petals are broader than in other mallows, more deeply coloured towards the middle, and have a column of purplish red anthers in the centre. The leaves, which are soft to the touch, are broadly triangular in outline and noticeably greyish, with a covering of downy hairs.

GROWS *in salt marshes and damp meadows, by brackish ditches, and on the banks of tidal rivers, usually by the sea.*

PERENNIAL

flowers in tight clusters

purplish red anthers

5 broad, slightly notched petals

NOTE

The root, with its high mucilage content, was ground with sugar, flour, and egg white to make marshmallow sweets. Do not attempt.

coarsely toothed margin

triangular leaf

downy leaf underside

calyx enclosing young fruit

PLANT HEIGHT *80–150cm.*
FLOWER SIZE *2.5–4cm wide.*
FLOWERING TIME *August–September.*
LEAVES *Alternate, triangular, three- to five-lobed, and long-stalked; softly hairy; greyish.*
FRUIT *Hairy mericarps in a ring, surrounded by the calyx.*
SIMILAR SPECIES *Hollyhock (A. rosea), which is a frequent garden escape, has flowers in many colours in a tall compact spike.*

Rosebay Willowherb

Chamerion angustifolium (Onagraceae)

Once established, this vigorous plant may form an extensive patch or colony, spreading by means of underground rhizomes, so a patch may really be a single plant. The flowers are borne in tall, narrow, pyramidal spikes; each has four broad, rounded rose-pink petals and eight drooping stamens. The flowers at the tip may still be in tight bud when the lower ones have formed long, ridged, cylindrical fruit. The leaves are narrow and pointed, with finely toothed, often rather wrinkled, margins.

THRIVES *in disturbed sites such as woodland clearings, river banks, and roadsides; also where the ground has been burned.*

tapered flower spikes

PERENNIAL

rose-pink flowers

wavy leaf margin

pale midrib

8 stamens

unequal petals

NOTE

The leaves of Rosebay and Great Willowherb used to be a substitute for tea. In Russia, Kaporie Tea is still made from the leaves of these plants.

PLANT HEIGHT *80–150cm.*
FLOWER SIZE *2–3cm wide.*
FLOWERING TIME *June–September.*
LEAVES *Alternate, lance-shaped, with slightly toothed margins.*
FRUIT *Slender, four-valved capsule, containing numerous fluffy seeds.*
SIMILAR SPECIES *Purple Loosestrife (p.243); Great Willowherb (p.212), which is hairy; River Beauty (C. latifolia), which is a shorter, and often prostrate plant, found only in Iceland.*

Great Willowherb

Epilobium hirsutum (Onagraceae)

PROLIFERATES *in damp, open sites, such as river banks, reedbeds, lake margins, ditches, and marshes.*

This tall, hairy plant forms large patches at the edges of wet areas. Born in racemes, the saucer-shaped flowers are deep pink with four-lobed creamy white stigmas. They give rise to long, downy fruit capsules that peel back to reveal many light, hairy seeds. The narrow leaves are stalkless or clasp the stem.

PERENNIAL

saucer-like flowers

shallowly notched petals

lance-shaped leaf

capsules split lengthwise

PLANT HEIGHT *1–1.8m.*
FLOWER SIZE *1.5–2.5cm wide.*
FLOWERING TIME *June–September.*
LEAVES *Mostly opposite, occasionally whorled, lance-shaped, coarsely toothed.*
FRUIT *Capsule with four segments.*
SIMILAR SPECIES *Rosebay Willowherb (p.211), which has flowers in distinct spikes.*

Broad-leaved Willowherb

Epilobium montanum (Onagraceae)

INHABITS *sheltered spots on woodland margins, along ditches, hedgerows, and old walls; also in gardens.*

A slender plant of semi-shaded places, this willowherb usually has just a few pale pink flowers with four deeply notched petals arranged in a cross. Despite the plant's name, the oval leaves are not particularly wide, but are broader than those of similar species. The rounded, slender stems are reddish.

PERENNIAL

oval leaves

few flowers in loose clusters

toothed margin

4-lobed stigma

notched petals

strongly veined leaf

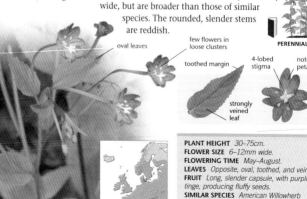

PLANT HEIGHT *30–75cm.*
FLOWER SIZE *6–12mm wide.*
FLOWERING TIME *May–August.*
LEAVES *Opposite, oval, toothed, and veined.*
FRUIT *Long, slender capsule, with purplish tinge, producing fluffy seeds.*
SIMILAR SPECIES *American Willowherb (E. ciliatum), which has narrower leaves.*

Heather

Calluna vulgaris (Ericaceae)

With its woody stems and scale-like leaves, Heather is well adapted to habitats with low-nutrient soil; it may grow slowly, but it lives a long time. The tiny leaves, in pairs on small branches, are leathery, becoming rough to the touch as they mature. Each flower has prominent sepals and a protruding style, with eight hidden anthers.

FORMS *carpets on heaths, moors, bogs, and dry, sandy banks, and in pine or birch woods, on acid soil.*

numerous flowers

PERENNIAL

very dense flowerheads

leaves crowded on stem

pale pink to purple flowers

PLANT HEIGHT *20–80cm.*
FLOWER SIZE *3–4mm long.*
FLOWERING TIME *July–September.*
LEAVES *Opposite, closely pressed on short branches, tiny and scale-like.*
FRUIT *Small, many-seeded capsule.*
SIMILAR SPECIES *Bell Heather (p.244), which has larger, darker flowers.*

Bog Rosemary

Andromeda polifolia (Ericaceae)

A small, evergreen, shrubby plant of upland areas, Bog Rosemary has narrow leaves that are dark green above but silvery white below, with the margins rolled under. The flowers are borne at the tips of the stems in small clusters, each on a long, curved stalk. The fruit is a dry capsule, unlike the fleshy berry of related plants.

OCCURS *in moist, acid habitats such as bogs and moors; associated with sphagnum moss.*

narrow leaves

PERENNIAL

nodding, bell-like flowers

pink flowers

spear-shaped leaf

PLANT HEIGHT *15–40cm.*
FLOWER SIZE *8–10mm long.*
FLOWERING TIME *May–September.*
LEAVES *Alternate; spear-shaped with in-rolled margins, whitish underneath.*
FRUIT *Erect, greyish capsule.*
SIMILAR SPECIES *Cowberry (p.75) and Bearberry (p.214), which have oval leaves.*

Bearberry

Arctostaphylos uva-ursi (Ericaceae)

This short, evergreen shrub, with its sprawling, rooting branches, has oval leaves that are broadest near the tip and have a finely stippled surface like leather. The small, pale pink flowers are borne in clusters, and are formed of petals fused together. The fruit is a shiny red berry.

FORMS *mats on acid peaty soil of moors, heaths, mountains, open woodland, scrub, and rocky places.*

fused petals

glossy, dark green leaves

PERENNIAL

flat leaf margin

urn-shaped flowers

woody stems

shiny red berries

PLANT HEIGHT *10–30cm.*
FLOWER SIZE *5–6mm long.*
FLOWERING TIME *July–September.*
LEAVES *Alternate, oval and leathery.*
FRUIT *Glossy red berry, 6–8mm wide.*
SIMILAR SPECIES *Cowberry (p.75) is taller; Bog Rosemary (p.213); Black Bearberry (A. alpina), which has black berries.*

Cranberry

Vaccinium oxycoccus (Ericaceae)

A straggling plant that can be easily missed, Cranberry has slender, creeping stems and small, oval leaves with whitish undersides. The curious shape of the pink flowers, with their recurved petals and columns of purple and yellow anthers, recall that of the unrelated Bittersweet (p.271). The large berries are orange-red, with brown speckles.

CREEPS *over sphagnum and other mosses in bogs, moors, heaths, and damp woodland.*

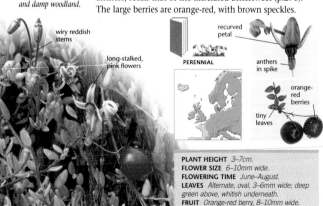

wiry reddish stems

long-stalked, pink flowers

recurved petal

PERENNIAL

anthers in spike

orange-red berries

tiny leaves

PLANT HEIGHT *3–7cm.*
FLOWER SIZE *6–10mm wide.*
FLOWERING TIME *June–August.*
LEAVES *Alternate, oval, 3–6mm wide; deep green above, whitish underneath.*
FRUIT *Orange-red berry, 8–10mm wide.*
SIMILAR SPECIES *Small Cranberry (V. microcarpa), which has smaller leaves.*

Bird's-eye Primrose

Primula farinosa (Primulaceae)

The delicate flowers of the Bird's-eye Primrose are borne in an umbel on top of a single, slender stem. The stalked flowers have five, bright pink petals, purple-tinged sepals, and a yellow centre or "eye". The leaves are in a tight rosette at the base. Each leaf has a green, wrinkled surface but a white underside with a floury "meal" that can be rubbed off.

FOUND *in tufts in short, usually grazed grassland, on peaty or stony ground, in damp habitats to 3,000m. May be abundant.*

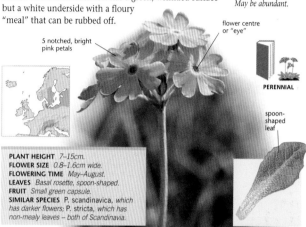

flower centre or "eye"

5 notched, bright pink petals

PERENNIAL

spoon-shaped leaf

PLANT HEIGHT	*7–15cm.*
FLOWER SIZE	*0.8–1.6cm wide.*
FLOWERING TIME	*May–August.*
LEAVES	*Basal rosette, spoon-shaped.*
FRUIT	*Small green capsule.*
SIMILAR SPECIES	P. scandinavica, *which has darker flowers;* P. stricta, *which has non-mealy leaves – both of Scandinavia.*

Water Violet

Hottonia palustris (Primulaceae)

This aquatic plant may go unnoticed before flowering time, as its leaves do not show above the water surface. However, dense whorls of fern-like, bright green fronds may be seen floating below. In summer, a single stem rises above the water surface, bearing several whorls of five-petalled, pale-pink to lilac flowers, each with a yellow centre.

GROWS *in colonies, in still, shallow water of lowland ditches, lakes, and ponds; prefers neutral soil.*

yellow centre of flower

finely divided leaves

PERENNIAL

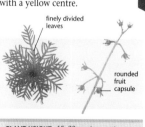

rounded fruit capsule

flowers in whorls

leafless stem

PLANT HEIGHT	*15–30cm above water.*
FLOWER SIZE	*2–2.5cm wide.*
FLOWERING TIME	*May–July.*
LEAVES	*Whorled, submerged or floating, finely pinnately divided, fern-like.*
FRUIT	*Rounded, pendent capsule within persistent calyx.*
SIMILAR SPECIES	*Bogbean (p.76).*

Sea Milkwort

Glaux maritima (Primulaceae)

A plant that has adapted well to the dry conditions of a coastal habitat, Sea Milkwort keeps low, hugging the ground, and has small, fleshy leaves on succulent stems that help to conserve moisture. The numerous tiny, short-stalked flowers are tucked in close to the leaf bases. Each flower consists of five pink to red sepals only, the petals being absent.

GROWS *in mats in rocky places, on salt marshes, coastal sands, and shingle.*

PERENNIAL

solitary flowers in leaf axils

unstalked, fleshy leaf

5-lobed flower

PLANT HEIGHT *5–15cm.*
FLOWER SIZE *3–6mm wide.*
FLOWERING TIME *May–August.*
LEAVES *Alternate and opposite, elliptical, fleshy; up to 1.2cm long.*
FRUIT *Small, round capsule at the leaf base.*
SIMILAR SPECIES *Bog Pimpernel (Anagallis tenella), which has rounded leaves.*

Thrift

Armeria maritima (Plumbaginaceae)

This plant forms cushions of narrow grey-green leaves that persist throughout the year. In summer, it produces long-stalked, bright pink flowerheads, each with papery scales surrounding the base, transforming the coastal scenery with extensive patches of colour. The plant is variable in height, with taller forms on inland sites.

FORMS *mats on cliffs, coastal rocks, and salt marshes, and inland on sandy grassland.*

grass-like leaves

spherical flowerheads

sheath below flowerhead

pink flowers

PERENNIAL

PLANT HEIGHT *5–30cm.*
FLOWER SIZE *Flowerhead 1.5–3cm wide.*
FLOWERING TIME *April–August.*
LEAVES *Basal, linear.*
FRUIT *Small, one-seeded capsule, with a papery wall.*
SIMILAR SPECIES *Common Sea-lavender (right), which has oblong to elliptical leaves.*

Common Sea-lavender

Limonium vulgare (Plumbaginaceae)

The wiry stems of this plant branch at the top and bear tight heads of pink to lilac flowers, each flower surrounded by papery bracts. The cut flowers retain their colour well and are commonly used in dried flower arrangements. The narrow, basal leaves, each with a single prominent vein, taper to a stalk about half the length of the leaf blade.

FOUND *in extensive carpets on the mud of salt marshes, colouring large areas with its flowers.*

tight clusters of flowers

tough, leafless stems

single-veined leaf

long leaf stalk

5-petalled flowers

PERENNIAL

PLANT HEIGHT *20–40cm.*
FLOWER SIZE *6–8mm long.*
FLOWERING TIME *July–September.*
LEAVES *Basal, oblong to elliptical.*
FRUIT *Small capsule, surrounded by a persistent papery calyx.*
SIMILAR SPECIES *Thrift (left), which has unbranched stems.*

Common Centaury

Centaurium erythraea (Gentianaceae)

The pink flowers of Common Centaury stand out among the grasses of the plant's natural habitat. They each have five elliptical petals, which are fused below into a tube about twice as long as the narrow sepals, and are borne in flat-topped clusters. The waxy, pale green leaves are arranged in a basal rosette, and in opposite pairs on the branching stems.

FLOURISHES *in grassy habitats on chalky or sandy soils, such as pastures, heaths, and among scrub.*

flowers in clusters

petals fused into long tube

untoothed leaf margin

yellow-orange anthers

BIENNIAL

PLANT HEIGHT *10–40cm.*
FLOWER SIZE *1–1.5cm wide.*
FLOWERING TIME *June–September.*
LEAVES *Basal rosette and opposite, elliptical, three-veined stem leaves.*
FRUIT *Two-parted capsule, with waxy seeds.*
SIMILAR SPECIES *Lesser Centaury (C. pulchellum), which has no basal rosette.*

Field Madder

Sherardia arvensis (Rubiaceae)

This low, bristly plant often goes unnoticed among taller vegetation. The pointed, oval leaves have prickly margins, and, as in other bedstraws, are borne in distinct whorls around square stems. The stems have downward-pointing bristles, and the pink flowers are borne in small clusters at the tip, with a ruff of green bracts below each cluster.

SPRAWLS *close to the ground in grassy places and on bare ground, preferring chalky soil.*

whorl of 4–6 leaves

leaf-like bracts

tiny, 4-petalled flowers

ANNUAL

PLANT HEIGHT *5–30cm.*
FLOWER SIZE *3mm wide.*
FLOWERING TIME *May–September.*
LEAVES *Whorled, oval to elliptical.*
FRUIT *Bristly nutlets, in pairs.*
SIMILAR SPECIES *Squinancywort (p.77), which has narrow leaves; Blue Woodruff (Asperula arvensis), which has blue flowers.*

Field Bindweed

Convolvulus arvensis (Convolvulaceae)

A fast-growing plant, this bindweed twines itself around other plants in an anti-clockwise direction, or sprawls along the ground. The leaves are either arrow-shaped with sharp, backward-pointing lobes at the base, or oblong. The trumpet-shaped flowers are usually pink with white stripes, but may be pure white or dark pink.

TWINES *around stems of other plants, fences, and other objects, and along hedgerows; on waste or arable land.*

striped petals

PERENNIAL

rounded or arrow-shaped leaves

untoothed leaf

yellow centre

PLANT HEIGHT *Up to 1.5m.*
FLOWER SIZE *2–2.5cm wide.*
FLOWERING TIME *June–September.*
LEAVES *Alternate; arrow-shaped or oblong.*
FRUIT *Rounded, many-seeded capsule.*
SIMILAR SPECIES *Hedge Bindweed (p.79); Sea Bindweed (Calystegia soldanella), which has fleshy leaves.*

Vervain

Verbena officinalis (Verbenaceae)

A wiry, hairy, and rather rough plant, Vervain has long,
square, branching stems bearing tall spikes of surprisingly
small flowers. These are pink with white centres,
and each have five asymmetric lobes, appearing
almost two-lipped. The opposite leaves are strongly
pinnately lobed, and coarsely toothed. Vervain,
once used as a charm against snake bites, has a
long history of medicinal and sacred uses.

GROWS in bare, rocky
places, on wasteland
and roadsides,
avoiding acid soil.

deeply lobed
leaf

narrow flower
spikes

pink
flowers

tough,
wiry
stems

PERENNIAL

PLANT HEIGHT 50–75cm.
FLOWER SIZE 4–5mm wide.
FLOWERING TIME June–September.
LEAVES Opposite; pinnately lobed and
coarsely toothed, the lower leaves more
strongly lobed than the upper.
FRUIT Four ribbed nutlets.
SIMILAR SPECIES None.

Wall Germander

Teucrium chamaedrys (Lamiaceae)

In most members of the mint family, the flowers have two
lips, but in this plant they have only one. This comprises
a broad lower lobe and four thin, finger-like lobes, two of
which point straight upwards, with the stamens and style
arching over them. The oblong leaves are shiny, deep
green, each lobed or toothed, and somewhat resembling
an oak leaf.

FOUND in dry, bare
places, on or alongside
old walls, and in open
woods; on chalky soil.

4 finger-like
petal lobes

broad
lower
lobe

purplish pink
flowers

PERENNIAL

dark green
leaves

PLANT HEIGHT 20–40cm.
FLOWER SIZE 1–1.5cm long.
FLOWERING TIME May–September.
LEAVES Opposite, oblong.
FRUIT Four single-seeded nutlets.
SIMILAR SPECIES Betony (p.220), which
has two-lipped flowers; Water Germander
(T. scordium), which has hairy leaves.

Bastard Balm

Melittis melissophyllum (Lamiaceae)

PERENNIAL

Easily recognized by its large, multi-coloured flowers, which range from white to pink or purple, this plant is covered with soft hairs. The pale green calyx is soft and non-bristly; and the pointed, hairy leaves are strong-smelling.

INHABITS *woodland margins, hedgerows, rocky places, and semi-shaded, sheltered sites; dislikes acid soil.*

neatly toothed margin

short-stalked, oval leaves

purple-blotched flower

3-lobed lower lip

PLANT HEIGHT *40–70cm.*
FLOWER SIZE *2.5–4cm long.*
FLOWERING TIME *May–July.*
LEAVES *Opposite, oval, softly hairy.*
FRUIT *Four nutlets held within the calyx.*
SIMILAR SPECIES *Large-flowered Hemp-nettle (Galeopsis speciosa), which has yellow and purple flowers and a spiky calyx.*

Betony

Stachys officinalis (Lamiaceae)

The bright magenta flowerheads of Betony, with leaf-like bracts drooping below them, are hard to miss among the grasses with which it grows. The plant has a neater appearance than many of its relatives in the mint family, with square stems bearing 2–4 pairs of narrowly oval, deep green leaves, with rounded teeth. Betony was used medicinally for centuries and as a protective charm by the Anglo-Saxons.

GROWS *in dry, grassy places, in heaths, woodland, and hedgerows.*

tapered flower spike

whorls of magenta flowers

PERENNIAL

rounded teeth

2-lipped flower

PLANT HEIGHT *20–75cm.*
FLOWER SIZE *1.2–1.8cm long.*
FLOWERING TIME *June–October.*
LEAVES *Opposite, narrowly oval, toothed.*
FRUIT *Four small nutlets within the calyx.*
SIMILAR SPECIES *Common Hemp-nettle (p.175); Wall Germander (p.219); Wild Basil (p.222); Hedge Woundwort (p.246).*

Wild Marjoram

Origanum vulgare (Lamiaceae)

Commonly cultivated as the herb oregano, this hairy, bushy plant often grows in large colonies, filling the air with its strong scent. The culinary herb marjoram comes from two similar, related plants of the Mediterranean, *O. majorana* and *O. onites*. The leaves are a simple oval shape, untoothed and short-stalked, and covered with tiny glands. Numerous flowers, with protruding stamens, are borne in dense clusters on the much-branched reddish stems. The two-lipped, pink petals are surrounded by prominent crimson sepals and bracts.

FOUND *in rough, dry grassland, woodland, and scrub; also along roadsides, hedgerows, and embankments, and often on slopes; prefers chalky soil.*

tough red-purple stems

flat-topped clusters of flowers

PERENNIAL

NOTE

The scientific name of this plant comes from the Greek oros *(mountain) and* ganos *(joy). It was used by Greeks and Romans to crown brides and grooms.*

untoothed leaf margin

red-flushed bracts

PLANT HEIGHT *30–50cm.*
FLOWER SIZE *4–7mm long.*
FLOWERING TIME *July–September.*
LEAVES *Opposite, untoothed, strongly aromatic; bright green.*
FRUIT *Four nutlets within the calyx.*
SIMILAR SPECIES *Wild Thyme (p.222) and Large Thyme (Thymus pulegioides), which are smaller and have a distinctly different scent.*

Wild Basil

Clinopodium vulgare (Lamiaceae)

GROWS *in dry, grassy places along woodland margins, hedgerows, and on embankments; prefers chalky soil.*

Although Wild Basil is not the culinary herb, it is faintly aromatic, with a scent similar to thyme. A rather weak and straggly plant, it has dense whorls of deep pink flowers clustered around the upper leaf bases. The lower sepals of the calyx are slightly longer and more slender than the upper ones. The hairy leaves are oval and gently toothed.

flowers in dense whorls

oval leaves

bluntly toothed margin

2-lipped flower

PERENNIAL

spiky calyx

PLANT HEIGHT *40–75cm.*
FLOWER SIZE *1.2–2cm long.*
FLOWERING TIME *July–September.*
LEAVES *Opposite, toothed, and hairy.*
FRUIT *Four nutlets at the base of calyx.*
SIMILAR SPECIES *Red Dead-nettle (p.175), which has purple-flushed leaves; Betony (p.220) has darker leaves with larger teeth.*

Wild Thyme

Thymus polytrichus (Lamiaceae)

FORMS *creeping mats, often in the short, grazed turf of chalk grassland; also heaths, banks, and dunes.*

The scent of thyme is released when the leaves of this plant are crushed, although it is not the species grown for culinary use. The slender, hairy, square stems bear tiny, oval leaves, and dense clusters of pink flowers with red sepals at their tips. In eastern and northern Europe this species is replaced by *T. serpyllum,* almost identical but with rounded stems.

oval leaf

2-lipped flower

pink flowers in dense heads

red sepals

PERENNIAL

PLANT HEIGHT *4–10cm.*
FLOWER SIZE *5–6mm long.*
FLOWERING TIME *May–September.*
LEAVES *Opposite, oval, up to 8mm long.*
FRUIT *Four nutlets in the persistent calyx.*
SIMILAR SPECIES *Wild Marjoram (p.221); Large Thyme (T. pulegioides) has hairs only on the angles of the square stems.*

Water Mint

Mentha aquatica (Lamiaceae)

The strong, sickly sweet scent of this plant is noticeable even without bruising the leaves. Its large flowerheads are bunched on top of one another, the flowers having two-lipped lilac-pink petals and crimson sepals, the prominent, protruding stamens giving them a fluffy appearance. The leaves are oval and toothed, the lower ones short-stalked, and often tinged with red.

FLOURISHES *at the edges of ponds, ditches, and lakes, often in the water, or in the damp parts of freshwater marshes and swamps.*

fluffy flowerhead

red-tinged leaf

toothed leaf margin

long stamens

2-lipped flower

PERENNIAL

PLANT HEIGHT *4–8m.*
FLOWER SIZE *4–6mm long.*
FLOWERING TIME *July–September.*
LEAVES *Opposite, oval, coarsely toothed.*
FRUIT *Four nutlets at the base of the calyx.*
SIMILAR SPECIES *Corn Mint (M. arvensis), which has stems ending in leaves, not flowers; hybrids also frequently occur.*

Common Valerian

Valeriana officinalis (Valerianaceae)

This plant of damp places has white flowerheads that may be flushed with pink. Each flower is five-lobed, narrowing to a tube with a pouched base. The leaves comprise long, narrow leaflets giving a ladder-like appearance, although the upper leaves are much smaller.

OCCURS *along river and stream margins, in wet meadows, ditches, pastures, and damp woodland.*

slender leaflets

ladder-like leaves

5-lobed flower

dense, branched flowerheads

pinkish white flowers

PERENNIAL

PLANT HEIGHT *1–1.8m.*
FLOWER SIZE *3–5mm long.*
FLOWERING TIME *June–August.*
LEAVES *Opposite, pinnately divided into lance-shaped, toothed leaflets.*
FRUIT *Achene with a pappus of hairs.*
SIMILAR SPECIES *Dwarf Elder (p.85), which has larger leaves.*

Foxglove

Digitalis purpurea (Scrophulariaceae)

Recognizable even in its first year, before it flowers, by the rosettes of large, wrinkled, hairy leaves, Foxglove is unmistakable in the following year when the tall flower stems are formed. As many as 60 or more pink to purple flowers droop in one-sided spikes, the petals opening from the bottom of the stems first. Each tubular flower has dark spots or rings inside the prominent lower lip and forms a wide funnel that is large enough for a bumblebee to enter. After flowering, the stems bear ranks of fruit capsules, ripening from green to black, with their persistent styles drooping down. The whole plant is poisonous.

PROLIFERATES *on heaths, in woodland clearings and margins, and along road verges, hedgerows, and banks; mostly on acid soil.*

tapered flower spikes

tubular flowers

NOTE

Foxglove leaves contain digitoxin, a chemical that increases blood flow to the heart muscle and is used in cases of heart failure to regulate the pulse. The plant's use is restricted because all parts of it are poisonous.

BIENNIAL/ PERENNIAL

wrinkled leaf surface

blunt, hairy leaf

many-seeded fruit capsule

PLANT HEIGHT *1–2m.*
FLOWER SIZE *4–5.5cm long.*
FLOWERING TIME *June–September.*
LEAVES *Basal rosette at first, followed by alternate stem leaves; oval, densely hairy.*
FRUIT *Capsule expelling numerous seeds through three slits at the tip.*
SIMILAR SPECIES *Great Mullein (p.141), which has a similar, though more hairy, leaf rosette in the first year.*

Red Bartsia

Odontites verna (Scrophulariaceae)

This wiry, hairy plant with slender, arching stems, is often flushed red. The pink flowers, borne in one-sided spikes, each have a three-lobed lower lip and a hooded upper lip from which the stamens protrude. Long, leaf-like bracts spread below each flower. The paired, narrow leaves have long veins and a few short teeth.

THRIVES *in fields, meadows, pastures, wasteland, and trampled ground; also along footpaths.*

flowers in leafy spikes

pink flowers

lance-shaped leaf

2-lipped flower

ANNUAL

PLANT HEIGHT *15–40cm.*
FLOWER SIZE *8–10mm long.*
FLOWERING TIME *June–September.*
LEAVES *Opposite, spear-shaped.*
FRUIT *Hairy capsule, with ridged, oval seeds.*
SIMILAR SPECIES *Common Lousewort (below) has pinnate leaves; Alpine Bartsia (Bartsia alpina) has dark purple flowers.*

Common Lousewort

Pedicularis sylvatica (Scrophulariaceae)

This tufted, compact plant has densely crowded leaves and flowers. The flowers are pale pink, each with a three-lobed lower lip and a hooded upper lip, emerging from a papery calyx that expands in fruit. The leaves are divided into small, "frilly" leaflets with crisped edges.

GROWS *in clumps in damp areas of heaths, bogs, moors, grassy places, and woodland.*

elongated upper lip

wavy leaf margins

BIENNIAL/ PERENNIAL

3-lobed lower lip

red-veined calyx

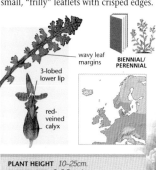

PLANT HEIGHT *10–25cm.*
FLOWER SIZE *2–2.5cm long.*
FLOWERING TIME *April–July.*
LEAVES *Alternate, pinnately lobed, fern-like.*
FRUIT *Capsule in the inflated, hairless calyx.*
SIMILAR SPECIES *Red Bartsia (above); Marsh Lousewort (P. palustris), which has longer leaves.*

Hemp Agrimony

Eupatorium cannabinum (Asteraceae)

Tall and robust, Hemp Agrimony has characteristic lobed leaves and red stems, which begin growing long before the flowerheads open. Short-stalked and hairy, the leaves are palmately lobed into three or five spear-shaped, toothed leaflets that droop down from the stems. The flowers are easily spotted when they do eventually open: distinctive, flat-topped, fluffy heads are composed of tubular pink florets with long, protruding stamens. Each group of five to six florets is enclosed by crimson-tipped bracts. Rich in nectar, the flowers attract numerous bees and butterflies.

FORMS *clumps on road verges, in spaces left by tree clearance, and in damp areas such as margins of rivers, streams, and ditches.*

protruding stamens

many-branched flower clusters

PERENNIAL

stout red stems

spear-shaped leaflet

3-lobed upper leaves

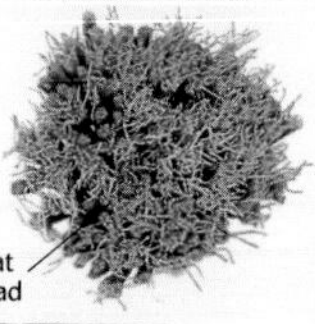

broad, flat flowerhead

PLANT HEIGHT *90–150cm.*
FLOWER SIZE *2–5mm wide.*
FLOWERING TIME *July–September.*
LEAVES *Opposite, palmately lobed into lance-shaped, toothed leaflets – lower leaves with five lobes and upper leaves with three lobes or undivided.*
FRUIT *Achene with a hairy pappus.*
SIMILAR SPECIES *None.*

Mountain Everlasting

Antennaria dioica (Asteraceae)

This upland species bears flowers in clusters on its long, downy stems, males and females on separate plants. The male flowers are surrounded by papery white bracts, resembling the rays of a daisy, while the female flowers have much smaller pink bracts. The Mountain Everlasting plant spreads by rooting runners, producing rosettes of spoon-shaped leaves, which are green above, and covered with downy white hairs below.

GROWS *on rocky slopes, heaths, and moors, and in mountain meadows, on base-rich soils.*

white male flower

downy white leaf underside

cluster of flowerheads

ray-like bracts

pink female flower

upright flowering stem

PERENNIAL

PLANT HEIGHT *12–20cm.*
FLOWER SIZE *Female flowerhead 1.2cm wide; male flowerhead 6mm wide.*
FLOWERING TIME *June–August.*
LEAVES *Spoon-shaped basal, lance-shaped stem; green above and white below.*
FRUIT *Achene with a hairy pappus.*
SIMILAR SPECIES *Edelweiss (p.87).*

Butterbur

Petasites hybridus (Asteraceae)

The leaves of this plant, although small at flowering time, grow up to a metre wide, and were once used for wrapping butter. The white or pink flowerheads are borne in dense, cone-like spikes, female and male flowers on separate plants; male flowers have short stalks.

PERENNIAL

OCCURS *in colonies alongside streams, rivers, ditches, and in damp woodland and meadows.*

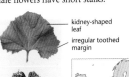

kidney-shaped leaf

irregular toothed margin

conical spike of flowers

tight flowerheads

PLANT HEIGHT *70–150cm.*
FLOWER SIZE *Female flowerhead 3–6mm wide; male flowerhead 7–12mm wide.*
FLOWERING TIME *March–May.*
LEAVES *Basal, kidney-shaped, felty beneath.*
FRUIT *Clock of achenes with a hairy pappus.*
SIMILAR SPECIES *White Butterbur (P. albus), which has white flowers and leaves to 30cm.*

Winter Heliotrope

Petasites fragrans (Asteraceae)

SPREADS *by means of underground runners, to form large clumps on road verges, footpaths, stream margins, and disturbed ground; in damp, semi-shaded sites.*

An introduced species from the central Mediterranean region, Winter Heliotrope is becoming increasingly common along roadsides and paths. It is perhaps the only wild flower in the region whose main flowering period is midwinter. During this time, spikes of loosely clustered lilac-pink flowerheads appear, made up mainly of tubular florets, but often with a few ray-like florets, and dark purple stamens. They smell pleasantly of vanilla. Lance-shaped bracts grow along the flowering stem. The rounded or kidney-shaped leaves are quite small when the plant flowers, but grow throughout the summer to a width of about 20cm.

lilac-pink flowers

loosely clustered flowerheads

PERENNIAL

NOTE

Although male and female flowers are borne on separate plants, the females are unknown in the region, so the plant spreads by vegetative means.

long stalk

branched flowerhead

PLANT HEIGHT *15–40cm.*
FLOWER SIZE *Spikes up to 25cm long.*
FLOWERING TIME *November–February.*
LEAVES *Basal, rounded or kidney-shaped with toothed margin; green above, paler below.*
FRUIT *Clock formed from achenes with a pappus.*
SIMILAR SPECIES *Butterbur (p.227), which has denser flower spikes and much larger leaves.*

Greater Burdock

Arctium lappa (Asteraceae)

This robust plant, with thick, branched stems, has large, rough leaves that appear longer than the flowers. Resembling those of thistles, the flowers themselves are reddish purple or pink and are surrounded by numerous hooked green spines or bracts, which form a much larger, spiny ball. These readily attach themselves to fur or clothing thereby helping to distribute the seed. The fruit is an achene with a pappus of rough yellowish hairs. The similar Lesser Burdock is a generally smaller plant that has a purple flowerhead of roughly the same size as the ball of spiny bracts beneath it.

FORMS *large clumps in woodland clearings and wasteland, and alongside roads and hedgerows; dislikes deep shade.*

NOTE

The scientific name Arctium *is derived from the Greek word* arktos, *which means "a bear", and refers to the roughness of the spiny burs.*

BIENNIAL

hooked bracts surround flowerhead

rounded flowerhead

large, stalked leaves

slightly toothed margin

spiny bracts

PLANT HEIGHT *80–160cm.*
FLOWER SIZE *Flowerhead 2–2.5cm wide.*
FLOWERING TIME *July–September.*
LEAVES *Basal and alternate, oval to heart-shaped, with a rough surface.*
FRUIT *Achene with a pappus of hairs.*
SIMILAR SPECIES *Spear Thistle (p.180), which has bristly leaves; Lesser Burdock (A. minor), which is smaller, with purple flowerheads and hollow leaf stalks.*

Flowering Rush

Butomus umbellatus (Butomaceae)

GROWS in shallow water at the edges of rivers, streams, ditches, and ponds; prefers recently cleared areas and dislikes acid soil.

PERENNIAL

Although the narrow leaves of this aquatic plant are superficially similar to those of a rush or sedge, the Flowering Rush is quite unrelated and, unlike them, it produces elegant umbels of reddish flower stalks. Each umbel looks like an upturned umbrella, with a pink flower at the tip of each spoke. The flowers have three petals, red-striped beneath, with three smaller sepals in between, and several dark-tipped stamens. In cross-section, the leaves are triangular at the bottom, thinning out to a flat blade at the top.

crimson flower bud

cup-shaped flower

umbrella-like flowerhead

leaf tapers to a point

blade-like leaf

dark-tipped stamens

NOTE

The seeds of the Flowering Rush contain air-filled tissue. This means that they will float when they fall into the water and may be carried along by the current to a suitable germination site away from the main plant.

PLANT HEIGHT *80–150cm.*
FLOWER SIZE *1.6–2.6cm wide.*
FLOWERING TIME *July–August.*
LEAVES *Basal, linear, triangular in cross-section in the lower half, with a broad sheath at the base.*
FRUIT *Six follicles, fused together, red to purple.*
SIMILAR SPECIES *Water-plantain (p.91), which has smaller flowers and broad leaves.*

Chives

Allium schoenoprasum (Liliaceae)

A familiar sight in herb gardens, Chives also occurs as a
true native in Europe. The very thin grey-green leaves are
cylindrical and hollow inside, as is the main flowering
stem (scape). At the tip of the stem, two or three papery
spathes open to reveal a tight, rounded mass of pink to
lilac six-petalled flowers on short stalks.

FORMS *tufts in rocky
places and meadows;
also along streams and
river banks.*

PERENNIAL

rounded
flowerheads

cylindrical
leaves

slender
flowering
stem

single
flower

PLANT HEIGHT *30–50cm.*
FLOWER SIZE *Flowerhead 2–4cm wide.*
FLOWERING TIME *June–August.*
LEAVES *Basal, narrow-cylindrical; grey-green.*
FRUIT *Small capsule.*
SIMILAR SPECIES *German Garlic (A.
senescens) has flat leaves; Round-headed
Leek (A. sphaerocephalum) has stem leaves.*

Meadow Saffron

Colchicum autumnale (Liliaceae)

The flowers and leaves of this poisonous plant are never
seen together. In autumn, large, crocus-like flowers appear
from a single papery spathe at ground level, the six petals
often flopping open. The flowers have six stamens, unlike
true crocuses, which have three. In spring, the large, shiny
green leaves are pushed up along with the fruit capsule.

APPEARS *in damp,
grassy meadows and
on roadsides; often
planted in gardens
from where it spreads.*

bright
green
leaf

large, crocus-
like flowers

dark to
light
pink
flower

PERENNIAL

PLANT HEIGHT *10–40cm.*
FLOWER SIZE *4–6cm wide.*
FLOWERING TIME *August–October.*
LEAVES *Basal, elliptical or lance-shaped.*
FRUIT *Fleshy, three-parted capsule.*
SIMILAR SPECIES *Autumn Crocus (Crocus
nudiflorus), which is occasionally naturalized
and has purple flowers and three stamens.*

Martagon Lily

Lilium martagon (Liliaceae)

One of the most exotic-looking of all European wild plants outside the orchid family, this is a robust plant with tall, red-streaked stems. Large whorls of broadly oval, deep green leaves are arranged in tiers up the stem, each ridged with 7–9 veins. Ranks of alternate flower buds droop down, each with a small, simple bract at the base. They persist for some weeks before finally opening, and when they do, the dark-spotted pink petals curve right back on themselves, the orange anthers and long stigma hanging like a pendent carousel.

OCCURS *in mountain meadows and pastures, and among scrub or open woodland, often on slopes, preferring chalky soil.*

bract at leaf stalk base

drooping flower buds

PERENNIAL

flowers at bottom open first

whorled leaves around stem

NOTE

Lilies grow from large underground bulbs, which are swollen leaf bases used to store food. This enables them to grow rapidly in a short season.

recurved petals

pendent orange anthers

PLANT HEIGHT *1–1.8m.*
FLOWER SIZE *3–4cm wide.*
FLOWERING TIME *June–July.*
LEAVES *Whorled, broadly oval to elliptical, ridged, with 7–9 veins; deep green.*
FRUIT *Three-lobed capsule, splitting to the base.*
SIMILAR SPECIES *L. bulbiferum, which has large, upright orange flowers and narrow, alternate leaves with bulbils at their bases.*

Marsh Gladiolus

Gladiolus palustris (Iridaceae)

This plant is hard to miss when in full bloom, with 3–6 flowers facing the same way along an elegant, one-sided spike. Each flower has five petals, four drooping, one upright and beneath which the stamens are hidden. The lower three petals have a distinct crimson-edged white stripe. The narrow leaves are difficult to spot before the flowers open.

FORMS *loose colonies among grass in damp meadows, pastures, and fields; found also in open scrub.*

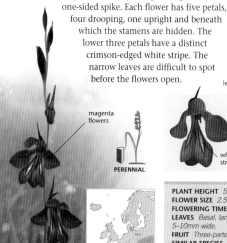

magenta flowers

PERENNIAL

upper petal covers anthers and stigma

leaf-like bracts

white stripe

drooping petals

PLANT HEIGHT *50–90cm.*
FLOWER SIZE *2.5–4.5cm long.*
FLOWERING TIME *June–July.*
LEAVES *Basal, lance-shaped and pointed, 5–10mm wide.*
FRUIT *Three-parted capsule.*
SIMILAR SPECIES *Wild Gladiolus (G. illyricus) has opposite facing flowers.*

Astrantia

Astrantia major (Apiaceae)

A distinctive member of the carrot family, Astrantia has very tight flower umbels that look like pincushions. The tiny flowers may be white or pink, and are surrounded by a ruff of narrow whitish bracts, often tinged green or red. Mostly basal, the distinctive leaves are long-stalked and palmately lobed, with toothed and strongly veined lobes.

INHABITS *semi-shaded places in woodland clearings and margins; also in scrub and mountain meadows.*

3–5 toothed leaf lobes

pincushion flowerhead

PERENNIAL

ruff of whitish bracts

tiny white flowers

PLANT HEIGHT *50–80cm.*
FLOWER SIZE *2–3.5cm wide.*
FLOWERING TIME *May–July.*
LEAVES *Mostly basal, palmately lobed with coarsely toothed margins.*
FRUIT *Mericarp, ridged and two-parted, 6–8mm long.*
SIMILAR SPECIES *None.*

Broad-leaved Helleborine

Epipactis helleborine (Orchidaceae)

This *Epipactis* species is unusual in that it grows and flowers at the darkest, shadiest time of year, when most other woodland plants are dormant. These orchids are able to do this with the help of a fungus around their roots that provides them with extra nourishment, a partnership from which the fungus appears to derive no benefit. Up to 50 flowers are borne in long spikes, each a complex shape of greenish sepals and petals, with a large pink or crimson, occasionally white, lower lip, recurved at the tip. Found mainly near the bottom of the stem, the strongly veined leaves are broadly oval.

OCCURS in shady areas of deciduous woodland, scrub, roadsides, and banks, preferring chalky soil. Sometimes found on sand dunes.

narrow bract under flower

greenish sepals

winged side petals

recurved lower lip

PERENNIAL

NOTE

The pollen of orchids forms in two waxy masses called pollinia, which stick to visiting insects to be deposited on the flowers of other plants.

broad, veined leaf

smooth fruit capsule

PLANT HEIGHT *50–80cm.*
FLOWER SIZE *Lower lip 1cm long.*
FLOWERING TIME *July–August.*
LEAVES *Spirally arranged, oval to elliptical, strongly veined.*
FRUIT *Pendent, many-seeded capsule.*
SIMILAR SPECIES *Marsh Helleborine (p.97) has narrower leaves; Violet Helleborine (E. purpurata), which has violet-grey stems and leaves; Dark Red Helleborine (E. atrorubens), which has dark crimson flowers.*

Purple-Blue

Purple and blue flowers may be seen as the same colour by some insects; for example, the red element in purple is invisible to a bee. However, such colours are frequently 'highlighted' by a yellow or white centre, and blue-flowered plants often grow among plants of other colours, providing further contrast, and helping them to compete for the attentions of pollinating insects. Some families, such as the Forget-me-nots, have predominantly blue-flowered species, while blue-flowered members of the Daisy family, such as Chicory (pictured), are very unusual.

PURPLE GROMWELL WILD PANSY PURPLE LOOSESTRIFE WOOD FORGET-ME-NOT

Cyclamen

Cyclamen purpurascens (Primulaceae)

FORMS *patches in woods, scrub, and open grassland, on chalky soil, persisting for many years.*

The fleshy leaves of this plant are evergreen and may last for several seasons. Their glossy, dark green upper surface is often marbled with pale green or grey; their undersides are usually purplish. The flowers, arising directly from underground tubers, have five bent-back, rose-pink petals, with a darker rim near the "mouth".

marbled, waxy leaf surface

PERENNIAL

reflexed petals

basal leaves

PLANT HEIGHT 10–20cm.
FLOWER SIZE 2cm long.
FLOWERING TIME June–September.
LEAVES *Basal; rounded or heart-shaped.*
FRUIT *Capsule, developing near ground on rolled-up flower stalk.*
SIMILAR SPECIES *Sowbread (C. hederifolium) has angular leaves.*

Bird-in-a-Bush

Corydalis solida (Fumariaceae)

GROWS *in open woods, and disturbed ground, alongside hedgerows, usually among grass.*

This attractive plant is, not surprisingly, grown in gardens. The purple flowers have the usual complex fumitory shape of two lips with a long horizontal spur at the back. The leaves are divided into three and then three again, and even the leaflets are three-lobed. The deeply divided bracts distinguish it from similar *Corydalis* species.

leaves divided into threes

flowers in dense racemes

PERENNIAL

long flower spur

PLANT HEIGHT 15–20cm.
FLOWER SIZE 1.5–3cm long.
FLOWERING TIME April–May.
LEAVES *Divided into three lobed leaflets.*
FRUIT *Oblong capsule, 1.5–2.5cm long.*
SIMILAR SPECIES *Bulbous Corydalis (C. cava) and C. intermedia, which have unlobed bracts.*

Common Fumitory

Fumaria officinalis (Fumariaceae)

This widespread weed has racemes of upright flowers, each flower with a pouched spur at the back, and two crimson-tipped lips at the front. The weak, straggly stems bear finely divided leaves, each leaflet on its own stalk. The feathery greyish green leaves look almost like smoke, hence the plant's scientific name.

SPRAWLS *over bare ground or grassy places in cultivated fields, wasteland, or pastures, and along roadsides.*

dark-tipped flowers

flowers in racemes

ANNUAL

feathery, divided leaves

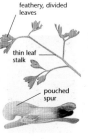

thin leaf stalk

pouched spur

> **PLANT HEIGHT** *10–30cm.*
> **FLOWER SIZE** *7–9mm long.*
> **FLOWERING TIME** *May–October.*
> **LEAVES** *Alternate, pinnately divided into lobed, stalked leaflets.*
> **FRUIT** *Single-seeded, round capsule.*
> **SIMILAR SPECIES** *Common Ramping-fumitory (F. muralis) has fewer flowers.*

Honesty

Lunaria annua (Brassicaceae)

Introduced from southeast Europe as a garden plant, Honesty is now naturalized in the countryside. The large purple or white flowers, the heart-shaped leaves, and particularly the fruit, are distinctive. The fruit splits to reveal a persistent silvery membrane, to which the seeds are attached.

OCCURS *on roadsides, banks, wasteland, rubbish tips, and cultivated land.*

coarsely toothed leaf

BIENNIAL

rounded fruit

flowers in clusters

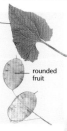

deep green foliage

4-petalled flowers

> **PLANT HEIGHT** *50–100cm.*
> **FLOWER SIZE** *2.5–3cm wide.*
> **FLOWERING TIME** *April–June.*
> **LEAVES** *Alternate, heart-shaped, coarsely toothed.*
> **FRUIT** *Round, flat silicula, 3–5cm wide.*
> **SIMILAR SPECIES** *Perennial Honesty (L. rediviva), which has pointed fruit.*

Purple Saxifrage

Saxifraga oppositifolia (Saxifragaceae)

Unmissable when in flower, this plant has creeping stems and, unusually for the saxifrage family, closely packed, tiny leaves in opposite pairs, which are often encrusted with lime excreted from pores at the leaf tip. The flowers, borne in masses on very short stems, are an extraordinary rosy-purple, with bluish stamens and orange anthers.

FORMS *mats on sea-cliffs, moraines, and damp rocks in mountainous areas or inaccessible spots.*

PERENNIAL

orange anthers

5-petalled flowers

tiny, crowded leaves

PLANT HEIGHT *4–10cm.*
FLOWER SIZE *1–2cm wide.*
FLOWERING TIME *March–August.*
LEAVES *Opposite pairs, oblong, thick; dark green.*
FRUIT *Capsule with numerous seeds.*
SIMILAR SPECIES *Moss Campion (Silene acaulis), which has linear leaves.*

Water Avens

Geum rivale (Rosaceae)

This graceful plant often hybridizes with the closely related Herb Bennet (p.117), resulting in flowers that have features of both plants. The flowers of Water Avens have pinkish cream petals and purplish brown sepals that become upright when the feathery fruit is formed. The leaves are divided into lobed leaflets; the stem leaves are smaller.

GROWS *in colonies in marshy grassland, ditches, meadows, and wet woodland. Prefers chalky soil.*

arched flower stalks

large terminal leaflet

toothed margin

PERENNIAL

pendent flowers

achenes with hooked styles

PLANT HEIGHT *30–50cm.*
FLOWER SIZE *8–15mm wide.*
FLOWERING TIME *April–September.*
LEAVES *Basal pinnate leaves, with 3–6 pairs of oval to round leaflets; stem leaves trifoliate.*
FRUIT *Collection of achenes.*
SIMILAR SPECIES *Herb Bennet (p.117), hybrids, which have pendent yellow flowers.*

Marsh Cinquefoil

Potentilla palustris (Rosaceae)

The short-stalked leaves of this plant are pinnately divided into 5–7 serrated leaflets. The distinctive flower has prominent, deep maroon or purplish sepals; the crimson petals are much smaller. The central core of immature achenes is surrounded by dark stamens.

FOUND in marshland, fens, bogs, and wet meadows, on acid soil.

serrated leaflet margin

PERENNIAL

strawberry-like flower centre

5 large sepals

PLANT HEIGHT *30–50cm.*
FLOWER SIZE *2–3cm wide.*
FLOWERING TIME *May–July.*
LEAVES *Alternate, 5–7 oblong, serrated leaflets with papery stipules at leaf stalk base.*
FRUIT *Head of achenes surrounded by persistent calyx.*
SIMILAR SPECIES *None.*

Bush Vetch

Vicia sepium (Fabaceae)

This plant uses its long tendrils to scramble over other vegetation. It produces small, tight clusters of peaflowers that vary in colour from a greyish blue to a purplish pink, the standard petal veined with streaks of dark purple. The flowers turn brown once pollinated. The leaves have neat rows of oblong leaflets.

CLAMBERS over other plants in woodland, scrub, meadows, and hedgerows, avoiding acid soil.

5–9 pairs of leaflets

PERENNIAL

short-stalked flower clusters

dark-veined petal

PLANT HEIGHT *20–60cm.*
FLOWER SIZE *1.2–1.5cm wide.*
FLOWERING TIME *May–October.*
LEAVES *Alternate, pinnate, toothed stipules.*
FRUIT *Black, hairless pod, 2–3.5cm long.*
SIMILAR SPECIES *Common Vetch (p.240), which has narrower leaflets; Wood Vetch (V. sylvatica), which has larger, paler flowers.*

Common Vetch

Vicia sativa (Fabaceae)

Introduced from southern Europe as a fodder crop for cattle, Common Vetch is now established throughout northern Europe. The ladder-like leaves are pinnately divided, each leaflet with a "needle" at the tip. Each leaf terminates in a long, branched tendril, and at the base are a pair of small, coarsely toothed stipules, each with a black spot. The flowers, usually paired but occasionally solitary, are vivid red to purple, the wing and keel petals usually being a shade darker than the standard petal.

SCRAMBLES *among grasses and other vegetation in cultivated fields, wasteland, roadsides, banks, and scrub.*

ANNUAL

NOTE

The spots on the stipules secrete a sugary substance that attracts ants, which, in turn, help to defend the plant against attack by other insects.

narrow, sharply tipped leaflets

flowers usually in pairs

terminal branched tendril

3–8 pairs of leaflets

red to purple peaflower

slender seed pod

PLANT HEIGHT *50–120cm.*
FLOWER SIZE *1.8–2.5cm long.*
FLOWERING TIME *April–September.*
LEAVES *Alternate, pinnately divided, with 3–8 pairs of oval to lance-shaped leaflets.*
FRUIT *Hairy pod, green, ripening to brown or black, 2.5–7cm long.*
SIMILAR SPECIES *Bush Vetch (p.239), which has broader leaflets; Bitter Vetch (right), which has larger leaves and no tendrils.*

Spring Pea

Lathyrus vernus (Fabaceae)

This upright, bushy pea has large leaves pinnately divided into 2–4 pairs of elliptical to lance-shaped leaflets, each tapering to a point. Each leaf ends in a tiny needle-like projection. The flowers, in loose clusters, are pinkish red at first, maturing through purple to blue.

FORMS *clumps in deciduous or mixed woodland, or among scrub, in semi-shaded places, preferring chalky soil.*

PERENNIAL

long flower stalk

widely spaced leaflets

prominent veins

PLANT HEIGHT 20–40cm.
FLOWER SIZE 1.4–2cm long.
FLOWERING TIME April–June.
LEAVES Alternate, pinnate with 2–4 pairs of elliptical to lance-shaped leaflets.
FRUIT Hairless brown pod, 4–6cm long.
SIMILAR SPECIES Bitter Vetch (below), which has smaller leaflets and winged stems.

Bitter Vetch

Lathyrus linifolius (Fabaceae)

Very similar to Spring Pea (above), Bitter Vetch is more delicate, with paler green, less obviously veined leaflets. The clearest distinguishing feature is that the stems are winged. The flowers turn from pink-purple to blue as they mature, and the leaves end in tiny points, rather than tendrils.

OCCURS *on heaths, road verges, grassy banks, woodland margins, and scrub, on neutral to acid soil.*

PERENNIAL

narrow, untoothed leaflets

pink-purple peaflower

loose clusters of 2–3 flowers

long flower stalk

PLANT HEIGHT 20–40cm.
FLOWER SIZE 1–1.6cm long.
FLOWERING TIME April–July.
LEAVES Alternate, pinnate with 2–4 pairs of elliptical or narrow leaflets.
FRUIT Hairless brown pod, 2.5–4.5cm long.
SIMILAR SPECIES Spring Pea (above), which has slender, unwinged stems.

Narrow-leaved Everlasting-pea

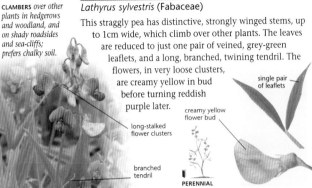

CLAMBERS *over other plants in hedgerows and woodland, and on shady roadsides and sea-cliffs; prefers chalky soil.*

Lathyrus sylvestris (Fabaceae)

This straggly pea has distinctive, strongly winged stems, up to 1cm wide, which climb over other plants. The leaves are reduced to just one pair of veined, grey-green leaflets, and a long, branched, twining tendril. The flowers, in very loose clusters, are creamy yellow in bud before turning reddish purple later.

single pair of leaflets

creamy yellow flower bud

long-stalked flower clusters

branched tendril

PERENNIAL

PLANT HEIGHT *1–2m.*
FLOWER SIZE *1.4–2cm long.*
FLOWERING TIME *June–August.*
LEAVES *Alternate, pinnate with one pair of leaflets, ending in tendrils.*
FRUIT *Brown hairless pod, 4–6cm long.*
SIMILAR SPECIES *Broad-leaved Everlasting-pea (L. latifolius), which has larger flowers.*

Tree Mallow

Lavatera arborea (Malvaceae)

Impossible to miss in its coastal habitat, this is a robust, tall plant with a woody stem. The large leaves are rounded, with 5–7 lobes that are wrinkled or wavy – an adaptation that helps the plant to conserve moisture in a dry environment. The cup-shaped flowers are a deep magenta-pink, with dark lines radiating out from a blackish centre, and pale pink anthers.

GROWS *on coasts, on shingle beaches, cliffs, wasteland, rocks, and sand dunes.*

BIENNIAL

wavy lobes

dark flower centre

dark-veined petals

stout stem

PLANT HEIGHT *1–2.5m.*
FLOWER SIZE *3–4cm wide.*
FLOWERING TIME *June–September.*
LEAVES *Alternate, palmate, lobed, downy when young, with pale undersides.*
FRUIT *Cluster of nutlets in a ring.*
SIMILAR SPECIES *Common Mallow (p.209), which has pink-centred flowers.*

Purple Loosestrife

Lythrum salicaria (Lythraceae)

Marshes and ditches are often enhanced by the tall,
purple spires of this plant towering over other
waterside vegetation. The square, ridged stems are
robust and erect, bearing stalkless leaves in whorls
of three lower down but in opposite pairs above.
They branch towards the top, bearing tiered ranks
of flowers in tight whorls, each flower with five
purple petals that are wrinkled and rather tissue-
like. The plant often grows with the unrelated
Yellow Loosestrife (p.134).

FORMS *clumps in
damp sites such as
marshes and wet
meadows, alongside
rivers, ponds, and
ditches; also at the
edges of reedbeds.*

PERENNIAL

tall flower
spikes

bright purple
flowers

NOTE

*This plant is a pest
in New Zealand and
other places where
it is introduced, as
it colonizes large
areas to the
detriment of
native species.*

lance-shaped,
stalkless leaf

12 stamens

5 narrow
petals

PLANT HEIGHT *70–150cm.*
FLOWER SIZE *1–1.5cm wide.*
FLOWERING TIME *June–August.*
LEAVES *Whorled below, opposite above, lance-shaped,
untoothed and stalkless.*
FRUIT *Capsule containing many seeds.*
SIMILAR SPECIES *Rosebay Willowherb (p.211), which has larger
flowers and alternate leaves.*

Bell Heather

Erica cinerea (Ericaceae)

FORMS *small or extensive colonies on the dry, acid, sandy soil of heaths and moors, or in clearings in open pine woodland.*

This evergreen shrub often grows scattered among other plants in the same family, such as Heather (p.213), but also forms large expanses on its own. An entire landscape of hills and low mountains may be coloured with the rich magenta-purple of its flowers, which usually open one or two weeks earlier than the paler pink flowers of Heather. The bell-shaped flowers are slightly flared at the mouth and are borne in whorls or clusters on short stems. The tiny, leathery leaves are in whorls of three on very short stems, so they appear bunched together.

PERENNIAL

NOTE

The stamens are hidden within the petals, but if insect pollination does not take place, they protrude, so that wind pollination may occur.

magenta-purple flowers

flowers in whorls

tiny, linear leaves

short leaf stems

bell-shaped flowers

woody stems

PLANT HEIGHT *20–60cm.*
FLOWER SIZE *5–7mm long.*
FLOWERING TIME *July–September.*
LEAVES *Whorled, tough, needle-like, and hairless, on very short stems; green to bronze.*
FRUIT *Small, dry, hairless capsule.*
SIMILAR SPECIES *Heather (p.213); Cross-leaved Heath (E. tetralix), which has pale pink flowers and hairy leaves in whorls of four.*

Hound's-tongue

Cynoglossum officinale (Boraginaceae)

This is a roughly hairy plant, with soft, hairy, greyish green leaves with a coarse texture. It forms a distinct tuft, sending up long branching cymes that uncoil to reveal a row of five-petalled, very dark crimson or dull purplish flowers, which have a characteristic smell of mice. Four large, bristly nutlets are squeezed tightly into the outspread calyx.

OCCURS *in rough grassland, among scrub, or alongside hedgerows, on chalky soil.*

funnel-shaped flowers

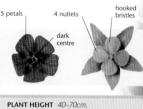

BIENNIAL

untoothed leaves

5 petals

4 nutlets

hooked bristles

dark centre

PLANT HEIGHT *40–70cm.*
FLOWER SIZE *6–10mm wide.*
FLOWERING TIME *May–August.*
LEAVES *Alternate, lance-shaped.*
FRUIT *Four nutlets, with hooked bristles.*
SIMILAR SPECIES *Green Hound's-tongue (C. germanicum), which has hairs only on the undersides of its leaves.*

Common Figwort

Scrophularia nodosa (Scrophulariaceae)

A tall, robust plant, Common Figwort has surprisingly small flowers, which in bud look like beads on stalks. They are borne on square stems, usually opening one at a time within a cluster. Each flower has a notched, purplish brown upper lip, which forms a little hood over the pouched lower lip, with two of the four stamens protruding.

GROWS *in damp places, along stream and river banks, in meadows and open woodland.*

bead-like flower buds

oval leaf

PERENNIAL

hooded upper lip

branching stems

yellow stamens

PLANT HEIGHT *60–100cm.*
FLOWER SIZE *7–9mm long.*
FLOWERING TIME *June–September.*
LEAVES *Opposite, oval, with finely toothed margins and wrinkled surface.*
FRUIT *Two-parted, rounded capsule.*
SIMILAR SPECIES *Water Figwort (S. auriculata), which has winged stems.*

Hedge Woundwort

Stachys sylvatica (Lamiaceae)

The dark claret or dull purple flowers of Hedge Woundwort do not seem bright enough to attract insects in their shady woodland habitat, but they do have some white markings that guide bees and flies to the throat of the flower to help pollination. The leaves give off a strong, foetid smell that may also entice insects. They are distinctly heart-shaped, with a wrinkled surface and toothed margin. The square stems have crimson ridges on the corners and are clothed in glandular hairs.

FOUND *in woodland margins, cultivated or waste land, and along hedgerows and footpaths, in semi-shaded situations.*

NOTE

The Hedge Woundwort and other Stachys *species have a long medicinal history. They have been used since the time of the ancient Greeks in poultices for wounds and to help staunch bleeding.*

PERENNIAL

flowers in whorled spike

dull purple petals

calyx with equal teeth

square stems

toothed margin

heart-shaped base

pale markings on lower lip

2-lipped flower

PLANT HEIGHT *60–100cm.*
FLOWER SIZE *1.3–1.8cm long.*
FLOWERING TIME *June–September.*
LEAVES *Opposite, heart-shaped, with toothed margins; short-stalked upper leaves, long-stalked lower leaves.*
FRUIT *Four nutlets at the base of the calyx.*
SIMILAR SPECIES *Black Horehound (p.174); Betony (p.220); Marsh Woundwort (S. palustris) has pink flowers and grows in marshes.*

Ivy-leaved Toadflax

Cymbalaria muralis (Scrophulariaceae)

Originally from southern Europe, this plant is now found further afield. The long, trailing stems are reddish, with fleshy, lobed leaves similar in shape to those of Ivy (p.24). The long-stemmed flowers have two lilac or violet lips, with two central yellow patches and a short spur.

LIVES *in nooks and crannies, old walls, pavements, and rocky places, generally on vertical surfaces, in full or partial shade.*

PERENNIAL

5–9 broad lobes

slender reddish stems

yellow patch

lilac or violet petals

short spur

PLANT HEIGHT *10–25cm.*
FLOWER SIZE *9–15mm long.*
FLOWERING TIME *May–September.*
LEAVES *Alternate, palmately lobed, fleshy.*
FRUIT *Small capsule, opens by irregular slits.*
SIMILAR SPECIES *Ivy (p.24) has similar leaves; Round-leaved Fluellen (p.143), which has oval leaves.*

Hepatica

Hepatica nobilis (Ranunculaceae)

An evergreen plant, Hepatica has distinctive leaves, recognizable long after the flowers die down. They are deep green and mottled brownish purple beneath, with three oval lobes and strongly marked veins. The flowers have six or seven petals which range from deep pink to blue, and are borne on hairy, unbranched stems.

PERENNIAL

FORMS *carpets among leaf-litter in woods and in rocky places, on chalky soil.*

shiny, deep green leaves

deep pink to blue flowers

3-lobed leaves

whitish anthers

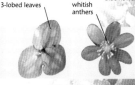

PLANT HEIGHT *10–20cm.*
FLOWER SIZE *1.5–2.5cm wide.*
FLOWERING TIME *March–May.*
LEAVES *Basal, three-lobed, fleshy, with heart-shaped base; glossy, deep green, purplish mottled beneath.*
FRUIT *Cluster of achenes.*
SIMILAR SPECIES *None.*

Monkshood

Aconitum napellus (Ranunculaceae)

The tall spikes of hooded deep violet or blue flowers, resembling a monk's cowl, are highly distinctive. However, they give little clue that Monkshood is a member of the buttercup family. Each flower has numerous stamens and five petal-like parts, the upper part larger and forming the characteristic hood. The large leaves, which are rounded in outline, are deeply divided into many narrow lobes. The entire plant, particularly the root, is extremely poisonous. Monkshood is frequently grown in gardens and is used in floristry. Northern Wolfsbane, found in Scandinavia, is similar, but has violet or yellow flowers with a more tapered hood, and less deeply divided leaves.

OCCURS *in patches or grows sporadically in meadows and damp woodland, or along the margins of streams and ditches.*

long spike of flowers

erect, unbranched stem

PERENNIAL

petals form hood

finely pointed leaves

deeply divided leaves

NOTE

A homeopathic medicine used to treat fever is derived from this plant. The poison from the root of Monkshood was used to tip arrows and also as a death drink for condemned criminals.

PLANT HEIGHT *80–150cm.*
FLOWER SIZE *1.5–2cm wide.*
FLOWERING TIME *June–September.*
LEAVES *Alternate, divided into 5–7 finely toothed lobes.*
FRUIT *A group of follicles.*
SIMILAR SPECIES *Meadow Clary (p.270), which has larger flowers and oval to oblong leaves; Northern Wolfsbane (A. lycoctonum subsp. lycoctonum), which has a more tapered hood.*

Columbine

Aquilegia vulgaris (Ranunculaceae)

The rounded, broadly lobed leaves of this member of the buttercup family are a good aid to identification, and the deep blue to purple flowers are unmistakable. The five narrow sepals are the same colour as the broader petals, each of which has a long, hooked spur containing nectar to attract long-tongued bees. Columbine is widely grown in gardens, and escaped plants of different colours frequently become naturalized. It has been used medicinally in the past but is now considered too poisonous, except as a homeopathic remedy.

FORMS *loose colonies in damp meadows, fens, and scrub, and alongside hedgerows and woodland margins; generally on chalky soil.*

PERENNIAL

petals end in hooked spurs

nodding flowers

sepals same colour as petals

erect, branched stems

unstalked stem leaves

rounded lobes

3–9 main leaflets

fruit of clustered follicles

NOTE

The scientific name Aquilegia is derived from the Latin word "aquila" (eagle), the spurs of the flowers being likened to an eagle's talons.

PLANT HEIGHT *50–90cm.*
FLOWER SIZE *3–5cm wide.*
FLOWERING TIME *May–July.*
LEAVES *Mostly basal, with broad, two- to three-lobed leaflets; dull green but paler beneath.*
FRUIT *Collection of five pod-like follicles.*
SIMILAR SPECIES *Dark Columbine (A. atrata), which has dark purple-violet flowers, and is found in the C. European mountains.*

Pasque-flower

Pulsatilla vulgaris (Ranunculaceae)

The clue to the identity of this member of the buttercup family are the numerous yellow stamens, surrounded by deep violet-purple sepals. Flowers open from within downy, leaf-like bracts, and are upright at first, but nodding later. The basal leaves are pinnately divided into fine, linear segments.

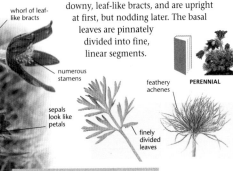

OCCURS *in open meadows and short turf, preferring well-drained, chalky soil.*

whorl of leaf-like bracts

numerous stamens

sepals look like petals

feathery achenes

PERENNIAL

finely divided leaves

PLANT HEIGHT *15–30cm.*	
FLOWER SIZE *5.5–8cm wide.*	
FLOWERING TIME *April–May.*	
LEAVES *Basal, pinnately divided into linear segments, long-stalked.*	
FRUIT *Dense head of achenes.*	
SIMILAR SPECIES *Small Pasque-flower (P. pratensis), which has smaller flowers.*	

Garden Lupin

Lupinus polyphyllus (Fabaceae)

Introduced from North America, this plant has become widely naturalized. Blue, pink, white, yellow, or bicoloured peaflowers are borne in tight spirals up the stem. The long-stalked, finger-like leaves, covered with tiny hairs, radiate from a single point.

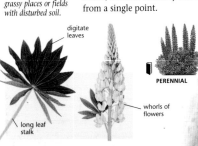

GROWS *sporadically along roadsides, on embankments, and in grassy places or fields with disturbed soil.*

tall, pyramidal flower spikes

digitate leaves

PERENNIAL

whorls of flowers

long leaf stalk

PLANT HEIGHT *70–120cm.*	
FLOWER SIZE *1.2–1.4cm long.*	
FLOWERING TIME *June–August.*	
LEAVES *Mostly basal with some stem leaves; digitate with 9–17 lance-shaped leaflets.*	
FRUIT *Black, hairy pod, 2.5–4cm long.*	
SIMILAR SPECIES *Nootka Lupin (L. nootkatensis), which has 6–8 leaflets.*	

Purple Milk-vetch

Astragalus danicus (Fabaceae)

The peaflowers clustered on the long, erect stalks of this plant are worth a close look. The violet or purple standard petal and the central white keel petal are flushed pink. Blunt, neatly divided leaves are ladder-like and covered in dense hairs, with a pair of small stipules joined at the bases.

INHABITS *meadows and other grassy places, on chalky soil, as well as on coastal sand dunes.*

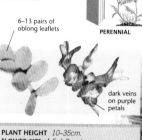

flowers in tight clusters

PERENNIAL

6–13 pairs of oblong leaflets

dark veins on purple petals

PLANT HEIGHT *10–35cm.*
FLOWER SIZE *1.5–1.8cm long.*
FLOWERING TIME *May–July.*
LEAVES *Alternate, pinnate.*
FRUIT *Dark brown swollen pods, 7–8mm long, covered with white hairs.*
SIMILAR SPECIES *Alpine Milk-vetch (A. alpinus) has loosely clustered flowers.*

Smooth Tare

Vicia tetrasperma (Fabaceae)

This plant is so fine and dainty that it gives a misty look to grasses and other vegetation over which it clambers by means of its long leaf tendrils. The tiny peaflowers are veined with purple or pale blue, and develop into small seed pods that contain four seeds.

SPRAWLS *over grasses in old meadows and along hedgerows and arable fields.*

veined petals

long, narrow leaflets

paired peaflowers

fine, slender stems

oblong seed pods

ANNUAL

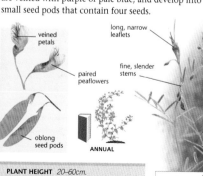

PLANT HEIGHT *20–60cm.*
FLOWER SIZE *4–8mm long.*
FLOWERING TIME *May–August.*
LEAVES *Alternate, pinnate with 3–6 pairs of linear leaflets, ending in tendrils.*
FRUIT *Green or brown four-seeded pod.*
SIMILAR SPECIES *Hairy Tare (V. hirsuta), which has whitish flowers and hairy pods.*

Tufted Vetch

Vicia cracca (Fabaceae)

CLAMBERS *among tall grasses in meadows, hedgerows, woodland margins, scrub, roadsides, and over coastal rocks and shingle.*

The deep violet-blue flowers of Tufted Vetch are produced in such profusion that they can be seen from some distance, often alongside roads and motorways. Up to 40 bluish violet flowers are clustered into long racemes, with each flower on a tiny stalk, arranged on one side of the stem. The leaves are divided into many pairs of narrow leaflets, sometimes with a fine covering of downy hairs. Each leaf terminates in a long, branching tendril, which can support the plant to a considerable height when it would otherwise flop on to the ground.

NOTE

Plants with tendrils exploit other plants by climbing up them to reach better light, without committing food resources into building robust stems.

flowers in one-sided racemes

slender stems

PERENNIAL

twining tendrils

paired leaflets

bluish violet petals

PLANT HEIGHT *0.8–1.8m.*
FLOWER SIZE *8–12mm wide.*
FLOWERING TIME *June–August.*
LEAVES *Alternate, pinnate, with 6–15 pairs of linear-oblong leaflets.*
FRUIT *Three-lobed capsule, splitting to the base.*
SIMILAR SPECIES *Lucerne (right), which has smaller flower clusters; Wood Vetch (V. sylvatica) has purple-veined white flowers; Fine-leaved Vetch (V. tenuifolia), which has narrower leaflets and larger flowers.*

Lucerne

Medicago sativa (Fabaceae)

Also known as Alfalfa, this plant was introduced throughout Europe as a fodder crop for cattle. Its trifoliate leaves are divided into long, slender leaflets, each toothed at the tip. The flowers, in loose clusters, vary in colour from pale pink to deep violet.

FORMS *colonies on cultivated and waste ground, roadsides, and disturbed, rough, grassy areas.*

pink to violet flowers

toothed leaflet tip

flowers in clusters

PERENNIAL

coiled seed pod

long, narrow leaflets

PLANT HEIGHT *40–90cm.*
FLOWER SIZE *7–11mm long.*
FLOWERING TIME *June–July.*
LEAVES *Alternate, trifoliate, elliptical leaflets.*
FRUIT *Spiralled pod, 5–6mm wide, with a hole in the centre.*
SIMILAR SPECIES *Tufted Vetch (left), which has pinnate leaves and longer flower clusters.*

Pale Flax

Linum bienne (Linaceae)

Although the flowers of Pale Flax have five petals, they are often seen with fewer in the afternoon, for after midday these begin to fall off. They are a delicate lilac shade with violet veins, and form a flat or saucer-shaped flower. The slender, erect stems bear just a few stalkless, linear leaves, which have one or three veins.

GROWS *in dry grassy places such as cliff slopes, field margins, old quarries; near the sea on neutral to chalky soils.*

BIENNIAL/PERENNIAL

slender stem

saucer-shaped flower

narrow leaf

rounded petals

PLANT HEIGHT *30–60cm.*
FLOWER SIZE *1.6–2.4cm wide.*
FLOWERING TIME *May–September.*
LEAVES *Alternate, linear, untoothed.*
FRUIT *Rounded capsule, 4–6mm wide, with a small beak at the top.*
SIMILAR SPECIES *Flax (L. usitatissimum), which has deep blue flowers.*

Meadow Crane's-bill

Geranium pratense (Geraniaceae)

GROWS *in meadows, pastures, hedgebanks, and road verges on rich or chalky soil. Garden cultivars of this species sometimes escape into the countryside.*

Distinctive among the geraniums, this plant has violet-blue flowers rather than the more usual pink. The petals are large, and often veined with white or crimson, and make an attractive sight along the verges of country lanes. Also large, the leaves are more or less rounded in outline but very deeply cut, almost to the base, into slender segments, giving them a rather tattered look and differentiating them from many garden cultivars.

toothed leaf segments

PERENNIAL

beaked fruit

hairy stems

petals rounded at tip

lighter veins on petals

NOTE

The beak of geranium fruit is formed from the elongated styles of the flowers. As they dry, they pull on the seeds, which are suddenly released and catapulted away from the plant.

PLANT HEIGHT *60–100cm.*
FLOWER SIZE *2.5–3cm wide.*
FLOWERING TIME *June–September.*
LEAVES *Basal and alternate, palmately lobed into many slender, deeply cut segments.*
FRUIT *Beaked fruit, splitting into five one-seeded portions.*
SIMILAR SPECIES *Wood Crane's-bill (p.204), which has pinker flowers and less deeply cut leaves.*

Common Milkwort

Polygala vulgaris (Polygalaceae)

The dainty blue flowers of Common Milkwort are the easiest to spot in the grass of its habitat, although it often has magenta or even white flowers. The coloured parts are actually three of the five sepals forming two wings and a hood, while the true petals are tiny, forming a frilly white tuft in the centre.

OCCURS *on short, often grazed grassland over chalk and limestone, on heaths, commons, and sand dunes.*

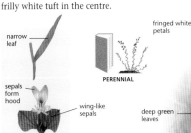

narrow leaf

fringed white petals

sepals form hood

wing-like sepals

deep green leaves

PERENNIAL

PLANT HEIGHT *10–30cm.*
FLOWER SIZE *5–8mm long.*
FLOWERING TIME *May–September.*
LEAVES *Alternate, oval-elliptic, untoothed.*
FRUIT *Small, two-lobed capsule.*
SIMILAR SPECIES *Heath Milkwort (P. serpyllifolia) has opposite lower leaves, and is found on acid soil.*

Common Dog-violet

Viola riviniana (Violaceae)

This is the one of the commonest violets, and may be identified by the distinctly heart-shaped leaves, each ending in a blunt point. The petals are generally spread widely, and there is a stout, gently curved spur at the back, paler in colour than the petals and slightly grooved at the tip. There is a pair of tiny bracts about one third of the way down the flower stem.

FOUND *in deciduous woodland, grassy heaths, and old pastures, on a variety of soils.*

widely spread petals

darker veins in centre of flower

heart-shaped leaf

PERENNIAL

PLANT HEIGHT *8–20cm.*
FLOWER SIZE *1.4–2.5cm wide.*
FLOWERING TIME *April–June.*
LEAVES *Basal, alternate, and long-stalked.*
FRUIT *Three-parted capsule.*
SIMILAR SPECIES *Sweet Violet (p.256); Heath Dog-violet (p.257); Early Dog-violet (V. reichenbachiana) has narrower petals.*

Sweet Violet

Viola odorata (Violaceae)

GROWS *in patches in hedgerows, woods, coppices, plantations, and scrub on chalky or neutral soils.*

One of the clues to identifying this tuft-forming species is its early flowering time, when the flowers add a splash of colour to the arrival of spring. They may be deep violet with a spur of the same shade or white with a pink spur, and are sweetly scented. Another important clue to identification are the two tiny, triangular bracts more than halfway down the stem. The kidney-shaped, bright green leaves are much more rounded than those of Common Dog-violet (p.255), but sometimes taper to a slight point.

NOTE

Since the flowers appear so early in the year and insects often fail to pollinate them, the plant forms cleistogamous (closed) flowers that self-pollinate.

deep violet spur

solitary flower

rounded leaves

separate petals

bluntly toothed margin

PERENNIAL

PLANT HEIGHT *8–15cm.*
FLOWER SIZE *1.3–1.5cm wide.*
FLOWERING TIME *February–May.*
LEAVES *Basal tufts, kidney-shaped with blunt teeth.*
FRUIT *Three-valved, hairy capsule.*
SIMILAR SPECIES *Common Dog-violet (p.255) has more pointed leaves; Marsh Violet (p.258) has darker flowers; Early Dog-violet (V. reicenbachiana) has more pointed leaves and narrow upper petals.*

Heath Dog-violet

Viola canina (Violaceae)

Very similar to Common Dog-violet (p.255), this plant is more likely to be found on acid soil and in open places, away from shade. The delicate, pale slate-blue, occasionally violet, flower has dark veins on the lower petal. The flower spur is usually straight and has a greenish tinge. The heart-shaped leaves are bluntly toothed.

FORMS *small patches on grassy heaths, fens, commons, woodland, and coastal dunes, on acid soil.*

dark-veined lower petal

PERENNIAL

bluntly toothed leaf

5-petalled flower

PLANT HEIGHT *5–20cm.*
FLOWER SIZE *1–1.8cm wide.*
FLOWERING TIME *April–July.*
LEAVES *Alternate, heart-shaped, toothed.*
FRUIT *Three-valved, hairless capsule.*
SIMILAR SPECIES *Common Dog-violet (p.255), which has broader leaves; Fen Violet (V. persicifolia) has lance-shaped leaves.*

Wild Pansy

Viola tricolor (Violaceae)

Also known as Heartsease, this plant sometimes hybridizes with garden pansies. Its flowers are variable in colour, appearing in combinations of yellow, purple, and white, but always with a few dark veins pointing to the centre of the flower. The petals are larger than the sepals.

FOUND *in rough grassland, neglected and cultivated arable fields, on neutral or acid soils.*

5-petalled flower

ANNUAL/PERENNIAL

narrow, toothed leaf

dark veins on petals

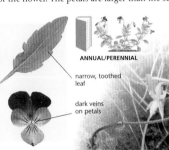

PLANT HEIGHT *10–30cm.*
FLOWER SIZE *1–2.5cm wide.*
FLOWERING TIME *April–October.*
LEAVES *Alternate, oval to elliptical; large, pinnately lobed stipules at the base.*
FRUIT *Three-parted capsule.*
SIMILAR SPECIES *Field Pansy (p.62); Mountain Pansy (V. lutea) has yellow flowers.*

Marsh Violet

Viola palustris (Violaceae)

Although easily missed among the lush vegetation of marshes, this violet is, once seen, simple to identify. The small flowers are a distinctive pinkish violet colour, with dark purple veins that guide insects to the pollen. The leaves, persisting for many weeks after flowering time, are kidney-shaped, with tiny stipules at the base.

CREEPS *low along the ground among wetland vegetation, in marshes, bogs, and woodland, on acid soil.*

PERENNIAL

pale green leaves

solitary flower

heart-shaped base

dark veins on petal

> **PLANT HEIGHT** *4–8cm.*
> **FLOWER SIZE** *1–1.5cm wide.*
> **FLOWERING TIME** *April–July.*
> **LEAVES** *Basal, heart- to kidney-shaped, long-stalked, toothed margins.*
> **FRUIT** *Three-parted capsule.*
> **SIMILAR SPECIES** *Sweet Violet (p.256), which has similar leaves but darker flowers.*

Lesser Periwinkle

Vinca minor (Apocynaceae)

The shiny, deep green leaves and trailing stems of this plant may carpet large areas of woodland in spring – only a few flowers may occur in such shaded places. The flowers are violet-purple, occasionally white, with each petal twisted and blunt-ended, resembling a ship's propeller. The calyx at the base of the long petal tube has tiny, triangular teeth.

FORMS *extensive mats in woodland, coppices, hedgerows, banks, and rocky ground, often in deep shade.*

glossy, deep green leaves

violet-purple flower

blunt-edged petals

PERENNIAL

oval leaf

slightly twisted petals

tiny sepals

> **PLANT HEIGHT** *15–40cm.*
> **FLOWER SIZE** *2.5–3cm wide.*
> **FLOWERING TIME** *March–May.*
> **LEAVES** *Opposite, oval to elliptic, short-stalked.*
> **FRUIT** *Forked capsule, 2.5cm wide, but rare.*
> **SIMILAR SPECIES** *Greater Periwinkle (V. major) has larger flowers with long sepals.*

Sea Holly

Eryngium maritimum (Apiaceae)

This member of the carrot family is unmistakable for many reasons. Most distinctive are its bluish or greenish grey leaves. They are stiff and waxy, undulating like dried leather, and are coarsely toothed, with each tooth ending in a sharp spine. The upper leaves are unstalked while the lower leaves are long-stalked. A tight ruff of bracts below the flowerhead is similarly spined, but may have a blue-violet tint, reflecting the colour of the blue flowers. The final clue to identity is the habitat, for the plant is restricted to sandy coasts.

GROWS *in small patches or extensive colonies along the coast, chiefly on sand dunes and sometimes on shingle.*

PERENNIAL

waxy, grey-green leaves

tiny blue flowers

spiny bracts below flowerhead

whitish leaf veins

rounded flowerhead

NOTE

The root of this plant was popular in the 17th century as a candied sweetmeat; the candied root was also used as an expectorant.

PLANT HEIGHT *30–60cm.*
FLOWER SIZE *Flowerhead 1.5–3cm wide.*
FLOWERING TIME *June–September.*
LEAVES *Basal and alternate, roughly rounded, lobed and toothed into spines; bluish or greenish grey.*
FRUIT *Mericarp with overlapping scales.*
SIMILAR SPECIES *Field Eryngo (p.37) has smaller flowerheads; Blue Eryngo (E. planum), which has narrow bracts and spineless leaves.*

Willow Gentian

Gentiana asclepiadea (Gentianaceae)

Not surprisingly, this graceful mountain wildflower has been adopted by gardeners and florists for its stunning blue flowers. These are produced in profusion on long, slender stems that arch over like the branches of a willow tree. Each flower is shaped like a long trumpet, with five pointed lobes, and faint whitish stripes inside and out. The leaves are arranged in well-spaced opposite pairs, each pair at right angles to the one next to it along the stem.

INHABITS *mountain meadows and open woodland; also found in damp places, alongside streams and in rocky places.*

whitish stripes on flower

trumpet-shaped flowers

PERENNIAL

NOTE

Gentians are named after Illyria's King Gentius of the 1st century BC who was reputedly the first to discover their value as a digestive tonic.

lance-shaped leaf

3–5 veins on leaf

pointed flower lobes

PLANT HEIGHT *30–60cm.*
FLOWER SIZE *3.5–5cm long.*
FLOWERING TIME *August–October.*
LEAVES *Opposite, lance-shaped, unstalked and untoothed; dark green.*
FRUIT *Capsule splitting into two parts, releasing dust-like seeds.*
SIMILAR SPECIES *Marsh Gentian (right), which is much shorter, has narrower leaves, and greenish spots on the petals.*

Spring Gentian

Gentiana verna (Gentianaceae)

Most European gentians flower in the autumn, but this one produces vivid, deep blue trumpet-shaped flowers in the spring, once the snows have melted in the mountains. Each flower has five spreading petals, which form a long tube at the base. The throat of the tube is white, with a fringe of hairs around it. Most of the leaves form basal rosettes.

FORMS *tufts in mountain meadows, wet flushes, and glacial deposits, on acid to chalky soils.*

deep blue flowers

white centre of flower

PERENNIAL

oval leaf

5 petals

PLANT HEIGHT *4–8 cm.*
FLOWER SIZE *1.2–1.8cm wide.*
FLOWERING TIME *April–June.*
LEAVES *Basal rosette, opposite pairs, oval, unstalked; bright green,*
FRUIT *Capsule containing many seeds*
SIMILAR SPECIES *Alpine Gentian (G. nivalis), which has smaller flowers later in the year.*

Marsh Gentian

Gentiana pneumonanthe (Gentianaceae)

Sometimes partly concealed among the grasses of peaty bogs, the violet-blue petals of this plant are flushed with olive green on the outside, and spotted greyish white on the inside. The flowers are trumpet-shaped and large in comparison to the leaves, which are exceptionally narrow for a gentian.

5-lobed flowers

OCCURS *in loose colonies in marshy areas, bogs, and wet heaths, on thin peaty acid soil; avoids shade.*

linear, unstalked leaves

whitish spots

PERENNIAL

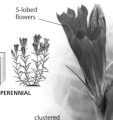

clustered flowers

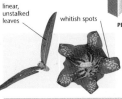

PLANT HEIGHT *20–50cm.*
FLOWER SIZE *2.5–4.5cm long.*
FLOWERING TIME *July–October.*
LEAVES *Opposite, lance-shaped.*
FRUIT *Capsule that splits to release seeds.*
SIMILAR SPECIES *Willow Gentian (left), which is taller; Cross Gentian (G. cruciata), which has broader leaves.*

Autumn Gentian

Gentianella amarella (Gentianaceae)

GROWS in short turf in pastures and other dry, grassy areas, and on dunes; on chalky soil and slopes.

Flowers of this small gentian usually have five short petal lobes which form a long tube at the base, but occasionally there are only four. Usually bluish violet, they may also be dull purple or magenta. The calyx also has four or five lobes of equal width.

clustered flowers

BIENNIAL

5 petal lobes

clearly veined leaves

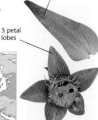

PLANT HEIGHT *10–30cm.*
FLOWER SIZE *1.4–2cm long.*
FLOWERING TIME *June–October.*
LEAVES *Basal rosette and opposite, lance-shaped; deep grey-green.*
FRUIT *Capsule, splitting into two parts.*
SIMILAR SPECIES *Field Gentian (G. campestris) has bluish lilac flowers.*

Jacob's-ladder

Polemonium caeruleum (Polemoniaceae)

OCCURS in rocky places, limestone screes, damp meadows, hedgerows, scrub, and roadsides.

This is a neat-looking plant, with characteristically ladder-like leaves. The flowers are clustered towards the top of the stems, each with five separate, pale blue-violet petals forming a cup shape. There are five long stamens with bright orange anthers, and an even longer purple style. The whole plant forms an erect tuft, but rarely forms colonies.

up to 12 pairs of leaflets

PERENNIAL

erect stem

orange anthers

PLANT HEIGHT *50–100cm.*
FLOWER SIZE *2–3cm wide.*
FLOWERING TIME *May–August.*
LEAVES *Alternate, pinnate, with many pairs of lance-shaped leaflets.*
FRUIT *Small capsule containing many seeds.*
SIMILAR SPECIES *P. acutifolium, which has fewer than eight pairs of leaflets.*

Viper's-bugloss

Echium vulgare (Boraginaceae)

An instantly recognizable plant, Viper's-bugloss grows in a wide variety of habitats. Its long, stout stems, covered in bristly speckles, arise from a rosette of leaves formed in the first year, and are clothed in masses of five-petalled, deep purple flowers, with long, protruding scarlet stamens. Each cluster or cyme of flowers unfurls along the stem like a scorpion's tail, the buds gradually changing from pink to violet as they mature. The narrow leaves and bracts are also rough and hairy.

coiled flower buds

FLOURISHES *in dry, open places, road verges, cliffs, shingle, sand dunes, heaths, and grassy banks, often on disturbed soil.*

BIENNIAL

funnel-shaped flowers

NOTE

The seeds seem to resemble a snake's head, giving rise to the belief that the plant cured snake poisoning. The scientific name Echium *is derived from 'Echis', which means a viper.*

narrow, stalkless leaves

scarlet protruding stamens

PLANT HEIGHT *50–100cm.*
FLOWER SIZE *1.5–2cm wide.*
FLOWERING TIME *June–September.*
LEAVES *Basal rosette and alternate, narrow-elliptical to lance-shaped, unstalked; bristly stem leaves.*
FRUIT *Four nutlets at base of persistent calyx.*
SIMILAR SPECIES *Meadow's Clary (p.270); Purple Viper's-bugloss (E. plantagineum) is a shorter plant, with purple flowers.*

Purple Gromwell

Lithospermum purpurocaeruleum (Boraginaceae)

INHABITS *semi-shaded areas such as chalky woodland margins, hedgerows, and banks.*

Leafy, non-flowering as well as flower-bearing shoots are produced on this plant. The flowers are clustered together with many narrow bracts, and are pinkish violet at first or in bud but soon change to a deep violet. The fruit, like those of Common Gromwell (p.81), are tiny white nutlets, like porcelain beads, that remain attached to the hairy stems into the late summer.

flowers in small clusters

narrow, untoothed leaf

5 deep violet petals

dark green leaves

woody stem

PERENNIAL

PLANT HEIGHT *40–60cm.*
FLOWER SIZE *1.4–1.9cm long.*
FLOWERING TIME *April–June.*
LEAVES *Alternate, lance-shaped, hairy.*
FRUIT *Up to four hard, shiny white nutlets.*
SIMILAR SPECIES *Alkanet (Anchusa officinalis), which is rough and bristly, with blue flowers.*

Common Lungwort

Pulmonaria officinalis (Boraginaceae)

FORMS *clumps in damp woodland and hedgebanks, in semi-shade on humus-rich soil; dislikes acid soil.*

This plant can be instantly recognized by its oval, heavily spotted leaves, which were once thought to resemble lungs and therefore to act as a cure for lung diseases. The flowers are borne in dense, branched clusters, pink in bud but maturing to a range of colours from reddish violet to blue. Each flower has five rounded, tissue-like petals fused into a tube at the base.

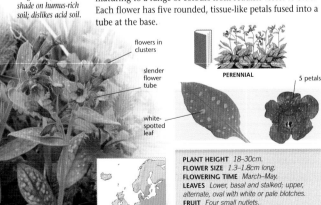

flowers in clusters

slender flower tube

PERENNIAL

5 petals

white-spotted leaf

PLANT HEIGHT *18–30cm.*
FLOWER SIZE *1.3–1.8cm long.*
FLOWERING TIME *March–May.*
LEAVES *Lower, basal and stalked; upper, alternate, oval with white or pale blotches.*
FRUIT *Four small nutlets.*
SIMILAR SPECIES *P. angustifolia, which has narrower, unspotted leaves.*

Bugloss

Anchusa arvensis (Boraginaceae)

This erect, extremely bristly plant has rough, alternate leaves with undulating and slightly toothed margins. The lower leaves are stalked, but the smaller upper leaves are unstalked and clasp the stem with heart-shaped bases. The tiny, five-petalled blue flowers are borne in clusters, each with a white centre and a curved tube at the base. A common plant in farmland, it may grow hidden among rows of cereal crops.

GROWS *on arable fields, field margins, waste and bare land, and sandy heaths, especially near the sea.*

fine bristles

5-petalled blue flower

unstalked upper leaf

white centre

ANNUAL

PLANT HEIGHT *15–60cm.*
FLOWER SIZE *4–6mm wide.*
FLOWERING TIME *May–September.*
LEAVES *Alternate, rough and bristly.*
FRUIT *Four nutlets at the base of the calyx.*
SIMILAR SPECIES *Green Alkanet (p.266), which has larger flowers; forget-me-nots (p.267), which have untoothed leaves.*

Borage

Borago officinalis (Boraginaceae)

Borne in loose, branched clusters, the nodding, ultramarine blue flowers of this plant have a curious appearance as the black stamens form a cone inside the white centre of the flower. The whole plant is bristly and hairy, giving it a frosted appearance. It originates from the Mediterranean but is widely naturalized.

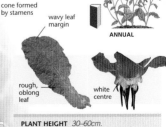

OCCURS *in arable fields, wasteland, and disturbed soil; favours dry, sunny places.*

bristly flower stems

cone formed by stamens

wavy leaf margin

ANNUAL

rough, oblong leaf

white centre

PLANT HEIGHT *30–60cm.*
FLOWER SIZE *2–2.5cm wide.*
FLOWERING TIME *May–September.*
LEAVES *Alternate, basal, oval to oblong, untoothed, stalked.*
FRUIT *Four nutlets at the base of the calyx.*
SIMILAR SPECIES *Green Alkanet (p.266), which lacks prominent black stamens.*

Green Alkanet

Pentaglottis sempervirens (Boraginaceae)

The large, slightly bristly, basal leaves of Green Alkanet are formed early in the year and may be mistaken for those of Foxglove (p.224) at first. Covered with fine hairs, they are somewhat wrinkled, and paler beneath. The flowering shoots are distinctive, bearing coiled clusters of blue flowers, darker than those of the related forget-me-nots (right), each with a pure white throat and spreading, rounded petals. The plant was introduced from southwestern Europe, but has naturalized in other regions of Europe as a result of its escape from gardens.

PROLIFERATES *in damp, semi-shaded sites along woodland margins, hedgebanks, and roadsides, often close to habitation.*

PERENNIAL

flowers in small clusters

5 well-separated petals

long, leafy stem

untoothed leaves

oval basal leaf

long stalk of basal leaf

white centre

NOTE

The fine, bristly hairs on the stems and leaves of this and other members of the borage family can cause skin irritation if handled without protection.

PLANT HEIGHT *40–80cm.*
FLOWER SIZE *8–10mm wide.*
FLOWERING TIME *April–July.*
LEAVES *Basal leaves, oval to oblong, long-stalked and hairy; alternate stem leaves, unstalked.*
FRUIT *Four nutlets, rough, netted on surface.*
SIMILAR SPECIES *Bugloss (p.265) is shorter and more bristly, with smaller flowers; Borage (p.265) has prominent, black stamens.*

Wood Forget-me-not

Myosotis sylvatica (Boraginaceae)

There are several species of forget-me-nots in Europe, all of which have the same basic flower structure of sky-blue petals with a yellow centre, as well as hairy leaves (the name *Myosotis* means "mouse's ear"). The chief differences are the size of the flowers and the preferred habitat. The Wood Forget-me-not has the largest flowers and is found in woodland.

GROWS *in semi-shaded situations in woodland rides and clearings, road verges, and damp meadows.*

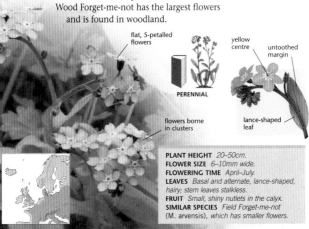

flat, 5-petalled flowers

yellow centre

untoothed margin

PERENNIAL

flowers borne in clusters

lance-shaped leaf

PLANT HEIGHT *20–50cm.*
FLOWER SIZE *6–10mm wide.*
FLOWERING TIME *April–July.*
LEAVES *Basal and alternate, lance-shaped, hairy; stem leaves stalkless.*
FRUIT *Small, shiny nutlets in the calyx.*
SIMILAR SPECIES *Field Forget-me-not (M. arvensis), which has smaller flowers.*

Water Forget-me-not

Myosotis scorpioides (Boraginaceae)

This species appears less hairy than most forget-me-nots, as the hairs lie very flat on the stems and leaves. The stems look fleshy, befitting its moist habitat. The flower cluster, a cyme, is coiled in bud and resembles a scorpion's tail when it uncoils. Pink in bud, the flowers open sky-blue.

FORMS *colonies in wet places along rivers and streams, in marshes, ditches, and meadows, on neutral soil.*

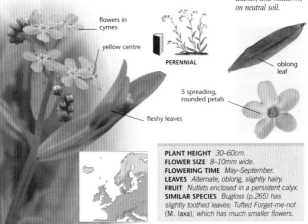

flowers in cymes

yellow centre

PERENNIAL

oblong leaf

5 spreading, rounded petals

fleshy leaves

PLANT HEIGHT *30–60cm.*
FLOWER SIZE *8–10mm wide.*
FLOWERING TIME *May–September.*
LEAVES *Alternate, oblong, slightly hairy.*
FRUIT *Nutlets enclosed in a persistent calyx.*
SIMILAR SPECIES *Bugloss (p.265) has slightly toothed leaves; Tufted Forget-me-not (M. laxa), which has much smaller flowers.*

Bugle

Ajuga reptans (Lamiaceae)

FOUND *in mats in damp areas of woodland rides and shady grassland, or along hedgerows.*

This erect, hairy plant spreads by runners to form mats of leaves, but it is the tall, densely flowered spikes that distinguish it from other plants. The flowers are blue, each with a reduced upper lip. The plant's oval leaves and bracts are often flushed with violet or bronze. The square stems are hairy on two opposite sides.

flowers in whorls

oval leaf

prominent flower lobes

violet-flushed leaves

square stem

PERENNIAL

PLANT HEIGHT *10–25cm.*
FLOWER SIZE *1.4–1.7cm long.*
FLOWERING TIME *April–June.*
LEAVES *Opposite, oval.*
FRUIT *Four small nutlets.*
SIMILAR SPECIES *Self-heal (right); Ground Ivy (right); Pyramidal Bugle (A. pyramidalis), which has hairy stems all round.*

Skullcap

Scutellaria galericulata (Lamiaceae)

OCCURS *in damp places, wet meadows, marshes, margins of rivers, streams, and ditches, often among taller vegetation.*

Not easy to spot among the taller vegetation of its marshy habitat, this member of the mint family produces just a few flowers, always in pairs, often quite low down on the square stem, at the base of the leaves. The bright violet-blue flowers have a distinctive shape, especially in bud, when they look like a pair of tiny, downy boxing gloves. The bluntly toothed leaves are oval to lance-shaped.

leafy stems

violet-blue flowers

opposite leaves

toothed leaf margin

2-lipped flowers in pairs

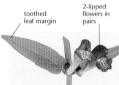

PERENNIAL

PLANT HEIGHT *30–50cm.*
FLOWER SIZE *1–1.8cm long.*
FLOWERING TIME *June–September.*
LEAVES *Opposite, oval to lance-shaped, with blunt teeth.*
FRUIT *Four nutlets at base of calyx.*
SIMILAR SPECIES *Lesser Skullcap (S. minor), which has smaller, pink flowers.*

Ground Ivy

Glechoma hederacea (Lamiaceae)

Although this plant may flower throughout summer, it is in early spring that extensive mats bloom with bluish mauve, sometimes pink, two-lipped flowers with pink spots on the lower lip. In summer, the plant spreads by sending long, leafy runners over the ground, much like Ivy (p.24).

GROWS *in mats on bare ground, field margins, woodland rides and clearings, and along hedgerows; prefers damp places.*

PERENNIAL

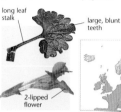

long leaf stalk — large, blunt teeth

2-lipped flower

red-tinged upper leaves

flowers in whorls

PLANT HEIGHT *10–25cm.*
FLOWER SIZE *1.5–2.2cm long.*
FLOWERING TIME *March–September.*
LEAVES *Opposite, kidney-shaped or rounded, long-stalked, coarsely toothed.*
FRUIT *Four nutlets in persistent calyx.*
SIMILAR SPECIES *Bugle (left), which has untoothed leaves and one-lipped flowers.*

Self-heal

Prunella vulgaris (Lamiaceae)

This plant forms distinctive oblong flowerheads, tightly packed with often purplish calyces. A pair of sharp bracts and rounded, dark-margined leaves below each flower, make the whole flowerhead look like a fir-cone. The flowers, each with a long, hooded upper lip, are usually deep blue, but colonies of pure pink flowers are often seen.

FORMS *patches in grassy places, lawns wasteland, and woodland clearings, or among scrub.*

dark bracts below each flower

dark lines on square stems

fine pointed teeth on calyx

PERENNIAL

oval leaf

hooded upper lip

PLANT HEIGHT *15–30cm.*
FLOWER SIZE *1.3–1.5cm long.*
FLOWERING TIME *June–November.*
LEAVES *Opposite, oval to lance-shaped, very slightly toothed.*
FRUIT *Four nutlets at base of calyx.*
SIMILAR SPECIES *Bugle (left); Large Self-heal (P. grandiflora) has much larger flowers.*

Meadow Clary

Salvia pratensis (Lamiaceae)

This imposing plant has some of the largest flowers in the mint family. They are a deep violet-blue, and are arranged in whorls on tall spikes, the lowermost opening first. The flower's upper lip is distinctive, forming a large curved hood from which the forked style protrudes. The leaves are oval or oblong, with an irregularly toothed margin and a rough, wrinkled surface.

INHABITS *dry grassland, hay meadows, grassy paths, and roadsides, on chalky soil.*

toothed margin

oblong leaf

hooded lip

long, forked style

PERENNIAL

tall spike

flowers in whorls

PLANT HEIGHT *50–80cm.*
FLOWER SIZE *2–3cm long.*
FLOWERING TIME *May–July.*
LEAVES *Basal leaves stalked and in a rosette; stem leaves unstalked.*
FRUIT *Four nutlets held within the calyx.*
SIMILAR SPECIES *Monkshood (p.248); Viper's-bugloss (p.263) has tubular flowers.*

Purple Toadflax

Linaria purpurea (Scrophulariaceae)

A robust plant, originating from southern Italy, Purple Toadflax is becoming increasingly naturalized in wasteland close to human habitation. The long, slender, almost wiry spikes are composed of whorls of two-lipped, purple flowers, each with a slender spur at the back, reminiscent of a snapdragon. The grey-green leaves are linear, whorled at the bottom, but alternate at the top.

GROWS *on cultivated and waste ground, on or along old walls and pavements, close to human habitation.*

slender flower spikes

PERENNIAL

deep purple flowers

dark-veined flower

linear leaf

slender spur

PLANT HEIGHT *60–100cm.*
FLOWER SIZE *0.9–1.5cm long.*
FLOWERING TIME *June–August.*
LEAVES *Whorls at bottom, alternate higher up, linear.*
FRUIT *Small, rounded capsule.*
SIMILAR SPECIES *Pale Toadflax (L. repens), which has pale lilac flowers with darker veins.*

Bittersweet

Solanum dulcamara (Solanaceae)

The flowers of this woody climber are instantly recognizable since they are similar to those of the related tomato and potato. The five slender, deep purple petals are often swept back, revealing the cone-shaped collection of bright yellow anthers. These later form clusters of egg-shaped fruit, green at first, but ripening to orange and finally to red. They persist long after the leaves have withered. The leaves are almost arrow-shaped, usually with three or five deeply cut lobes. In common with other members of its family, the entire plant is poisonous.

CLAMBERS *over hedges and other vegetation in scrub, marsh, and fens; also sprawls over shingle beaches.*

PERENNIAL

cone of yellow stamens

swept-back purple petals

NOTE

Although poisonous, the plant was used in the past for a variety of medicinal applications, and is said to taste bitter at first and then sweet, hence its name.

large terminal lobe

egg-shaped berries

PLANT HEIGHT *1–2.5m (20cm on shingle).*
FLOWER SIZE *1–1.5cm wide.*
FLOWERING TIME *May–September.*
LEAVES *Alternate, arrow-shaped, untoothed, 3–5 lobes, short stalks.*
FRUIT *Red, egg-shaped berry.*
SIMILAR SPECIES *Black Nightshade (p.83), which has white petals and grows as an annual on cultivated land; Potato (S. tuberosum), which may have larger purple flowers but grows as a low bushy plant.*

Brooklime

Veronica beccabunga (Scrophulariaceae)

Brooklime is a distinctive plant, with its fat, succulent stems flushed red around the leaf-joints. The flowers form loose clusters on long stalks that arise from the leaf bases. Each flower is a rich blue, with a small white "eye" ringed with scarlet. The hairless leaves are also a little succulent and have a wavy margin.

INHABITS *margins of ponds, ditches, rivers, and permanently damp parts of marshes and wet meadows.*

wavy-edged leaf

red ring around white centre

deep blue flowers

red-tinged succulent stems

PERENNIAL

PLANT HEIGHT *20–60cm.*
FLOWER SIZE *5–8mm wide.*
FLOWERING TIME *May–September.*
LEAVES *Opposite, oval to elliptical, slightly fleshy, toothed; deep green.*
FRUIT *Small, round capsule.*
SIMILAR SPECIES *Blue Water-speedwell (V. anagallis-aquatica) has longer leaves.*

Germander Speedwell

Veronica chamaedrys (Scrophulariaceae)

The flowers of this plant are an exceptionally deep and vivid blue, with a contrasting white "eye" in the centre and two divergent protruding stamens. The flower stalks are produced from the base of hairy, stalkless leaves. Close examination of the hairy stems reveals that the hairs are in two neat, opposite rows.

PROLIFERATES *in shady grassy areas, alongside woodland, hedgerows, among scrub, and on embankments.*

PERENNIAL

4 petals of unequal size

white centre

coarsely toothed leaves

PLANT HEIGHT *20–40cm.*
FLOWER SIZE *9–12mm wide.*
FLOWERING TIME *March–July.*
LEAVES *Opposite, oval, coarsely toothed, and unstalked.*
FRUIT *Small heart-shaped capsules.*
SIMILAR SPECIES *Common Field Speedwell (right) has flowers with a white petal.*

Common Field Speedwell

Veronica persica (Scrophulariaceae)

Introduced into Europe in the early 19th century, this species has become a common sight on farmland in many places. The lowest of the four petals is smaller than the others and is usually white, the others being violet with dark radiating veins. The oval, hairy leaves are very short-stalked, with just a few coarse teeth.

FLOURISHES *on disturbed soil such as wasteland, and particularly among farmland crops.*

coarsely toothed leaves

dark-veined flower

ANNUAL

lower petal usually white

oval leaf

PLANT HEIGHT *5–20cm.*
FLOWER SIZE *8–12mm wide.*
FLOWERING TIME *Year round.*
LEAVES *Mostly alternate, lower ones opposite.*
FRUIT *Heart-shaped capsule.*
SIMILAR SPECIES *Germander Speedwell (left); Green Field Speedwell (V. agrestis) has smaller white flowers with a blue upper petal.*

Heath Speedwell

Veronica officinalis (Scrophulariaceae)

This speedwell may be recognized by its small spikes of lilac flowers. The plant sends out runners which root at intervals, so the flowering stems arch upwards from the ground. The opposite, deep green leaves are neater in appearance than those of most speedwells.

CREEPS *over the ground on heaths, open woods, and grassy places; on well-drained, acid soil.*

serrated leaf margin

flowers in short spike

deep green leaves

PERENNIAL

dark veins on petals

hairy stem

PLANT HEIGHT *10–40cm.*
FLOWER SIZE *5–9mm wide.*
FLOWERING TIME *May–August.*
LEAVES *Opposite, oblong, with neatly serrated margin.*
FRUIT *Hairy, heart-shaped capsule.*
SIMILAR SPECIES *Wood Speedwell (V. montana), has flowers in loose clusters.*

Spiked Speedwell

Veronica spicata (Scrophulariaceae)

This erect, tufted speedwell has tall spikes of flowers that are deep violet-blue, with prominent stamens ending in large, dark anthers. The narrow, hairy leaves have neat, blunt teeth. Hybrids with Garden Speedwell may escape and be naturalized.

FOUND *in dry grassland, woodland margins, among scrub and rocky outcrops, on dry, chalky soil; also grown in gardens.*

tall, narrow flower spike

violet-blue flowers

narrow leaf

PERENNIAL

dark anthers

PLANT HEIGHT *20–60cm.*
FLOWER SIZE *4–8mm wide.*
FLOWERING TIME *July–October.*
LEAVES *Opposite pairs, narrow above, oval below, hairy, with toothed margin.*
FRUIT *Small, notched capsule.*
SIMILAR SPECIES *Garden Speedwell (V. longifolia), which is taller.*

Common Butterwort

Pinguicula vulgaris (Lentibulariaceae)

The pale yellow-green leaves of Common Butterwort have a very sticky surface that attracts small insects. These become trapped when they alight and are digested by the plant, as the leaf margins roll in slightly. The solitary purple flowers have a whitish centre and a spur at the back.

FORMS *small colonies in wet, acid locations such as bogs, moors, heaths, and damp rocks, often along streams.*

flower spur

leafless stem

PERENNIAL

rounded petals

pale yellow-green leaf

PLANT HEIGHT *8–18cm.*
FLOWER SIZE *1.5–2cm wide.*
FLOWERING TIME *May–July.*
LEAVES *Basal rosette, elliptical with in-rolled margin, fleshy and sticky; yellow-green.*
FRUIT *Small, erect, many-seeded capsule.*
SIMILAR SPECIES *Alpine Butterwort (P. alpina), which has white flowers.*

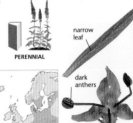

Common Cornsalad

Valarianella locusta (Valerianaceae)

The flowers of Common Cornsalad are so tiny and profuse that they give the impression, at a distance, of a bluish mist. They are borne in dense clusters, with a little ruff of bracts below each cluster, at the top of the many branched stems. Also known as Lamb's Lettuce, the plant is often cultivated as a salad crop.

GROWS *in colonies on rocky outcrops, old walls, cultivated or waste ground, shingle, and sandy places, often near the sea.*

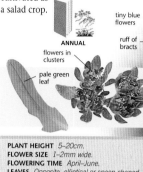

ANNUAL

tiny blue flowers

ruff of bracts

flowers in clusters

pale green leaf

PLANT HEIGHT *5–20cm.*
FLOWER SIZE *1–2mm wide.*
FLOWERING TIME *April–June.*
LEAVES *Opposite, elliptical or spoon-shaped, slightly toothed; pale green.*
FRUIT *Tiny one-seeded nutlet.*
SIMILAR SPECIES *Other species occur, but are different only in the shape of the fruit.*

Small Scabious

Scabiosa columbaria (Dipsacaceae)

The flowerhead of this pretty grassland plant is a cluster of lilac-blue tubular florets, each with five tiny petals. The outer florets have an enlarged petal which gives the flowerhead a lacy appearance. The upper leaves are very finely divided into linear segments; the lower leaves are long-stalked, with fine teeth.

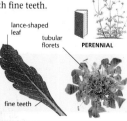

OCCURS *on dry, chalky soil on embankments, roadsides, downland and coastal areas.*

lilac-blue flowerhead

lance-shaped leaf

tubular florets

PERENNIAL

enlarged petal

fine teeth

PLANT HEIGHT *10–70cm.*
FLOWER SIZE *2–4cm wide.*
FLOWERING TIME *July–August.*
LEAVES *Basal leaves oval to lance-shaped, upper leaves finely pinnately divided.*
FRUIT *Achene with a feathery calyx.*
SIMILAR SPECIES *Field Scabious (p.277), which is taller with larger pinnate leaves.*

Devil's-bit Scabious

Succisa pratensis (Dipsacaceae)

Entire meadows may be coloured purple by swathes of this plant in late summer. The flowers are generally darker than other scabious species, and form a rounded rather than flat-topped head. Each tubular floret is the same in shape and size, without larger petals on the outside. When in bud, the flowerhead is like a collection of green or purple beads but later, when the flowers open and the stamens protrude, it comes to resemble a pincushion.

FLOURISHES *in meadows and heaths, in dry or moist conditions, in the open or in light shade of scrub, on chalky to slightly acid soils.*

PERENNIAL

NOTE

The long root of this plant formed in the first year, was thought to have been bitten off by the devil, as it later withers away when the side-roots are formed.

florets of equal size

small linear bracts below flowers

rounded flowerhead in bud

prominent pale midrib

protruding stamens

PLANT HEIGHT *50–100cm.*
FLOWER SIZE *Flowerhead 1.5–2cm wide.*
FLOWERING TIME *July–October.*
LEAVES *Basal leaves, lance-shaped with prominent white midrib; stem leaves opposite and toothed.*
FRUIT *One-seeded achene.*
SIMILAR SPECIES *Sheep's-bit (p.279), which does not have protruding stamens; Round-headed Rampion (p.282), which has curved florets.*

Field Scabious

Knautia arvensis (Dipsacaceae)

This is the largest and most robust of the scabious family flowers and may be recognized by its large leaves dissected into narrow, pointed lobes, though the basal ones are usually undivided. The flowerhead is a collection of tubular florets, in some ways similar to a dandelion-type member of the daisy family. Each of the pinkish lilac florets has four petals fused at the base, with an enlarged petal on the outer florets contributing to its rather untidy appearance. The narrow bracts below the flowerhead are about the same length as the florets.

GROWS *in meadows, pastures, open woodland, hedgerows, and roadside verges; generally on chalky soil.*

PERENNIAL

tubular florets

long, slender flower stem

pinnately lobed leaf

ruff of bracts below flowerhead

enlarged outer petals

NOTE

This species was called Scabious arvensis, but has been renamed after the 17th-century Saxon botanist, Dr Knaut. The juice and roots of Field Scabious and related plants were once used to treat scabies and other skin disorders.

PLANT HEIGHT *50–100cm.*
FLOWER SIZE *Flowerhead 2–4cm wide.*
FLOWERING TIME *July–September.*
LEAVES *Basal rosettes; upper leaves opposite and pinnately lobed.*
FRUIT *Achene with a feathery calyx attached.*
SIMILAR SPECIES *Small Scabious (p.275), which has finely divided leaves; Wood Scabious (K. dipsacifolia), which has toothed rather than lobed stem leaves, and is found in C. Europe.*

Teasel

Dipsacus fullonum (Dipsacaeae)

FLOURISHES *in rough, grassy places and along embankments, roadsides, river and stream banks, hedgerows, and woodland margins.*

Shaped like the blade of a spear, the leaves of Teasel are unmistakable, with a bold white midrib armed with long prickles underneath, and many lateral veins creating a rather wavy margin. The opposite leaves are joined together around the stem, and may collect pools of rainwater in wet weather. The flowerhead is a dense collection of stiff, straight spines, between which the lilac-blue flowers emerge. They open in a concentric ring about one third of the way up the head, and then spread upwards and downwards simultaneously.

BIENNIAL

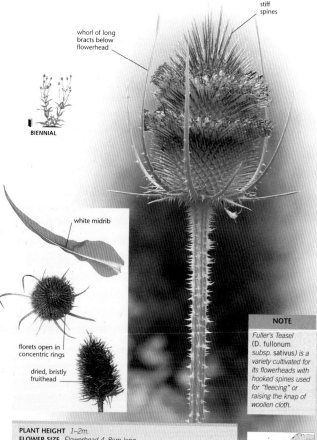

stiff spines

whorl of long bracts below flowerhead

white midrib

florets open in concentric rings

dried, bristly fruithead

NOTE

Fuller's Teasel (D. fullonum subsp. sativus) is a variety cultivated for its flowerheads with hooked spines used for "fleecing" or raising the knap of woollen cloth.

PLANT HEIGHT 1–2m.
FLOWER SIZE *Flowerhead 4–8cm long.*
FLOWERING TIME July–October.
LEAVES *Basal rosette in first year; opposite stem leaves, lance-shaped with spines on lower midrib, fused around stem.*
FRUIT *Small achene.*
SIMILAR SPECIES *Small Teasel (p.85) has white flowerheads; Cut-leaved Teasel (D. laciniatus) has pink flowers and pinnate leaves.*

Sheep's-bit

Jasione montana (Campanulaceae)

There are no obvious clues that this is a member of the bellflower family, but the small, alternate, hairy leaves show that it is not scabious, although apparently similar. The flowerhead is made up of tiny florets with five narrow petals, usually deep blue though sometimes pink or white, with a prominent pink style. There is a neat ruff of oval or triangular bracts below.

FORMS *on heaths, hills, meadows, dry, rough grassland, coastal rocks, and sand-cliffs, on light sandy soil.*

PERENNIAL

very compact flowerhead

small, wavy-edged leaves

oval bracts

PLANT HEIGHT *20–50cm.*
FLOWER SIZE *Flowerhead 1–2.5cm wide.*
FLOWERING TIME *July–October.*
LEAVES *Alternate, lance-shaped, hairy, with wavy margins; grey-green.*
FRUIT *Capsule opens by two valves at apex.*
SIMILAR SPECIES *Devil's-bit Scabious (p.276) is taller with protruding stamens.*

Harebell

Campanula rotundifolia (Campanulaceae)

The scientific name *rotundifolia* refers to the round basal leaves, which have almost always withered away by flowering time. By contrast, the stem leaves are linear, the lowest ones lance-shaped. It is the dainty nodding bells, however, that are the noticeable feature of the plant: a rich sky-blue with five pointed lobes, usually in a very loose cluster.

GROWS *in dry, grassy places, such as commons, heaths, banks and hills; on rocky ground and sand dunes.*

PERENNIAL

5-lobed corolla

tiny calyx

nodding bells

linear stem leaf

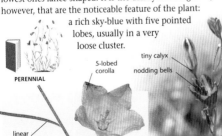

PLANT HEIGHT *20–50cm.*
FLOWER SIZE *1.2–2cm long.*
FLOWERING TIME *July–September.*
LEAVES *Basal leaves rounded, usually withered by flowering time; stem leaves alternate, narrow, and untoothed.*
FRUIT *Pendent capsule.*
SIMILAR SPECIES *None.*

Clustered Bellflower

Campanula glomerata (Campanulaceae)

INHABITS *dry, rough grassland, pastures, and meadows; also along roadsides and among scrub, on chalky soil.*

This plant is easily identified by the close grouping of the flowers at the top of the stems, giving it a rather top-heavy look. Each upright flower is deep blue-violet in colour, the five petals fused into a long bell shape but with pointed lobes at the mouth and a fold along the length of each. The slightly toothed stems and leaves are roughly hairy.

flowers clustered at top of stem

5 narrow lobes

bell-shaped flowers

PERENNIAL

PLANT HEIGHT *15–30cm.*
FLOWER SIZE *1.5–2cm long.*
FLOWERING TIME *July–September.*
LEAVES *Basal leaves oval to lance-shaped, stem leaves narrower and clasping the stem.*
FRUIT *Capsule containing many seeds.*
SIMILAR SPECIES *Nettle-leaved Bellflower (right) is taller, with loose racemes of flowers.*

Peach-leaved Bellflower

Campanula persicifolia (Campanulaceae)

OCCURS *in meadows, woodland edges, rough grassland, and along road verges.*

This familiar garden plant sometimes forms extensive loose colonies. It produces widely open bell-shaped flowers with broad petals, which open upright but mature to a horizontal position, though not drooping. The calyx has rather narrow, pointed sepals. The basal leaves are lance-shaped to oval and stalked, while the stem leaves are almost linear and more finely toothed.

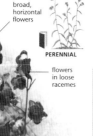

broad, horizontal flowers

PERENNIAL

flowers in loose racemes

flower bud

linear bract

PLANT HEIGHT *40–80cm.*
FLOWER SIZE *3–4cm long.*
FLOWERING TIME *June–August.*
LEAVES *Basal leaves lance-shaped and stalked, upper leaves linear and toothed.*
FRUIT *Capsule splitting lengthwise.*
SIMILAR SPECIES *Creeping Bellflower (C. rapunculoides) has narrow, drooping bells.*

Nettle-leaved Bellflower

Campanula trachelium (Campanulaceae)

Coarsely toothed, very hairy, triangular, and sometimes with a heart-shaped base, the leaves of this plant resemble those of a stinging nettle, though they carry no stinging hairs. When the sun catches them, the deep violet-blue flowers show up brightly against the shady gloom of dense woodland, the edges of which are its favoured habitat. The flowers are upright or horizontal, which prevents pollen falling from the short stamens onto the style, but when the fruit begins to ripen the calyx droops down.

FOUND *on the margins of woodland, tracks, hedgerows, and scrub, sometimes in the shade, preferring chalky soil.*

PERENNIAL

prominent white style

horizontal or upright flowers

coarsely toothed leaf

petals spreading at tip

PLANT HEIGHT *40–80cm.*
FLOWER SIZE *2.5–5cm long.*
FLOWERING TIME *July–September.*
LEAVES *Basal and alternate, triangular to heart-shaped; deep green above, paler beneath.*
FRUIT *Pendent capsule.*
SIMILAR SPECIES *Giant Bellflower (C. latifolia), which is taller with larger, more profuse flowers.*

NOTE

This and other bellflowers have a protruding style, which is longer than the stamens, to prevent self-pollination as a bee enters. Hairs inside the bell afford extra grip for the bee.

Round-headed Rampion

Phyteuma orbiculare (Campanulaceae)

GROWS *in rough pastures and meadows, on embankments and on grazed slopes, on chalky soil.*

The spherical heads of Round-headed Rampion are a collection of strongly incurved, narrow, deep violet florets, the petals of which split down to the base when they open to reveal the styles. They may be hidden by tall grasses as the stems are quite short. Most of the leaves are basal, the stem leaves being reduced to very narrow bract-like scales.

lance-shaped leaf

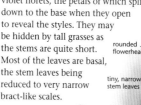

rounded flowerhead

tiny, narrow stem leaves

incurved florets

PERENNIAL

PLANT HEIGHT *20–40cm.*
FLOWER SIZE *Flowerhead 1–2cm wide.*
FLOWERING TIME *June–August.*
LEAVES *Lance-shaped, and slightly toothed.*
FRUIT *Capsule splitting into two or three pores.*
SIMILAR SPECIES *Devil's-bit Scabious (p.276); Sheep's-bit (p.279).*

Sea Aster

Aster tripolium (Asteraceae)

FORMS *large colonies in salt marshes and estuaries, often inundated by high tide.*

Most easily observed at low tide, this plant may be almost engulfed by the incoming sea over salt marshes. The daisy-like flowers have narrow, rather untidy, pale lilac or purple ray florets, though sometimes these are missing altogether, leaving only the bright yellow disc florets on the short column of bracts. The leaves are fleshy and rounded in cross-section.

linear stem leaf

yellow disc florets

BIENNIAL

fleshy stems

pale lilac ray florets

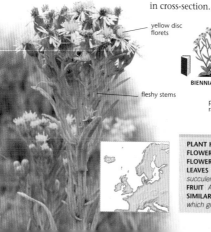

PLANT HEIGHT *30–70cm.*
FLOWER SIZE *1–2cm wide.*
FLOWERING TIME *July–October.*
LEAVES *Alternate, linear to lance-shaped, succulent.*
FRUIT *Achene with a hairy pappus.*
SIMILAR SPECIES *Michaelmas-daisy (right), which grows inland.*

Michaelmas-daisy

Aster novi-belgii (Asteraceae)

This garden plant was introduced into Europe from North America along with several other *Aster* species which have since hybridized, making identification difficult. However, they are all robust plants with white to blue or purple ray florets and yellow centres, and small leaves that clasp the wiry stems.

PROLIFERATES *on fens, wasteland, commons, roadsides, and river or stream banks.*

branched clusters of flowers

PERENNIAL

red-tinged stems

ray florets around yellow centre

unstalked stem leaf

PLANT HEIGHT *80–150cm.*
FLOWER SIZE *2.5–4cm wide.*
FLOWERING TIME *September–October.*
LEAVES *Alternate, oval to lance-shaped, hairy.*
FRUIT *Achene with a hairy pappus.*
SIMILAR SPECIES *Sea Aster (left) grows near the sea; Narrow-leaved Michaelmas-daisy (A. lanceolatus) has short-stalked leaves.*

Blue Fleabane

Erigeron acer (Asteraceae)

Rather spindly and modest, this little daisy is easily missed among other vegetation, as it may grow very short if conditions are dry. The flowers are at the branched tops of erect, wiry stems. The ray florets are a pale bluish lilac, but instead of spreading outwards they remain upright, and are barely longer than the straw-coloured disc florets.

INHABITS *dry places such as embankments, rough grassland, field margins, and old walls.*

short, erect ray florets

stiff, red-spotted stems

ANNUAL/BIENNIAL

narrow, hairy leaves

dark-tipped bracts

PLANT HEIGHT *10–40cm.*
FLOWER SIZE *1–1.5cm wide.*
FLOWERING TIME *July–August.*
LEAVES *Basal, elliptical, and stalked; stem leaves alternate and lance-shaped, very hairy.*
FRUIT *Achenes with a yellowish pappus.*
SIMILAR SPECIES *Alpine Fleabane (E. borealis) has longer, purple ray florets.*

Cornflower

Centaurea cyanus (Asteraceae)

What used to be a common and beautiful flower of the farmed countryside has now, sadly, become scarce. The resilient, tough, and wiry stems would resist the reaper's sickle in cornfields, and it grew in such profusion that it drained valuable nutrients from the soil. The use of powerful herbicides has now eradicated it from many areas. Cornflower is rather like a blue form of Greater Knapweed (p.183), with broad and finely cut, spreading ray florets. The disc florets are blackish pink, and the overlapping bracts have a short fringe of brown hairs.

GROWS *on the cultivated soil of arable fields, but only where herbicides are not used. Grown in gardens and sometimes escapes to wasteland.*

NOTE

The juice from the petals is a brilliant blue and was once used as ink, as a watercolour, and to dye linen, although the colour is not permanent.

solitary flowerhead

brown-edged flower bracts

ANNUAL

linear leaf

large, spreading ray florets

blackish pink disc florets

PLANT HEIGHT *30–70cm.*
FLOWER SIZE *Flowerhead 2–4cm wide.*
FLOWERING TIME *June–August.*
LEAVES *Alternate, linear to lance-shaped, becoming toothed and lobed towards base of plant.*
FRUIT *Achene with short hairs.*
SIMILAR SPECIES *Greater Knapweed (p.183); Perennial Cornflower (C. montana), which has larger flowerheads and broader leaves.*

Chicory

Cichorium intybus (Asteraceae)

The tall, flowering spikes of Chicory are an unmistakable sight among the grass on road verges and wasteland. Each flower is made up of broad, strap-like ray florets that are sky-blue, an unusual colour for the daisy family. It is cultivated as a salad vegetable; the roots and young shoots are also roasted, ground, and then blended with coffee.

FOUND *in grassy places and fields, and on road verges, wasteland, and embankments, on chalky soil.*

lobed lower leaf

green flower bracts

spreading ray florets

flowers in tall spikes

PERENNIAL

stiff, upright stem

PLANT HEIGHT	*60–100cm.*
FLOWER SIZE	*2.5–4cm wide.*
FLOWERING TIME	*July–October.*
LEAVES	*Alternate; upper leaves spear-shaped and toothed, lower leaves pinnately lobed.*
FRUIT	*Achene without a pappus.*
SIMILAR SPECIES	*None.*

Tassel Hyacinth

Muscari comosum (Liliaceae)

There are two kinds of flowers on the fleshy, erect stems of this plant. The tassel of long-stemmed purple flowers, forming a top-knot, are sterile and serve to attract insects to the plant. The dark purplish brown flowers below droop downwards and become paler with a whitish rim. These are the fertile flowers that go on to develop three-lobed fruit capsules.

OCCURS *in well-drained or disturbed soil of roadsides, cultivated ground, and rough, grassy places.*

long flower stem

bell-shaped lower flowers

PERENNIAL

glossy, strap-like leaves

tassel of purple sterile flowers

pale brown fertile flowers

PLANT HEIGHT	*25–50cm.*
FLOWER SIZE	*Fertile flower 5–9mm long.*
FLOWERING TIME	*May–June.*
LEAVES	*Basal, strap-like and channelled.*
FRUIT	*Three-parted capsule.*
SIMILAR SPECIES	*Grape Hyacinth (M. neglectum), which has all-blue fertile flowers in a tight cluster.*

Bluebell

Scilla non-scripta (Liliaceae)

An easily recognizable plant, the Bluebell forms dense carpets of blue in woodland in western Europe, where it blooms just as the trees are coming into leaf. The fragrant, nodding, violet-blue (rarely white or pink) flowers have creamy white anthers. They are clustered on one side in groups of five to fifteen, each flower ending with two blue membranous bracts on its base. The narrow, dark green leaves, which rise from the base may persist for some weeks after flowering.

FORMS *carpets in woodland and scrub; found on hedgebanks and sea-cliffs in the far west of its range.*

PERENNIAL

NOTE

The "bluebell woods" of Britain and Ireland, often written about over the centuries, are considered to be some of the most spectacular floral displays in Europe.

fleshy, leafless
flower stalks

blue
bracts

strap-shaped,
dark green leaf

bell-shaped
flowers

6-parted flower
forms a tube

PLANT HEIGHT *25–50cm.*
FLOWER SIZE *1.5–2cm long.*
FLOWERING TIME *April–June.*
LEAVES *Basal, linear to lance-shaped.*
FRUIT *Small, three-parted capsule.*
SIMILAR SPECIES *Spanish Bluebell (S. hispanica), which is a more robust plant with broader bells and blue anthers; frequently escapes gardens.*

Stinking Iris

Iris foetidissima (Iridaceae)

The large tufts of narrow, strap-like leaves of this iris are evergreen, and most easily seen in winter, when most of the other woodland greenery has disappeared. They have a strong smell rather like that of roast meat, but give off a more offensive odour if crushed. The purple and yellow petals of the flowers sometimes occur as dull violet-brown. The purple fall petals, however, are always darkly veined and the inner yellowish and notched "petals" are actually modified styles. The red berries remain attached to the plant until early winter.

GROWS *in shady corners of woodland, alongside hedgerows, embankments, and paths, in dampish areas; dislikes acid soil.*

PERENNIAL

purple outer petals

notched, yellowish inner "petals"

NOTE

The thin flesh of the berries offers little nourishment to birds, but their bright colour attracts them in the gloom of woodland.

dark-veined purple petals

numerous bright red berries

3-parted fruit capsule

PLANT HEIGHT *40–70cm.*
FLOWER SIZE *5.5–8cm wide.*
FLOWERING TIME *May–July.*
LEAVES *Basal and alternate, sword-shaped, up to 2.5cm wide, strong-smelling.*
FRUIT *Three-parted capsule, containing red berries.*
SIMILAR SPECIES *Yellow Flag (p.162), which is larger; Iris foetidissima var. citrina, which has all yellowish petals.*

Siberian Iris

Iris sibirica (Iridaceae)

FORMS *tufts and sometimes extensive colonies in damp meadows and margins of lakes and ponds. Widely grown in gardens but often escaping.*

This statuesque iris has flowers on tall stems towering above the leaves. The stems branch to produce up to five flowers on short stalks, with a pair of papery spathes at the base. The drooping lower – fall – petals are golden yellow at the base, with a white blotch, and are delicately veined with dark purple. Both the standard petals and the arm-like modified style are purple, without any markings. The narrow leaves are grass-like, but are stiff and remain upright.

3-parted fruit capsule

narrow, grass-like leaf

flower bud on short stalk

PERENNIAL

wide style "arm"

plain standard petal

dark-veined fall petal

NOTE

As this species readily sets seed, horticulturalists have made it the parent of cultivars such as 'Sparkling Rose', 'Ruffled Velvet', and 'Cambridge'.

PLANT HEIGHT *80–120cm.*
FLOWER SIZE *5–7cm wide.*
FLOWERING TIME *June–July.*
LEAVES *Alternate, mostly basal, strap-like, very narrow, up to 1cm wide.*
FRUIT *Three-parted capsule, up to 5cm long.*
SIMILAR SPECIES *Blue Iris (I. spuria), which has stalkless flowers and broader leaves.*

Glossary

Many of the terms defined here are illustrated in the general introduction (pp. 8–13). For anatomical terms see also pp. 8–9. Words in *italics* are defined elsewhere in the glossary.

ACHENE A dry, one-seeded, non-splitting fruit, often with a *pappus*.

AXIL The angle between two structures, such as the leaf and stem or the midrib and a small vein.

BOSS A rounded projection on a petal.

BRACT A leaf-like organ at the base of a flower stalk.

BRACTEOLE A small leaf-like organ at the base of secondary branches of the flower stalk.

BULBIL A small, bulb-like organ that breaks off to form a new plant.

CLADODE A modified stem that looks like a leaf.

CLEISTOGAMOUS Used to describe self-pollinating flowers, whose petals and sepals never open.

CYME A flower cluster with lateral branches, each ending in a flower.

DISC FLORET In the Daisy family, a flower in the central part of the flower-head, whose petals are fused into a tube.

DRUPE A fleshy fruit whose seeds are surrounded by a tough coat.

DRUPELET One of several small *drupes* joined together.

EPICALYX A ring of sepal-like organs just below the true sepals (calyx).

ESCAPE A non-native plant, commonly cultivated and now established in the wild.

FALL PETAL In the Iris family, one of three outer petals that droop down.

FAMILY A classification unit, grouping one or more closely related *genera*.

FLORET One of a group of small or individual flowers usually clustered together to form a flowerhead.

FLOWERHEAD A cluster of florets.

GENUS (pl. **GENERA**) A unit of classification grouping together one or several closely related *species*.

KEEL PETAL The lower, fused petals of a *peaflower*, folded and curved like the keel of a boat.

LIP A protruding petal, as in members of the Orchid and Mint families.

MERICARP A one-seeded portion of a fruit formed by splitting from the rest.

NATURALIZED A non-native plant, introduced into a region, and now forming self-sustaining populations.

NECTARY A nectar-secreting gland.

OCHREA A papery, tubular sheath around the stem of some plants, notably docks.

PANICLE A branched flower cluster, with stalked flowers.

PAPPUS A tuft of hairs on *achenes* or other fruits, which aids wind dispersal.

PEAFLOWER A flower, usually from the Pea family, with sepals fused into a short tube, and with a usually erect upper petal, two *wing petals*, and two *keel petals*.

RACEME An unbranched flower cluster where each flower is clearly stalked.

RAY/RAY FLORET The outer, distinctively flattened flower of a daisy-type flowerhead.

RECURVED Curved backwards or splayed out.

RHIZOME A (usually underground) thickened stem which serves as a food storage organ.

RUNNER A stem which creeps along the ground, forming roots at intervals and eventually separate plants.

SAPROPHYTE A plant which feeds on rotting vegetation in the soil.

SCAPE A leafless stem bearing flowers.

SILICULA A fruit of the Cabbage family, less than three-times as long as broad, and often rounded.

SILIQUA A fruit of the Cabbage family, long and linear or pod-like.

SIMPLE Describes leaves not divided into leaflets.

SPADIX A fleshy *spike* with many unstalked flowers.

SPATHE The large, hooded *bract* that encloses a *spadix*.

SPECIES A classification unit defining a group of similar individuals that breed true in the wild.

SPECULUM A shiny, shield-like patch on the petals of some orchids.

SPIKE An unbranched flower cluster, with unstalked flowers.

SPUR A hollow, cylindrical or pouched structure projecting from a flower, usually containing nectar.

STAMINODE An infertile, modified stamen.

STANDARD PETAL The upright, upper petal of a *peaflower*, often larger than the others.

STEMLESS Describes a plant without an obvious stem; the flower stalk arising directly from the ground.

STIGMA The part of the flower that receives the pollen.

STIGMA-RAY A *stigma* that forms a star with radiating branches.

STIPULE A leaf-like organ at the base of a leaf stalk.

STYLE The part of the female reproductive organ that joins the ovary to the *stigma*.

SUBSHRUB A small perennial with some stems that become woody.

TEPAL Petals and sepals that cannot be distinguished.

TRIFOLIATE A leaf made up of three distinct leaflets.

UMBEL A flat-topped or domed flower cluster with all the stems originating at the same place.

WING PETAL The lateral petals of many flowers, particularly orchids and *peaflowers*.

Index

Acknowledgments

DORLING KINDERSLEY would like to thank Bridget Lloyd-Jones for her help with picture administration and editing. The author would like to thank his wife, Christine, for her constant support.

PICTURE CREDITS
Picture librarian: Richard Dabb, Claire Bowers
Abbreviations key: a = above, b = bottom, c = centre, f = far, l = left, t = top, r = right.

A D Schilling: 53 bl; 103 tr; 116 tl; 128 car; 192 bc; 213 bl. **Barry Hughes:** 19 cfr; 20 tl; 34 cr; 35 car; 38 bl; 48 cfl; 107 tr; 190 cra; 233 br; 235 bcl; 257 bcr; 265 cfr; 279 cla, tr. **Bernd Liebermann:** 199 tr; 219 cfr. **Carl Farmer:** 116 cra, cla. **Chris Gibson:** 13 cbl, cb; 19 br, cra; 21 br, cfr; 24 ca; 25 br, cfr; 30 cr; 34 tl; 35 br; 37 cra, tr; 38 cfl, cra; 48 bl; 54 bl, cla; 55 la; 63 tr; 67 ca; 77 ca; 85 cla, tr; 92 tl; 96 cra; 97 cr; 99 tr; 103 cla; 107 br; 110 cla, tl; 128 tl; 132 bl, cfl; 143 br, tr; 159 cra; 160 br, cra, tl; 167 br; 170 tl; 171 cfr; 176 tl; 178 bl, cfl; 184 cfl; 190 bl, cfl; 191 tr; 195 cra; 196 tl; 197 bl, cfr; 198 br, cla, clb; 200 tl; 201 cra; 205 tr; 214 cra; 215 ca, tr; 216 cla, tl; 219 br; 233 tr; 234 cl; 235 bl; 236 bl, cfl; 238 cra, tl; 241 cra; 247 bcr; 248 tl; 250 cla, tl; 253 br, cfr; 254 tl; 261 cla, tr; 262 cfl; 264 cla, tl; 274 cla; 280 cfl; 284 tl; 285 bl, cfr. **Dave Barlow:** 251 cla, cal. **David Lang:** 13 bc; 33 cbr, cfr; 53 cfr; 55 cra; 60 cl; 63 cla, cra; 96 cla; 97 tr; 98 cl; 99 cb, tr; 100 bcl; 112 ca, tl; 116 bl; 149 tr; 159 tr; 163 cfl, cr; 170 ca; 184 tl; 186 bl, tl, cfr, crb; br; 188 cra; 190 tl; 191 ca; 204 tl; 219 clb; 249 tr; 251 cla, cal; 251 cra, tr; 257 cfr; 274 bl, cfl. **Henriette Kress:** 74 bl, cfl, crb; 94 clb; 139 cbr; 233 cfr; 241 tr. **Jarmo Holopainen:** 58 cra. **Jens Schou:** 12 crb; 13 cal; 14 bcl; 19 tr; 35 cfr; 38 cal; 43 ca; 50 cla; 58 cla; 67 tr; 74 cla, tl; 75 bl, cfr, cla, tr; 81 cra; 86 car; 94 cfl; 98 tl; 100 bl; 109 tr; 130 car, cla, tl; 140 bc, cfl; 146 cra, tl; 158 bl; 160 bl, cfl; 171 br; 173 br, cfr, tl; 176 cl; 188 tl; 189 tr; 195 tr; 197 tr; 198 tl; 213 br, cfr; 214 tl; 227 cla, tr; 231 tr; 236 cla, crb, tl; 257 cfr, cla; 262 cla; 274 tl; 280 bl; 284 cl. **Neil Fletcher:** 1c 2; 3; 4; 5; 10 cla, cal, ca, car, cra, cfl, cr, cfr; 12 cr; 14 bcr, bl, br, ca; 13 tcr, tr, cla, car, cra, cfl, cl, c, cr, cfr, cbr, crb, bl, bc, bcr, br; 15 cb, fr, cra, tr; 16 cl, tl; 17 ca, cbr, cfr, tr; 18 bl, cfl, cra, tl; 20 bl, cfl, cla; 21 cla, tr; 22 cfr, crb, cl, tl; 23 br, cal, cfr, cra, cfr, tr; 24 tl; 25 ca, car, tr; 26 bl, cfl, cra, tl; 27 br, cfr, cra, tr; 28 bl, cfl, cla, cra, tl; 29 cr, tr; 30 cbl, tl; 31 cr, tr; 32 cr, tl; 33 ca, tr; 35 tr; 36 bl, cfl, cra, tl; 37 bc, cfr; 38 tl; 39 cr, tr; 40 bl, cfl, cla, cra, cfr, tl; 41 bl, cb, cfr, tr; 42 bl, cfl, cra, tl; 43 tr; 44 bl, cfl, cra, tl; 45 cbr, cfr, clb, cbl, cra, tr; 46 ca, tl; 47 br, car, cfr, tr; 48 cra, tl; 49 bc, ca, cfr, tr; 50 br, cfl, tl; 51 cr, tr; 52 car, cbl, cfl, tl; 53 ca, tr; cla; 55 br, cfr; 56 cl, tl; 57 cr, tr; 58 br, cfl; 59 br, cfr, cfr, cla, cra, tr; 60 br, cfl, tl; 61 cra, tr; 62 bl, cfl, cra, tl; 63 cbr, cfl, tl; 65 br, ca, cfr, tr; 66 cl, tl; 68 bcr, cfl, cla, crb, br, tl; 69 br, cfr, cla, cdb, cbl, tr; 70 bl, car, cfl, tl; 71 cr, tr; 72 bl, car, cfl, tl; 73 bl, cb, clb, tr; 76 cr, tl; 77 br, tr; 78 br, cfl, cla, tl; 79 ca, cbr, crb, tr; 80 cr, tl; 81 cb, cfr; 82 br, cfl, cra, tl; 83 br, ca, cfr, tr; 84 br, cfl, cla, tl;

85 bl, cfr; 86 cbl, cfl, cla, tl; 87 br, cfr; 88 cb, tl; 89 cr, tr; 90 br, cfl, cla, cra, tl; 91 br, ca, cfl, cfr, tr, br; 92 cfl, cra; 93 ca, tr; 94 cla, cra, tl; 95 br, car, cfr, tr; 96 bl, cfl, tl; 100 bcr, ca, br; 101 ca, tr; 102 cbl, tl; 103 cb, cfr, clb; cbl; 10 bl, ca, cfl, cla, tl; 105 br, ca, cfr, tr; 106 ca, crb, br, tl; 107 cb, cfr, cra, cra, tr; 108 ca, tl; 109 br, cfr; 110 cbl, cfl; 111 bl, ca, cfr; tr; 113 bl, ca, cfr, tr; 114 br, cfl; 115 br cfr, cra, tr; 116 cfl; 117 bl, cfr, cra, tr; 118 cr; tl; 119 bc, cfr, cla, tr; 120 ca, tl; 121 cb, cla, tr; 122 bl, cfl, cra; 123 br, ca, cfr, tr; 124 bl, cbr, cfl, tl; 125 br, cfr, cla, tr; 126 bl, cfl, cra, tl; 127 cbr, tr; 128 bl, cfl; 129 cbr, clb, cbl, tr; 130 bl cfl; 131 cr, tr; 132 cla, tl; 133 bcr, bl, car, tr; 134 cbr, cl, crb, tl; 135 bc, car, cfr, tr, br, cfr; 137 cla, tr; 138 bl, cfl, cra, tl; 140 cra, tl; 141 cr, tr; 142 bl, cfl, cra, tl; 143 car, cla, tr; 144 bl, cfl, cra, tl; 145 clb, bl, cr, tr; 146 bl, cfl; 147 br, cfr, cla, clb, cbl, cra, tr; 148 bl, cfl, cla cra, tl; 149 cr; 151 bl, ca, cfr, tr; 152 cr, tl; 15 cl, tr; 154 bl, car, cfl, cla, crb, tl; 155 bl, car, cfr, tr; 156 bcr, cfl, cla, tl; 157 bcr, cfr, cla, cra, tr; 158 cfl, cla, tl; 159 br, cfr, cla; 161 cr, tr; 162 cl, tl; 164 bl, cfl, cra, tl; 165 cr, tr; 166 bl br, cfl, cla, tl; 167 bcl, bcr, bl, ca; 168 bl, cfl, cra, tl; 169 cr, tr; 170 bl, cbr, cfl; 171 ca, tr; 172 bl, cfl, cra, tl; 173 cra, tr, bl, cfl, cra, tl; 175 bl, cfr, cra, tr; 177 cr, tr; 178 cra, tl; 179 cb, tr; 180 cb, tl; 181 br, ca, cfr, tr, bl, cfl, cra, tl; 183 ca, tr; 184 cra; 185 bc, car, cfr, tr; 187 bcr, cfr, cra, tr; 188 bl, cfl; 189 ca; 191 bl, br, cfr; 193 br, cfr, cra, tr; 194 bl, cfl, cla, cra, tl; 195 br, cfl, cla, tr; 199 br, cfr, cla, cra; 200 bl, cfl 201 br, cfr; 202 br, cfl, cla, tl; 203 cfl, cla, cr, tr; 204 cr; 205 bl, cf, cra; 206 cl, tl; 208 cl, tl; 209 br, cfr, cla, tr; 210 cr, tl; 211 cr, tr; 212 bl cfl, cra, tl; 213 cra, tl; 214 bl, cfl; 215 br, cfr, clb; 216 br, cfl; 217 bc, cfr, cla, tr; 218 bl, cra tl, tl; 219 cra, tr; 220 bl, cfl; 221 cr, tr; 222 br cfl, cla, tl; 223 bc, cfr, cla, tr; 224 cl, tl; 225 br, cfr, cra, tr; 226 cl, tl; 227 br, cfr; 228 cl, tl; 229 ca, tr; 230 ca, tl; 231 cra; 232 cl, crb, tl; 234 crb, tl; 235 bcr, bc, ca; 236 car; 237 br, cfr, cla, tr; 239 br, cfr, cra, tr; 240 cl, tl; 241 br, cfr; 242 br, cfl, cfr, cla, cra, tl; 243 cr, tr; 244 cr, tl; 245 br, cfr, cra, tr; 246 cr, tl; 247 cra; tr; 249 cl; 250 br, cfl; 251 br, cfr; 252 cr, tl; 253 cra, tr; 254 cl; 255 bl, cfr, cra, tr; 256 cl, tl; 258 bl, cfl, cra, crb, tl; 259 cr, tr; 261 br, cfr; 262 bl; 263 cr, tr; 264 bl, cfl; 265 bl, cra, tr; 266 cl, tl; 267 bl, cfr, cla, tr; 268 bl cfl, cra, tl; 269 bc, cfr, cra, tr; 270 bl, cfl, cra, tl; 271 ca, tr; 272 bl, cfl;, cra, tl; 273 br, cfr, cra, tr; 275 bl, cfr, cra, tr; 276 cr, tl; 277 cr, tr; 278 cr, tl; 279 br, cfr; 280 cra; 281 ca, tr; 282 bl, cfl, cra, tl; 283 bc, tr, cfr, cla, cal, cra, crb, br; 285 ca, tr, cla; 286 tl; 287 cl, tr; 288 cla; cal. **Ted Benton:** 10 c; 54 cfl; 58 car, tl; 61 br, cfr; 99 cra; 109 cla; 114 tl; 122 tl; 136 cl, tl; 184 bcl; 192 tl; 196 cl; 200 cra; 201 tr; 238 bl; 280 tl. **Thomas Schoepke:** 81 tr; 136 cr; 139 tr; 171 clb; 198 cfl. **Ulf Lieden:** 248cl. **Wendelin Dorn:** 13 ca; 54 tl; 87 cra, tr; 107 cfr; 150 tl; 163 tr; 233 car, cla, cra; 236 cra; 238 cfl; 247 cfr; 257 cra, tr; 260 tl; 288 bc, tl.

All other images © Dorling Kindersley